Future Trends in AI Banking: Decentralized Finance (DeFi), Central Bank Digital Currencies (CBDCs), and Beyond

RIVER PUBLISHERS SERIES IN COMPUTING AND INFORMATION SCIENCE AND TECHNOLOGY

The "River Publishers Series in Computing and Information Science and Technology" covers research which ushers the 21st Century into an Internet and multimedia era. Networking suggests transportation of such multimedia contents among nodes in communication and/or computer networks, to facilitate the ultimate Internet.

Theory, technologies, protocols and standards, applications/services, practice and implementation of wired/wireless networking are all within the scope of this series. Based on network and communication science, we further extend the scope for 21st Century life through the knowledge in machine learning, embedded systems, cognitive science, pattern recognition, quantum/biological/molecular computation and information processing, user behaviors and interface, and applications across healthcare and society.

Books published in the series include research monographs, edited volumes, handbooks and textbooks. The books provide professionals, researchers, educators, and advanced students in the field with an invaluable insight into the latest research and developments.

Topics included in the series are as follows:-

- Artificial intelligence
- Cognitive Science and Brian Science
- Communication/Computer Networking Technologies and Applications
- Computation and Information Processing
- Computer Architectures
- Computer networks
- Computer Science
- Embedded Systems
- Evolutionary computation
- Information Modelling
- Information Theory
- Machine Intelligence
- Neural computing and machine learning
- Parallel and Distributed Systems
- Programming Languages
- Reconfigurable Computing
- Research Informatics
- Soft computing techniques
- Software Development
- Software Engineering
- Software Maintenance

For a list of other books in this series, visit www.riverpublishers.com

Future Trends in AI Banking: Decentralized Finance (DeFi), Central Bank Digital Currencies (CBDCs), and Beyond

Editors

Jyoti Verma
Chitkara Business School, Chitkara University,
Punjab, India

Sarvjeet Kaur Chatrath
University of Canberra,
Australia

Gagandeep
Chitkara Business School, Chitkara University,
Punjab, India

River Publishers

Routledge
Taylor & Francis Group
NEW YORK AND LONDON

Published 2026 by River Publishers
River Publishers
Broagervej 10, 9260 Gistrup, Denmark
www.riverpublishers.com

Distributed exclusively by Routledge
605 Third Avenue, New York, NY 10017, USA
4 Park Square, Milton Park, Abingdon, Oxon OX14 4RN

Future Trends in AI Banking: Decentralized Finance (DeFi), Central Bank Digital Currencies (CBDCs), and Beyond / Jyoti Verma, Sarvjeet Kaur Chatrath and Gagandeep

Routledge is an imprint of the Taylor & Francis Group, an informa business

ISBN 978-87-438-1074-2 (Hardback)
ISBN 978-87-438-1080-3 (Paperback)
ISBN 978-87-438-1077-3 (E-book)
ISBN 978-87-438-1079-7 (E-pub)
ISBN 978-87-438-1076-6 (E-book master)

DOI: 10.1201/9788743810766

Contents

Preface

The idea for this book emerged from a simple but pressing observation: the financial sector is changing faster than our traditional frameworks for understanding it Artificial intelligence is no longer an auxiliary tool in banking; it is becoming the cognitive backbone of modern financial systems. At the same time, developments such as Decentralized Finance (DeFi) and Central Bank Digital Currencies (CBDCs) are challenging long-standing assumptions about intermediation, trust, regulation, and the very nature of money. This book is written to make sense of these converging transformations and to offer a coherent, forward-looking perspective on the future of AI-driven banking and finance.

The motivation to write this book is a sense of a developing disconnect between technology and conceptualization. Although fragmented studies and more practitioner-driven discourses on AI, fintech, blockchain, and digital currencies are abundant, they are discussed in isolation. As a matter of fact, though, they are closely related. Artificial intelligence creates the decision-making, automation and personalization; blockchain facilitates decentralization and transparency, and CBDCs bring a re-conceptualization of sovereign money in the digital era. Their interactive effect is critical to comprehend by scholars, policy makers, and other professionals seeking to move and influence their future financial environment.

The book has been multidisciplinary and balanced. It does not consider AI as a productivity-enhancement technology, nor does it consider DeFi and CBDCs as unconditionally disruptive forces. Rather, it considers the opportunities and constraints. In addition to covering the efficiency, innovation, and financial inclusion, the book also pays sufficient attention to ethical issues, data privacy, algorithmic bias, governance, and regulatory issues. It is not aimed at promoting blind technological implementation and adoption, but rather responsible, informed, and situation-specific application of AI in finance.

The chapters unite theoretical information, empirical evidences, and practical perspectives. They discuss the next-generation banking model, AI-powered customer interactions, risk management, and decision-making, the significance of agentic AI systems, and the increasing desire to have a strong AI governance. A specific focus is placed on Central Bank Digital Currencies, and the way artificial intelligence can be used to design, implement, and make them effective in policy, as well as the fact that the surveillance, the lack of trust, and financial privacy raise critical questions. It goes further to discuss sustainable finance, ESG integration, and inclusive financial architectures, pointing out the way in which AI can play into the wider socio-economic development.

The book is authored to a wide readership audience. It is aimed at scholars and other researchers interested in building knowledge in the field of finance and artificial intelligence; at banking and fintech practitioners who need to learn how to apply the latest technologies to the corporate strategy; at policy-makers and regulators who struggle with the challenge of how to govern and regulate the financial system; and at postgraduate learners who want to acquire a more rigorous and future-oriented view of modern finance. The language and form are established in such a way that they are easy to understand and follow without any loss of analytical complexity.

The responsibility to use artificial intelligence will become a marker of success over time as financial systems face more uncertainty, complexity and disruption. I hope that this book will help to become a valuable resource and a source of strategic wisdom that encourages interested to engage in AI-powered finance and helps to create a more efficient, inclusive, and sustainable global financial system.

Editors

List of Contributors

A, Veena, *School of Business, RV University, India*

Agarwal, Rachit, *Dr. Vishwanath Karad MIT World Peace University, India*

Arora, Ayushi, *Chandigarh College of Technology, Punjabi University, India*

Batra, G. S., *Jagat Guru Nanak Dev Punjab State Open University, India*

Chatrath, S. K., *School of Business, University of Canberra, Australia*

Choudhary, Vinita, *School of Leadership and Management, Manav Rachna International Institute of Research and Studies, India*

Choudhary, Vinita, *School of Management, IILM University, India*

Gagandeep, Chitkara Business School, *Chitkara University, India*

Geetika, School of Management & Commerce, *LPU, India*

Kalyani, Monika, *Mittal Business School, LPU, India*

Kamboj, Neha, *School of Management, IILM University, India*

Kamboj, Neha, *School of Management, IILM University, India*

Kaur, Amandeep, *Chitkara Business School, Chitkara University, India*

Kaur, Gurpreet, *Manav Rachna University, India*

Kumar, A., *Department of Commerce, University of Lucknow, India*

Kumar, Amit, *FABER, Department of Orthopaedics, PGIMER, India*

Kumar, Narinder, *School of Economics and Public Policy, RV University, India*

Kumar, Tanya, *Dr. Vishwanath Karad MIT World Peace University, Pune, India*

Pandit, Anirudh, *Assistant Professor, Chandigarh College of Technology (CGC Landran), India*

Singh, Hakim, *Department of Political Science, Lovely Professional University, India*

Singh, J., *ICSSR, Ministry of Education, India*

Singh, Puneet, *SAVP, EXL Services, India*

Srivasatav, Shalini, *Amity College of Commerce & Finance, Amity University, India*

Trivedi, Sonal, *School of Management and Commerce, Manav Rachna University, India*

Trivedi, Sonal, *School of Management, IILM University, India*

Verma, Jyoti, *Chitkara Business School, Chitkara University, Punjab, India*

List of Figures

List of Tables

List of Abbreviations

AI	Artificial intelligence
AML	Anti-money laundering
BFSI	Banking, financial services and insurance
CBDCs	Central bank digital currencies
CER	Corporate environmental responsibility
CSR	Corporate social responsibility
DeFi	Decentralized finance
DLT	Distributed ledger technology
DoS	Denial-of-service
ESG	Environmental, social, and governance
FRS	Financial reporting systems
ICO	Initial coin offering
IVAs	Intelligent virtual assistants
IVR	Interactive voice response
KYC	Know your customer
KYB	Know your business
LSTM	Long short-term memory
ML	Machine learning
NLP	Natural language processing
PbD	Privacy by design
PoW	Proof of work
RPA	Robotic process automation
SDGs	Sustainable development goals
SEM	Structural equation modelling
SIA	State bank intelligent assistant
SSI	Self-sovereign identity
SVM	Support vector machines
TAM	Technology acceptance model
UN	United nations
WEF	World economic forum

1

Next-gen Banking: Exploring the Impact and Future of Artificial Intelligence

Anirudh Pandit

Chandigarh College of Technology (CGC Landran), India

Email: Anirudh.5511@cgc.edu.in

Abstract

Banking firms are undergoing significant changes as a result of the rapid development of AI. This chapter reviews how improving technologies such as machine learning, natural language processing, and robotic process automation are making important changes in customer service, risk analysis, credit decisions, following compliance rules, and improving financial operations. The introduction of hyper-personalized services, AI systems that respond to human questions, autonomous finance services, and AI assistance in people's decisions is considered a major reason for progress and edge in the market. As a result, also, the merging of AI with DeFi and the establishment of AI-oriented banks are significantly altering the worldwide financial market. However, using AI in banking leads to great difficulties, such as data privacy, comprehending model decisions, biased algorithms, problems with the current technology, and answers to rules and guidelines. This provides insights and guidance into the challenges and possibilities caused by AI in banking, helping users achieve lasting growth in the AI-based financial sector.

1.1 Introduction

AI is driving the major changes happening in the banking industry due to fast technological advancements. Since there is more digital data available, customers require more, and new competitors in fintech are emerging, traditional banks need to change how they do business. The use of AI is helping banks

 DOI: 10.1201/9788743810766-1

engage with their customers, control risks, ensure compliance, and improve their profits.

Systems in AI use technologies such as machine learning (ML), natural language processing (NLP), robotic process automation (RPA), and computer vision to learn, change, and decide on their own without much help from humans. In the banking world, AI uses its capabilities in many areas, including checking for fraud, assisting with virtual support, scoring credit, recommending investments, and automated legal compliance.

AI is strongly affecting the experiences businesses provide to their customers. Currently, people expect fast and personal communications on various digital platforms. With AI, banks can console their customers, assuring they receive the right service suggestions, quick insights into their finances, and uninterrupted day-and-night help from bots.

AI is helping companies handle their procedures efficiently and are becoming more effective. Automating rule-based and everyday duties at banks allows them to reduce errors, reduce their spending, and boost the speed of their services. Nowadays, AI helps check loan applications, scrutinize identity documents for flaws, discover fraud, and comply with many regulations more efficiently and faithfully than before.

Even so, as banks adopt AI, they are faced with issues surrounding data confidentiality, ethical matters, stricter laws, and lucidity in their models. Ensure that AI systems are open, fair, and answerable, especially in situations that influence customers' financial matters or protection. Moving forward, AI is making it possible for banks to put AI at their core. Investing in AI by financial institutions leads to better customer service, enhanced risk management, and a more competitive position compared to others in the field.

1.2 Main Text

1.2.1 Future trends in AI within banking

Here are the key future trends in AI within banking that are shaping the industry over the next 5–10 years:

1.2.1.1 Hyper-personalized banking experiences

Artificial intelligence has made it possible for banks to provide highly personalized services to their clients. Unlike before, AI makes it possible for banks to create personal solutions for their customers, considering their individual financial activities, needs, and behaviors.

Predictive analytics allows banks to foresee when their users might require a loan, intend to invest or can profit from revising their savings plan.

With such insights, financial institutions ensure they provide the proper solution at the perfect time and see customers use those solutions more.

In addition, AI helps to offer personalized experiences on all types of digital channels. Automated mobile apps and online banking services may spotlight relevant information, advice, or warnings that relate to what you do and do not do with your money. So, a travel spender may receive travel card recommendations and someone nearing retirement can expect pension guidance.

Because of this, people enjoy using the app more and feel trusted and appreciated by the company. Banking companies use it to further involve their customers, keep them loyal, and increase the amount of money their customers spend [1].

1.2.1.2 Conversational AI and virtual assistants

Chatbots and voice assistants controlled by AI are changing the way bank customers get instant help when they need it. It can be improved through new methods like NLP and machine learning. AI can go much further than before by supporting content, interpreting emotions, and performing very complex banking tasks. A key advantage is that conversational AI can supply customers with smart support, all hours of the day. Virtual assistants are equipped to handle various tasks on their own, such as checking accounts, transferring funds, reporting a lost card, and updating a user's details. This makes customers happier as they get quick answer, decreasing the amount of work for the support team too.

Furthermore, Amazon Alexa, Google Assistant, and Siri can allow customers to carry out banking actions using their voices. Speaking to a bot is easier and more convenient for those who cannot read or see well. With technology progressing, some banks are starting to analyze emotions and sentiments to enhance their customer interactions. Analyzing what a person says and the way they communicate, conversational AI can detect both frustration and confusion and respond appropriately. As a result, people now use virtual assistants for more purposes than before and rely on their suggestions to choose services suited to them or for information about other possibilities from the bank [2].

1.2.1.3 AI-driven risk management and fraud detection

As we move closer to digital banking, risks regarding fraud and cybersecurity have increased drastically. Banks rely on AI to help detect, evaluate, and respond to risks as they occur in the present. With the help of big data and sophisticated algorithms, AI strengthens the company's ability to prevent and recognize threats, protecting its customers' faith in it.

Real-time detection of unusual activity in transactions is among the most helpful uses of AI. Such systems are unable to adapt quickly to the changing methods used by fraudsters. On the other hand, AI makes it possible for these systems to learn from any newly collected data, helping them detect suspicious activities more accurately and with fewer chances to misidentify anything noteworthy.

Extra security is being offered by using biometric methods, including face, fingerprint, and voice recognition. Unlike PINs and passwords, they offer enhanced security and are less likely to allow someone else to log in to your bank account.

Identifying unique habits related to typing, handling the mouse, using different devices, and navigating helps AI with behavioral biometrics.

1.2.1.4 Autonomous finance

The use of AI in banking is replacing human tasks and improving the management of funds for customers. This move is significant because AI can handle large sets of information, see patterns in them, and act quickly when needed.

With AI, people can have automated plans for budgeting and paying off debt. Intelligent systems are able to determine how much to save every month, manage payments to debts cautiously, and modify their plans without requiring the user to do anything manually.

Similarly, modern AI systems can always keep an eye on a user's money matters, spot areas where they waste resources, and making or helping them make appropriate changes. If someone spends too much in a specific area, the system could guide them by suggesting or applying spending rules, streamlining their subscriptions, or moving budget items to support their objectives in the coming years.

They are most needed when managing finances well is too difficult for customers because of time, lack of skill, or discipline. Users benefit from autonomous finance by having more control over their finances, as this approach sets a higher level of efficiency for banking systems.

1.2.1.5 AI in credit scoring and lending

Traditional methods for scoring credit generally depend only on limited details such as how much is on a credit card, how many loans there are, and proof of income. Adopting this method frequently means that many people living in neglected or cash-free areas cannot apply for bank credit.

AI is helping to change the field by allowing for more fair, reliable, and flexible credit scoring. AI is used to study information obtained from mobile phones, paying bills, online behavior, digital payment systems, and e-commerce. Alternative scoring helps to establish the credit score of those who do not have enough official credit history.

When AI is used, loans can be granted faster and more accurately. Algorithms can watch for any hidden risks and help discover minor patterns that are harder for humans to notice. This means gig workers, small entrepreneurs, and those living in rural areas are more likely to access credit than they were before.

Additionally, AI allows lenders to design loans that suit each customer's lifestyle and aims. With these services, financial institutions satisfy customers better, reduce defaults, and can serve markets they were unable to before.

AI scoring models are making finance more accessible, which in turn empowers many people and small businesses with opportunities for growth [5].

1.2.1.6 Enhanced regulatory compliance (RegTech)

Banking firms now rely on AI more and more to help with KYC, AML, and governance, as rules in these areas are becoming tougher. Automated systems help to quickly notice anything unusual in customers' activities or their payments. Using machine learning, they can spot threatening situations that are missed by other approaches. Through automated identity checks and matching several sources, AI facilitates the KYC and AML processes. Due to this, workers become more efficient, do their work more accurately, and maintain a solid adherence to rules as they are updated. In addition, NLP allows companies to automatically review complicated documents and communications to spot any possible risks or issues. It makes the process more efficient, faster, and guarantees all rules are followed [4].

1.2.1.7 AI-augmented human decision making

Rather than replacing human jobs, AI will join forces with people in the banking sector. Now, AI often acts as a partner, helping professionals deliver accurate and quick decisions concerning customer service, compliance, and investment decisions. AI is used by financial advisors and relationship managers to give them up-to-date insights on their clients' risks, additional needs, and relevant analysis in real time. They assist advisors in molding their suggestions to clients' purposes and making complicated portfolios simpler to handle. AI dashboards consolidate information from the risk, compliance, marketing, and operations departments throughout the organization and help leaders make well-informed decisions. When data silos are removed, AI encourages people to work more closely and share strategies. Importantly,

AI technology can be overridden by human experts, who are always the ones making the final decisions. Having checks and balances ensures everyone is accountable and that legal or ethical matters are considered [4].

1.2.1.8 Decentralized and AI-integrated finance (DeFi + AI)

Artificial Intelligence (AI) and blockchain technology interacting could make Decentralized Finance (DeFi) more transparent, safe, smart, and adaptable. This process opens doors for financial services to explore opportunities outside banks. AI-powered smart contracts, written on blockchains and whose terms are set in code, can update their function automatically when needed. They are able to quickly modify details of loans, collateral, or how and when payments are made, helping to follow new trends and laws and ensure flexibility and less risk. Because of AI, credit and lending can happen trustlessly using algorithms to measure borrower trust, rather than relying on banks or other central groups. This allows individuals worldwide to enjoy easier, safer, and more efficient credit access. Additionally, AI enables users to make decisions across all sectors in fintech with data collected from many blockchains and DeFi protocols to improve their investment and yield farming strategies in real time.

1.2.1.9 AI-first banks and fintechs

These new challenger banks are using AI from the start, rather than adding it later. They depend on AI to provide customers with effective, growing, and people-first financial services that rely very little on humans. When this happens, AI makes it possible for these banks to deliver experiences that meet the expectations of people who know how technology can work for them. AI ensures the identity is correct, manages risk, and offers useful products, all at once. Using AI technology, challenger banks with few staff spend less on operations and can provide low prices on products and services. Since they keep their operations lean, Apple can rapidly respond to new demands and introduce innovations. As a result, these banks are changing the industry, beating established competitors by using AI to provide banking for all, engage better with customers, and earn new income.

1.2.1.10 Ethical AI and explainability

Since AI is becoming involved in significant banking decisions, having XAI and effective rules is more important than ever. Today, there is no choice but to include transparency, fairness, and accountability in responsible AI use.[7] Explainable AI describes systems that are able to present clear explanations for what they do. Having openness in banking helps to earn the trust of customers and regulators, mainly when automatic AI processes are involved in financial matters. XAI can assist banks in explaining their decisions when they follow through on loan applications. Going along with being open, it is essential to make sure AI systems do not inadvertently discriminate based on race, gender, income, or various sensitive factors. Banks should perform thorough tests, look at their data carefully, and fix models to ensure bias has no effect on their customers. Increasingly, countries are telling regulators to require that financial institutions adhere to standards that guard privacy, maintain safe storage of data, and preserve fair treatment. To follow these requirements, companies must monitor regularly, have proper governance practices, and speak with people who have diverse skills. If they lead with explainable AI and ethical approaches, banks will be able to use artificial intelligence safely, make better decisions, and keep customers' and regulatory trust intact [7].

1.2.2 Challenges for AI in banking

Even though AI could greatly transform banking, there are still many important obstacles to using it in the industry. It is hard to get AI systems off the ground because the costs of building and using AI infrastructure, upgrading computers, and training staff can be very high. Many banks are still challenged by problems related to data, including incomplete datasets, data stored in multiple places, and difficulties gaining immediate access to information. Some employees and leaders resist adopting AI, which can cause delays, as they fear they will lose their jobs and are not informed about what AI offers. Having ethical and social risks in AI means being concerned about biases in algorithms, a reduction in human interactions, and AI control. Because AI is becoming increasingly advanced, it creates new cybersecurity threats, such as risks to system integrity that come from manipulating the system or carrying out adversarial attacks. Banks must handle these issues if they want to fully use AI in the future.

1.2.2.1 Data privacy and security concerns

As more AI is used in banking, it is increasingly necessary to keep data safe and secure. Because AI relies on lots of private and financial information, keeping it protected is important for both building customer trust and obeying laws. For your data to be secure, banks require advanced defenses such as regular encryption, safe storage, and proper rules for access. Because of these defenses, confidential information can be accessed only by those who are allowed. Even so, new security issues arise as a result of AI technologies.

Advanced cyber-attacks may be launched at them to corrupt algorithms, take information, or change transactions. One way to deal with these risks is through active cybersecurity measures that monitor systems in real time, identify threats rapidly, and have set plans for what to do if an incident occurs. In addition, making sure your data handling meets changing data protection regulations is necessary. In the EU, GDPR, in California, CCPA, and India, DPDP Act, individuals are protected by strict guidelines relating to how their data is collected and how it can be used. A bank that does not follow applicable laws can face tough monetary fines and a lowered standing among customers. When AI is used in banking, it needs to be done in a considered way that also respects responsibility. Any AI project relies on strong management of data, clarity, and surety to keep information safe, follow laws, and earn customers' trust [9].

1.2.2.2 Regulatory and compliance uncertainty

Because AI has spread quickly in the banking sector, clear, joined-up regulations have not been written, leaving the industry unsure about rules and regulations. Banks and other financial companies struggle to deal with a wide range of changing rules that often do not outline regulations for AI. All over the world, officials are making extra efforts to ensure credit scoring, fraud detection, and other sensitive processes involving automation are clear and open. It is important for banks to show that their AI models are equitable, unbiased, and easy to review so that they stay compliant and respected by their customers. Still, because each region sets its own rules, institutions have to interpret and adjust to those different requirements, complicating their multinational work. Furthermore, when regulations are always changing, companies can face problems with delays, higher costs, and difficulties scaling their AI systems smoothly. For banks to succeed, agile frameworks are necessary that quickly notice when regulations change and allow them to easily make adjustments in their use of artificial intelligence [9].

1.2.2.3 Explainability and transparency

A major obstacle in AI adoption in banking is that a lot of deep learning models are very complex and tend to be unclear about their results. Because of this lack of transparency, customers, regulators, and those inside the company may question the organization's trustworthiness. Banks are expected to create explanations for important decisions such as approving or denying loans, detecting fraud, and measuring risks, so that such decisions can be easily understood and shared. Making AI clear helps users learn the rationale behind a decision and allows regulators to ensure the AI is following fairness rules. Because of this, banks are now more likely to use Explainable AI (XAI) solutions. Examples include methods that make complex models simpler, help show how decisions are made, and produce explanations that anyone can read. XAI makes it easier for companies to explain their decisions, detect bias, and manage AI systems better. Including explainability in their AI processes helps banks win their customers' trust, improve their experiences, and adhere to regulations in the age of AI in finance.

1.2.2.4 Biasness and discrimination

Even as Artificial Intelligence offers many benefits to banking, it may also help perpetuate the biases inside the data used to teach the machines. As a result of such biases connected to things like race, gender, and so on; customer service, lending processes, and credit scores may not be fair. If left unnoticed, distorted AI in banking could contribute more to imbalanced finances and weaken a bank's credibility. A credit scoring algorithm that does not work correctly may wrongly prevent people from certain groups from getting a loan, though they are actually able and willing to pay it. It is important for financial institutions to have detailed methods for finding and preventing bias. To do this, companies must carry out recurring fairness reviews, design and build models using a range of representative data, and pay careful attention to results in different communities. When banks handle bias properly, they ensure they comply and also show how much they value ethical progress and fair treatment for all. Taking this approach grows public confidence, helps the brand build a good reputation, and provides financial services to all – making the banking ecosystem more responsible and accessible to all [9].

1.2.2.5 Infrastructure

Most traditional banks use IT systems that are old and not equipped for today's AI tools. AI-driven solutions often find it challenging to work smoothly with these legacy systems because their databases are separated and their software construction is inflexible. Integrating AI means setting up new systems so they easily connect with the bank's main programs for transactions, customer handling, and compliance. Usually, organizations face great challenges in this process, with high costs for transferring data, updating systems, and monitoring ongoing reliability and safety. In addition, banks that have more AI usually require major digital transformation projects to take place. These steps include modernizing infrastructure, using the cloud, refreshing staff skills, and looking at business processes differently to get the best use of AI. The initial cost can be large, but proper transformation makes an organization more flexible, boosts customer experiences, and sets it apart from other companies. So, working on legacy integration is very important for banks looking to use AI to its maximum benefit. Important tasks for this include planning, strong project management, and involving IT, business departments, and AI specialists [2].

1.2.2.6 Skill shortage

Banks are experiencing a shortage of people skilled in AI and data science, which is made worse by how fast AI is being adopted and how particular the financial industry is. Experts with plenty of skill and experience in banking management and regulations are not always available. There is a big demand for these experts and not enough can be found, which drives up their salaries and makes it difficult to retain them. The lack of ready talent can delay AI projects, make innovations hard to implement, and increase the need for outside support. For these issues to be handled, banks should form teams that mix fintech knowledge with knowledge about the domain. By cooperating, AI specialists, data scientists, compliance officers, and business leaders ensure that AI solutions are technically strong and follow what the financial industry needs and what regulators require. Furthermore, training present workers, working with educational institutes, and constructing strong career paths in AI can help banks have the skilled people they need for their ongoing change using AI [3].

1.2.2.7 High implementation costs

The early stages of using AI require a large investment, since information must be gathered, powerful computers must be used, and models must be trained well. Being that their ROI rarely appears in the near future, small banks must work harder to defend the initial cost. Apart from putting the system in place, using AI requires teaching staff to use it, upgrading current equipment, and handling the changes required in the organization.

1.2.2.8 Ethical and social risks

Using Artificial Intelligence in banking causes important ethical and social challenges. Concerns have arisen, especially because of the threat that robots may take away jobs and shrink the number of chances available in the industry. At the same time, customers are concerned about more algorithmic behavior and the loss of regular face-to-face contact that banks used to offer. To deal with these matters, banks need to find an ideal combination of both computerized and human processes. AI is best used alongside humans to boost productivity, help with smart choices, and allow employees to concentrate more on factors connected with relationships. It is important to keep people at the heart of our work. If banks are open, guard privacy and don't neglect customer relationships, they can trust AI and engage with their customers and employees [9].

1.2.2.9 Quality and availability of data

Most AI systems only work well when given plenty of clean, organized data. Yet, a lot of banks suffer from not linking data sources, duplication, and low quality because of poor data maintenance. If Al receives only limited access to suitable real-time information or sources, its performance can be limited because it cannot provide accurate and timely inputs [9].

1.2.2.10 Resistance to change

It is difficult for banks to move forward in AI because many resist the changes it brings. Many are concerned about being replaced by new technologies, so they say no to them. Occasionally, leadership does not fully see the need for digital transformation or isn't fully committed, which results in slower advancements. Changing these issues calls for a good strategy to encourage change, as well as wide-reaching AI knowledge training to develop interest, confidence, and motivation across the group [10].

1.2.2.11 Bonus: Cybersecurity threats

When banks rely on AI more, their exposure to cyber-attacks gets much broader. Because of this growth, we have to worry about new threats, including attempts to alter models, attacks meant to fool AI, and threats specific to AI technologies. Protecting these systems needs specific cybersecurity steps designed for these new risks and to keep AI-based operations reliable and secure [7].

1.3 Conclusion

Smart, fast, and customized banking is now becoming a reality thanks to Artificial Intelligence. With its ability to engage customers, control risks, and include more people in financial operations, AI is driving many new innovations. Banks need to address a range of major problems when moving to AI-first banking, such as handling sensitive data, updating dated systems, addressing bias in algorithms, and following regulatory rules. Moving ahead needs an approach with better technology while adding ethical standards, making solid plans, and helping workers gain new skills. Driving this transformation in all areas will allow banks and institutions to lead in digital financial markets and provide top customer trust and lasting value.

References

[1] K G Radhika, R. Shriraksha, "ARTIFICIAL INTELLIGENCE IN INDIAN BANKING SECTOR: AN OVERVIEW," MSNIM Management Review Vol. 2(2) Bi- Annual Journal July – December 2024.

[2] McKinsey & Company, "AI in banking: Can banks meet the challenge?," Oct. 2020.

[3] Accenture, "Reworking the Revolution: Are you ready to compete as intelligent technology meets human ingenuity to create the future workforce?," 2018.

[4] D. Arner, J. Barberis, and R. Buckley, "FinTech, RegTech, and the Reconceptualization of Financial Regulation," Northwestern Journal of International Law and Busines, vol. 37, no. 3, Dec. 2017.

[5] A Wilhelmena, N.A Adeola, and B.Binaebi, "AI in credit scoring: A comprehensive review of models and predictive analytics," Global Journal of Engineering and Advances, vol. 8, pp. 118-129, 2020.

[6] World Economic Forum, "The Future of Financial Infrastructure: An Ambitious Look at How Blockchain Can Reshape Financial Services," Aug. 2016.

[7] IBM Institute for Business Value, "The AI Bank of the Future," 2019.

[8] Deloitte, "AI and Risk Management: Innovating with Confidence," 2021.

[9] European Commission, "Ethics Guidelines for Trustworthy AI," Apr. 2019.

[10] J. Manyika et al., "Harnessing automation for a future that works," McKinsey Global Institute, Jan. 2017.

2

Blockchain Frameworks: Usability and Applications Across Domains

Neha Kamboj[1], Vinita Choudhary[2] and Sonal Trivedi[3]

[1]School of Management, IILM University, India
[2]School of Leadership and Management, Manav Rachna International Institute of Research and Studies, India
[3]School of Business, Manav Rachna University, India

Email: nehakamboj2000@gmail.com; postvinita@gmail.com; trivedi.sonal86@gmail.com

Abstract

Blockchain technology, initially developed as a backbone for cryptocurrencies, has rapidly expanded into broader domains of finance and business. Its unique attributes – transparency, decentralization, immutability, and enhanced security – offer solutions to persistent challenges in financial services. This chapter examines blockchain applications beyond cryptocurrency, focusing on its role in transforming financial services such as Know Your Customer (KYC), cross-border payments, and compliance. A case-based exploration of blockchain-enabled KYC demonstrates how distributed ledgers can streamline identity verification while ensuring trust and efficiency. The chapter also outlines benefits, limitations, and potential applications, contributing to a holistic understanding for policymakers, financial institutions, researchers, and practitioners.

2.1 Introduction

In recent years, blockchain technology has attracted significant attention due to its potential to drive innovation and create positive transformations in various industries. It has emerged as a prominent example of technological

 DOI: 10.1201/9788743810766-2

disruption in the financial sector. In 2016, the World Economic Forum (WEF), through its Future of 10 New Technologies report, highlighted blockchain as one of the most promising innovations, which encouraged many nations to channel substantial investments into this domain. Increased funding has, in turn, accelerated the pace of growth and experimentation within the blockchain ecosystem.

For the FinTech industry, blockchain offers solutions to several long-standing challenges. Among these, the Know Your Customer (KYC) process stands out as a critical issue where blockchain can deliver significant improvements. This chapter explores blockchain's role in addressing KYC challenges, with a detailed use case analysis providing further insights into its effectiveness [1].

Figure 2.1 illustrates the diverse applications of blockchain in financial services, including supply chain finance, cross-border payments, transparency enhancement, and data security. Beyond reducing transaction costs for banks, blockchain ensures consistency of records across systems, thereby enhancing security and minimizing risks of cyberattacks and data breaches. These capabilities highlight the urgent need to understand blockchain's potential and integration into finance.

This chapter particularly investigates how blockchain facilitates KYC in the banking sector by enabling distributed data management, secure

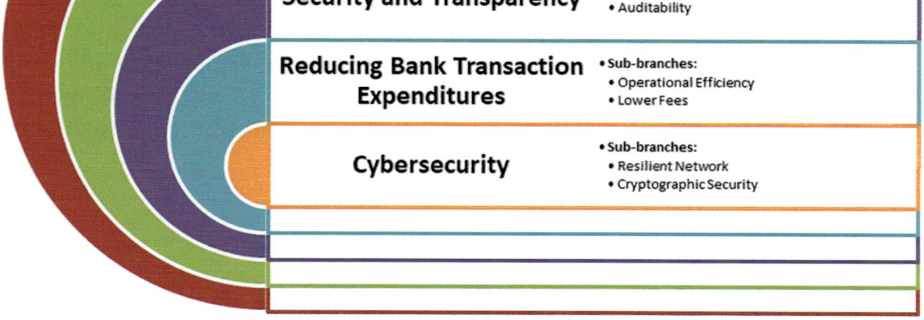

Figure 2.1 Blockchain for the Finance Sector, developed by Authors.

authentication, transparent communication, and enhanced trust. The discussion contributes to a broader understanding of how blockchain is reshaping financial services and promoting efficiency across the industry [2].

2.2 Literature Review

Blockchain, also referred to as distributed ledger technology (DLT), is a decentralized system that removes the need for a central authority by relying on algorithms for validation. It offers significant potential for cost reduction, the creation of new markets, and opportunities for innovative service models, attracting both established institutions and emerging players [3], [4]. Unlike conventional systems that depend on trusted intermediaries, blockchain achieves consensus among participants through mechanisms such as Proof of Work (PoW), in which a majority of nodes validate and confirm the authenticity of transactions.

Different categories of blockchain networks exist to address specific application requirements [5]. When a ledger is owned and managed by a defined group of entities, it is known as a permissioned private blockchain, often used within banking firms, such as Bankchains. In cases where only recognized participants can validate transactions but the network is publicly

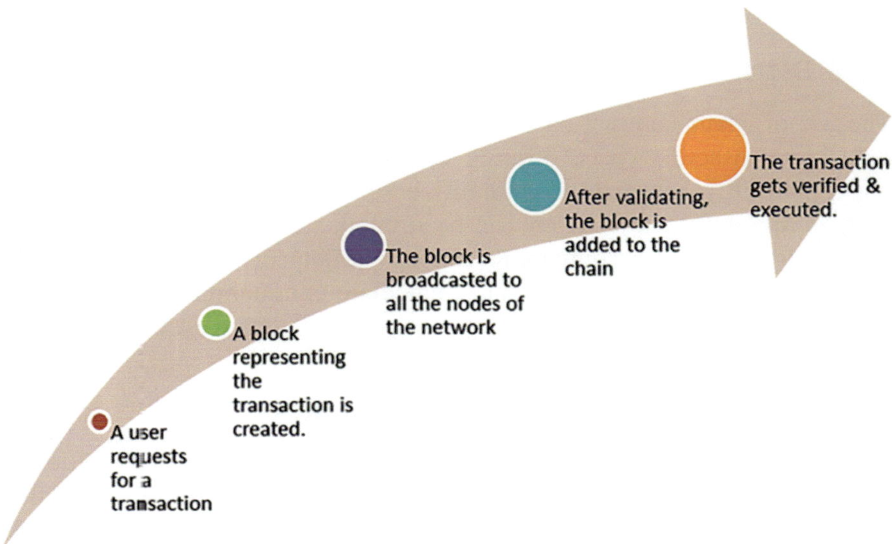

Figure 2.2 Working flow of blockchain, developed by authors.

accessible, it is referred to as a permissioned public blockchain, with Ripple serving as a well-known example in global financial transactions [6]. On the other hand, when the ledger is open to all participants, and anyone can contribute to consensus, it is termed an unpermissioned public blockchain, as seen in cryptocurrencies like Bitcoin [7], [8].

Bitcoin marked the first large-scale adoption of blockchain technology [9]. While it initially gained traction as the foundation for digital currencies such as Bitcoin, Ethereum, Litecoin, Primecoin, Namecoin, and Zcash, the underlying technology demonstrates far wider applicability. Beyond cryptocurrencies, blockchain shows strong potential in areas such as decentralized identity management, credit scoring, financial services, and broader banking applications [10].

2.3 Benefits of Blockchain in the Financial Sector

2.3.1 Instant settlements and reduced risk

Blockchain enables near real-time transaction processing, completing transfers within seconds instead of days as in conventional systems. By removing the need for multiple layers of verification in middle-office and back-office operations, blockchain minimizes operational delays and reduces the risk of settlement failures [11].

2.3.2 Better financial products and services

The use of smart contract-based crowdfunding ensures transparency while reducing transaction costs, offering new and innovative methods of raising capital [12]. Similarly, community-based savings and lending models, such as rotating money circles, can be strengthened through blockchain by improving trust and accountability among participants. Moreover, individuals can extend their reach beyond immediate communities to raise funds globally, overcoming traditional barriers associated with trust [13].

2.3.3 Improved performance of the contracts

Smart contracts accelerate transaction completion by automatically enforcing business rules. This is particularly advantageous for complex asset transactions, where automation reduces the need for manual intervention. However, businesses must remain mindful of strict regulatory compliance, particularly when transactions extend across multiple jurisdictions [14], [15].

2.3.4 Transparency

All monetary flows and transactions recorded on the blockchain are immutable and auditable, ensuring a high level of transparency across the network. However, complete disclosure of every data point is neither practical nor desirable. To balance transparency with privacy, advanced cryptographic solutions have been implemented. Examples include zero-knowledge proofs, which allow parties to verify necessary details without exposing sensitive data, and Enigma's secret contracts, which encrypt smart contract information for select participants. Confidential transactions, which encrypt transaction values while maintaining verifiability, further enhance privacy in blockchain ecosystems [16], [17].

2.3.5 Reduced fraud by using self-sovereign identity

Blockchain, when combined with self-sovereign identity (SSI) solutions, strengthens defenses against fraud, denial-of-service (DoS) attacks, and hacking attempts. A blockchain-enabled digital identity not only reduces risks of duplication and impersonation but also grants individuals greater control over their credentials compared to traditional identifiers, such as government-issued IDs. The adoption of SSI in financial services could significantly decrease disputes, errors, and fraudulent activities [18].

2.4 Drawbacks of Blockchain

Despite its transformative potential, blockchain faces significant limitations. Scalability remains a concern, as transaction throughput is still lower than traditional payment systems. Additionally, the energy demands of certain consensus mechanisms, such as Proof of Work, raise environmental sustainability issues. Another challenge is the concentration of mining power within a few large pools, which compromises decentralization.

Regulatory gaps also create vulnerabilities, as blockchain can be exploited for illicit activities such as money laundering when identity verification is weak. Security breaches and large-scale thefts from centralized cryptocurrency exchanges highlight persistent risks [19]. Moreover, the lightly regulated nature of cryptocurrency markets has led to instances of manipulation, fraudulent initial coin offerings (ICOs), and questionable practices in stablecoin ecosystems. For instance, nearly half of Bitcoin transactions are associated with Tether, a "stablecoin" claimed to be backed by U.S. dollars, yet its reserves have never been fully audited, raising concerns about potential misuse and suspicious activities [20].

2.5 Potential Applications of Blockchain in the Financial Sector

2.5.1 Digital fiat currency or cryptocurrency

Bitcoin and Ethereum are two very popular and widely accepted cryptocurrencies. Many online vendors and online payment applications accept digital payments in Bitcoin and investors and investment firms are investing in cryptocurrencies. Bitcoin has the potential to become the new world currency or even an intermediary for the new world currency, although its possibility is not foreseeable in the near future practically. But blockchain is set to disrupt the currencies of the world fundamentally, if not completely replace them [21]

2.5.2 ICO (initial coin offering)

Initial coin offering or initial currency offering is a type of funding by using cryptocurrencies. It can be public funding, like crowdfunding, or privately held funds for startups. A set quantity of cryptocurrency or "tokens" is sold to the investors or speculators, which can be exchanged for valuable cryptocurrencies like Bitcoin and Ethereum, or these tokens are realized in value when a set goal is met for the startup and the project launches successfully[22]. Many innovative projects and ideas are seeking ICOs for their initial funding. ICOs have a potential for truly innovative ideas to be implemented, and if done correctly, can disrupt many financial services [23], [24].

2.5.3 International market

Blockchain can fundamentally disrupt international money transfers. Banks and financial firms charge a fee of set percentage value to transfer funds across borders. With the help of blockchain, these fees can be eliminated, and the money can be directly transferred to anyone across the border [25], [26]. International banks require payments in gold while working with different fiat currencies. So instead of transferring gold now and then, they rely on third-party banks or firms to issue credits or contracts to the banks as payments. This payment can be done using smart contracts on the blockchain, and the need for the third firm can be eliminated, creating a trustless and robust system of contracts [27]. Even eliminating the gold transfers, as the contracts would be reflected across the member banks, and retain its true value throughout. Many big banks are forming a consortium to combat disruptive technology, reduce customer turnover, and reduce fees for providing essential services. With the help of blockchain, these banks are forming a private blockchain with the help of Hyperledger (a blockchain-based framework) and with the support of IBM-run Linux Foundation, to work with each other and protect their firms from technological disruption [28].

2.5.4 Blockchain in banking services

Know Your Customer (KYC) and Know Your Business (KYB) require many documents each time a customer or a business goes to a different financial firm or bank. Also, these documents are used to profile the data so that personalized services can be provided and future data points can be aggregated. Using blockchain to streamline the process can eliminate much of the paperwork for submitting documents every time a new account is created, and also the process instantly eliminates the wait for the approval of the documents. Credit scoring is another parameter that can be streamlined by using a common blockchain by banks and financial firms. All the firms participate in the same chain, and so the credit scoring of customers and businesses is transparent. Insurance claims are also ripe for disruption by blockchain [29]. Insurance claims management is a lengthy and complicated process involving many stakeholders and intermediaries participating to decide on the issuance of claims. Using blockchain, many of the intermediaries and stakeholders are eliminated, making the process fast and straightforward [3].

2.6 Research Methodology

Scope	Research problem	There are very few studies discussing how KYC in financial services (banks) is done using blockchain. Additionally, there are lack of studies explaining the transformation of the financial sector due to blockchain based on use cases.
	Research question	How KYC in finance services (banks) is done using blockchain
		Fintech use cases have been illustrated to understand deep about Fintech
		How the financial sector got transformed by the use of blockchain.

	Research objective	In this chapter, the author has discussed about blockchain and cryptocurrency. In addition, the author examines how KYC in financial services (banks) is done using blockchain. Furthermore, Fintech use cases have been illustrated to understand in-depth about fintech and how it has been transformed by the use of blockchain. This paper contributes to understanding the changes in the financial sector using this application.
Data Selection	Source	Science Direct
	Search term	Blockchain, financial sector, banks, KYC
	Process of screening	The abstract of selected papers was considered to eliminate the ineligible papers.
	Inclusion of studies	The papers with a focus on blockchain, financial sector, banks, KYC were considered for inclusion.
	Exclusion of studies	Grey papers, such as books, editorials, conference papers, etc., were excluded.
Data processing	Use case	KYC in finance services (banks) using blockchain was discussed on the basis of the use case of Corda.
Data reporting	Findings	Corda/R3 platform makes the KYC (Know Your Customer) service easier, reliable, and robust. The other side of blockchain is the negative thoughts arousing amongst the people and their governments related to Cryptocurrency. Its future in the long term remains to be seen, but at present, the above-listed use case is very fruitful with the help of blockchain, and it is one of the most optimistic technologies in the sector of fintech.
	Limitation	The study only discusses KYC, but the usage of blockchain in the financial sector in far more than this.
	Conclusion	Corda/R3 platform makes the KYC (Know Your Customer) service become easier, reliable, and robust.
	Implications for future research	The usage of blockchain in the financial sector will increase in future.

2.7 KYC in Finance Services (Banks) Using Blockchain

Corda, an open-source blockchain platform, enables direct transactions with enhanced privacy through the use of smart contracts. By reducing transaction and storage costs, Corda streamlines business processes across various sectors. R3 LLC, the enterprise blockchain company behind Corda, has established a collaborative environment of more than 300 firms developing distributed applications (CorDapps) for industries such as insurance, trade finance, banking, digital assets, and healthcare. Headquartered in New York City, R3 was founded in 2014 by David E. Rutter. Among its partners is Synechron, a New York–based IT and consulting firm specializing in financial services, including banking, capital markets, and insurance [30].

A blockchain-based KYC solution using Corda was first piloted globally in June 2018. The four-day trial successfully processed more than 300 KYC transactions across 19 countries. During the trial, participating banks could request permission to access a customer's KYC data. Customers were also able to modify their test data, which was instantly updated across all institutions with access rights. In total, 39 banks joined the trial, including ABN AMRO, Alfa Bank, Bank ABC, Deutsche Bank, BNP Paribas, ING, Natixis, U.S. Bank, Societe Generale, and Shinhan Bank, among others. Together, these institutions deployed and operated over 45 nodes on Microsoft Azure, showcasing the collaborative capabilities of Corda's distributed network.

The participating banks managed customer KYC information through a CorDapp designed by Synechron. This solution highlighted the potential of blockchain to reduce duplication, increase efficiency, and strengthen trust in KYC processes across the financial sector [31].

2.7.1 Case analysis

The analysis is done from the perspective of key features provided by the blockchain. The features simultaneously provide multiple benefits to both the users/customers and the banks.

2.7.2 Distributed ledger

This blockchain-based KYC utility system allows for the smooth identification and verification phase for the financial and banking sectors. That is because consumer data is actually collected and maintained in a distributed structure. KYC providers must share Client information with companies or organizations, or banks in order to obtain this data [32].

This blockchain KYC method also improves data security by requiring data access only after receiving confirmation or approval from the appropriate entity. This diminishes the chances of illegal access, giving customers or users greater control over their data.

2.7.3 Secure authentication process

A cryptographic verification aids financial organizations in swiftly authenticating the uniqueness of any entity. This is essential for data protection and preventing fraud. The growing demand for banks and other financial establishments to develop apps that allow users to conduct online transactions also poses new challenges. Flaws in security, bugs in applications, and theft of smart devices have created a need for a more secure decentralized solution that will specifically address the security concerns of all users [33].

The security suggested by R3's blockchain system significantly reduces the chances of fraud. Whereas a skilled hacker could be able to search for some confidential information if the computer is stolen. However, due to the blockchain's immutability, they will still not be able to alter the data [34].

2.7.4 Transparency

R3's KYC based on Corda's blockchain platform allows active real-time observation of everything ranging from opening of accounts to day-to-day transactions. Once linked with smart contracts that have a prearranged criterion to spot deceitful activity, the R3's Corda platform has the ability to alert banks of any mischief or suspicious activity [35].

The blockchain's immutability aspect helps in creating healthy trust between concerned entities involved in the process of KYC. The competence to have faith in data stored on a KYC blockchain software solution eliminates the requirement for cross-checking or verifying, or authentication mechanisms by secondary third-party companies. Also, a distributed ledger system makes the process of reporting and communication more efficient, which saves a lot of time and resources. As clients may quickly obtain credible and accurate data, suspicious procedures and fraud can be identified in less time [36].

2.7.5 Inferences

Blockchain is gaining attention as a future technology. It is bringing noticeable changes in the fintech sector. Related to this, we first provide an overview of the potential of blockchain and then how it brings a noteworthy change in the Fintech sector. Subsequently, we discussed some key issues that must be taken into consideration while developing any banking services with the use of blockchain.

Blockchain developers trust that these use cases are going to become conventional in the Fintech Sector in the upcoming years. We have shown how Corda/R3 platform makes the KYC (Know Your Customer) service easier, reliable, and robust. The other side of blockchain is the negative thoughts arousing amongst the people and their governments related to cryptocurrency. Its long-term future remains to be seen, but at present, the above-listed use case is highly effective due to the use of blockchain, and it is one of the most optimistic technologies in the fintech sector.

2.8 Implication for Future Research

While conducting the literature review, we have observed that lots of research has been done on the usage of blockchain technology and its effects in the financial sector, and the popular research is application-focused. And it is also evident that there are no appropriate rules and regulations available to govern the use of blockchain applications as a substitute for conventional financial transactions [37]. The government and relevant sectors should frame policies to enable the public to benefit from blockchain and strictly stop the unlawful usage of blockchain in money laundering, terrorist financing, and even wealth control events [38]. Investors still have preferences for the regulations which clearly define the type and scope of investments. Nonetheless, it looks as if they are in favor of the decentralized and independent transactions that this technology facilitates. We have identified a few important areas that need more investigation if blockchain technology in finance is to continue to succeed. There is no doubt that blockchain is an extremely competitive and "imaginative" technology that has the potential to transform our society's financial and commercial infrastructure in the future. To stay competitive, financial services should adopt a long-term perspective and investigate the application of blockchain technology. In the future, blockchain will play an important role, managing various activities in the finance sector.

References

[1] Kamboj, N., & Sharma, M. (2023). Analytical Study of Fin-Tech in Banking: A Utility Model. Fintech and Cryptocurrency, 157-172.

[2] Hassija, V., Bansal, G., Chamola, V., Kumar, N., &Guizani, M. (2020). Secure lending: Blockchain and prospect theory-based decentralized credit scoring model. IEEE Transactions on Network Science and Engineering, 7(4), 2566-2575.

[3] Chung, S. (2016). Legal issues for the introduction of distributed ledger based on blockchain technology-focused on the financial industry. Korea Financial Law Association, 13(2), 107-138.
[4] Xu, M., Chen, X., & Kou, G. (2019). A systematic review of blockchain. Financial innovation, 5(1), 1-14.
[5] FossoWamba, S., Kala Kamdjoug, J. R., EpieBawack, R., & Keogh, J. G. (2020). Bitcoin, Blockchain and Fintech: a systematic review and case studies in the supply chain. Production Planning & Control, 31(2-3), 115-142.
[6] Dorfleitner, G., & Braun, D. (2019). Fintech, digitalization and blockchain: possible applications for green finance. The rise of green finance in Europe: opportunities and challenges for issuers, investors and marketplaces, 207-237.
[7] Fanning, K., & Centers, D. P. (2016). Blockchain and its coming impact on financial services. Journal of Corporate Accounting & Finance, 27(5), 53-57.
[8] Akanfe, O., Lawong, D., & Rao, H. R. (2024). Blockchain technology and privacy regulation: Reviewing frictions and synthesizing opportunities. International Journal of Information Management, 76, 102753.
[9] Warmke, C. (2024). What is bitcoin. Inquiry, 67(1), 25-67.
[10] Kayani, U., & Hasan, F. (2024). Unveiling Cryptocurrency Impact on Financial Markets and Traditional Banking Systems: Lessons for Sustainable Blockchain and Interdisciplinary Collaborations. Journal of Risk and Financial Management, 17(2), 58.
[11] Trivedi, S., Choudhary, V., & Kamboj, N. (2023). AI and Blockchain for smart contract management in Digital world of IoT. In International Applied Social Sciences Congress (pp. 63-63).
[12] Choudhary, V., Kamboj, N., & Trivedi, S. (2023). Scoping Review of Literature on the Application of Blockchain in Finance. Perspectives on Blockchain Technology and Responsible Investing, 1-28.
[13] Zachariadis, M., Hileman, G., & Scott, S. V. (2019). Governance and control in distributed ledgers: Understanding the challenges facing blockchain technology in financial services. Information and Organization, 29(2), 105-117.
[14] Niranjanamurthy, M., Nithya, B. N., &Jagannatha, S. J. C. C. (2019). Analysis of Blockchain technology: pros, cons and SWOT. Cluster Computing, 22(6), 14743-14757.
[15] Martens, D., Tuyll van Serooskerken, A. V., &Steenhagen, M. (2017). Exploring the potential of blockchain for KYC. Journal of Digital Banking, 2(2), 123-131.

[16] Werth, O., Schwarzbach, C., Rodríguez Cardona, D., Breitner, M. H., & Graf von der Schulenburg, J. M. (2020). Influencing factors for the digital transformation in the financial services sector. Zeitschriftfür die gesamteVersicherungswissenschaft, 109(2), 155-179.

[17] Hughes, A., Park, A., Kietzmann, J., & Archer-Brown, C. (2019). Beyond Bitcoin: What blockchain and distributed ledger technologies mean for firms. Business Horizons, 62(3), 273-281.

[18] Jena, S. K., Barik, R. C., &Priyadarshini, R. (2024). A systematic state-of-art review on digital identity challenges with solutions using conjugation of IOT and blockchain in healthcare. Internet of Things, 101111.

[19] Ali, O., Krsteska, K., Said, D., &Momin, M. (2023). Advanced technologies enabled human resources functions: Benefits, challenges, and functionalities: A systematic review. Cogent Business & Management, 10(2), 2216430.

[20] Huberman, G., Leshno, J. D., &Moallemi, C. (2021). Monopoly without a monopolist: An economic analysis of the bitcoin payment system. The Review of Economic Studies, 88(6), 3011-3040.

[21] Alahmad, M., Alfouderi, A. D. E. L., Alonaizi, A. H. M. A. D., & Aldhamen, M. (2023). Comparison Study of the Top 5 Leading Cryptocurrencies based on General Consensus Protocol: Bitcoin, Ethereum, Tether, XRP and Bitcoin Cash. WSEAS Transactions on Computer Research, 11, 23-32.

[22] Kewell, B., Adams, R., & Parry, G. (2017). Blockchain for good?. Strategic Change, 26(5), 429-437.

[23] Chen, Y. (2018). Blockchain tokens and the potential democratization of entrepreneurship and innovation. Business horizons, 61(4), 567-575.

[24] Vincent, O., & Evans, O. (2019). Can cryptocurrency, mobile phones, and internet herald sustainable financial sector development in emerging markets?. Journal of Transnational Management, 24(3), 259-279.

[25] Al-Wreikat, A., Almasarwah, A., & Al-Sheyab, O. (2024). Blockchain technology, cryptocurrencies and transforming accounting fees. International Journal of Electronic Business, 19(1), 95-122.

[26] Martino, P. (2019). Blockchain technology: Challenges and opportunities for banks. International Journal of Financial Innovation in Banking, 2(4), 314-333.

[27] Parra Moyano, J., & Ross, O. (2017). KYC optimization using distributed ledger technology. Business & Information Systems Engineering, 59(6), 411-423.

[28] Hawlitschek, F., Notheisen, B., &Teubner, T. (2018). The limits of trust-free systems: A literature review on blockchain technology and trust

in the sharing economy. Electronic commerce research and applications, 29, 50-63.

[29] Wei, W. C. (2018). The impact of Tether grants on Bitcoin. Economics Letters, 171, 19-22.

[30] Yadav, A. K., &Bajpai, R. K. (2020). KYC optimization using blockchain smart contract technology. Int J Innov Res ApplSciEng (IJIRASE), 4(3), 669-674.

[31] Richard, G. B, The Corda Platform: An Introduction. https://www.corda.net/content/corda-platform-whitepaper.pdf , May, 2018.

[32] Hassani, H., Huang, X., & Silva, E. (2018). Banking with blockchain-ed big data. Journal of Management Analytics, 5(4), 256-275.

[33] Wang, H., Ma, S., Dai, H. N., Imran, M., & Wang, T. (2020). Blockchain-based data privacy management with nudge theory in open banking. Future Generation Computer Systems, 110, 812-823.

[34] Kirkby, R. (2018). Cryptocurrencies and digital fiat currencies. Australian Economic Review, 51(4), 527-539.

[35] Diniz, E. H., Cernev, A. K., Rodrigues, D. A., &Daneluzzi, F. (2021). Solidarity cryptocurrencies as digital community platforms. Information Technology for Development, 27(3), 524-538.

[36] Zhang, L., Xie, Y., Zheng, Y., Xue, W., Zheng, X., & Xu, X. (2020). The challenges and countermeasures of blockchain in finance and economics. Systems Research and Behavioral Science, 37(4), 691-698.

[37] Mangano, C., Luongo, F., Migliario, M., Mortellaro, C., & Mangano, F. G. (2018). Combining intraoral scans, cone beam computed tomography and face scans: the virtual patient. Journal of Craniofacial Surgery, 29(8), 2241-2246.

[38] Nguyen, P. K., Rhee, J. W., & Wu, J. C. (2016). Adult stem cell therapy and heart failure, 2000 to 2016: a systematic review. JAMA cardiology, 1(7), 831-841.

3

Smart Persuasion: The Influence of AI Nudges on Retirement Preparedness

Geetika[1], Kalani, M.[2] and Srivasatav, S.[3]

[1]School of Management & Commerce, LPU, India
[2]Mittal Business School, LPU, India
[3]Amity College of Commerce & Finance, Amity University, India

Email: geetika18dec@gmail.com; monika.kalani@lpu.co.in; ssrivastav@gn.amity.edu

Abstract

The rising impact of digital technologies on financial behavior has led to a rise in the use of artificial intelligence (AI) powered nudging strategies in influencing people's retirement planning strategies. This chapter explores the use of AI-based personalization and behavioral science by online platforms to gently help people become more prepared for retirement. In order to assess how well they work to encourage saving behaviors, investment choices, and long-term financial planning, it looks at a variety of digital nudging techniques, such as default settings, timely reminders, visual cues, and algorithmic recommendations. The chapter also discusses how ethics affects these methods. Additional focus is given to matters of user autonomy, transparency, and looking after those groups that need extra help. Results are based on studies that bring together different fields of investigation. All disciplines considered are here, such as financial planning, behavioral economics, and human-computer interaction. The chapter reviews in detail the changes "smart persuasion" is bringing to persuasion how people decide to retire. The last part includes suggestions for good design that AI nudging helps people become more informed, fair, and ready for what lies ahead.

 DOI: 10.1201/9788743810766-3

3.1 Introduction

The end of official employment and the start of a new chapter in one's identity, finances, and lifestyle are both significant life transitions that occur with retirement. Retirement, formerly thought of as a reward for years of hard work, is becoming more complicated because of factors like changing labor market dynamics, rising life expectancy, and evolving work and savings patterns. Retirement is no longer a single event or a set age, but rather a process that frequently includes unretirement, bridging employment, or staggered exits from the workforce.

When people or families feel ready and able to retire from active work, we say they have retirement preparedness. As people live longer and old pension plans change, workers have to take greater responsibility for having a pleasant retirement. Because of this change, early planning is now seen as important for lifestyle, social ties, health, and finances. Many people are unable to secure a solid retirement because they do not know much about finances, do not save enough, and incorrectly guess what their expenses and income will be once retired. All people concerned with retirement, such as politicians, financial professionals, and individuals, must understand what influences retirement planning opportunities to achieve retirement readiness and what they entail. Here, we establish the basics needed for exploring the ways to help different groups get ready for retirement.

When financial institutions use psychological ideas, personalized proofs, and technology to influence where people choose to invest, it is known as "smart persuasion" in investment. Some of the features include automatic portfolio management through app. The platform keeps you informed with messages and subtle reminders to help encourage diversification, long-term investing, and avoiding unwise decisions when investing with your emotions. Smart persuasion has become a powerful method for changing the way investors act in today's financial world. The most powerful methods in smart persuasion are behavioral economics, data analytics, and persuasive technologies. It relies on special, relevant messages and reminders to guide people toward better investment choices. Because of AI, machine learning, and real-time information, smart persuasion matches suggestions and messages to what an investor desires, their willingness to take risks, and their typical biases, differently from traditional marketing or financial advice.

As the world's population ages and life expectancy increases, people, governments, and financial institutions are becoming increasingly concerned about making sure people are well prepared for retirement. Behavioral biases, including present bias, inertia, and over-optimism, frequently prevent people from making the best long-term financial decisions, even if saving for retirement is widely acknowledged to be necessary. With new advances in artificial intelligence (AI), it has become possible to develop custom digital methods that gently change behavior. A way to become better at managing money and retirement is to make use of AI-driven "nudges" that prompt people to help them decide what's best without reducing their personal choices. AI nudges better influence behavior than traditional interventions because messages, schedules, and content are customized with machine learning, the way each user uses the system. For example, these technologies help users sign up for pensions, increase their savings for retirement, or revise their portfolio to stay on track with future goals. Despite how powerful AI nudges can be, there are worries about the impact of their use on retirement benefits, on their effectiveness for everyone, and about ethical concerns.

New strategies for preparation and planning are required in light of this changing environment. People have to deal with financial risks like inflation, healthcare expenditures, and the sustainability of their income. Retirees need to discover new sources of structure, connection, and purpose on a psychological and social level. Effective retirement planning is now a multifaceted task that extends beyond savings objectives and financial estimates. People's retirement planning and experiences are changing as a result of the combination of digital technology and behavioral tools, especially those driven by artificial intelligence (AI). These tools not only make financial information more accessible, but they also have a subtle but significant impact on decision-making.

As financial tasks move online, artificial intelligence has created entirely new and exciting options for retirement saving and investing. Adjusting how users behave to help them make better financial choices, driven by AI, has become very popular these days. AI-driven suggestions for retirement differ from regular methods because they are automatic and use behavioral information to direct people's decisions [1, 2].

Based on the ideas of behavioral economics, digital nudges exploit cognitive biases and heuristics to assist users in overcoming common obstacles to long-term planning and saving, including information overload, present bias, and inertia [3]. According to Brynjolfsson et al [4], artificial intelligence (AI) improves these interventions by allowing real-time customization and adjusting nudges to user behavior, preferences, and context. To encourage better financial practices and retirement readiness, for instance, internet platforms now use algorithmic recommendations, visual cues, defaults, and reminders [5].

Applying AI nudging is promising, although it raises some serious ethical problems. Since people might be harmed by poor or unclear decisions made by algorithms, users need to have enough control and awareness to avoid being manipulated in their actions [6]. Agarwal et el [7] note that these challenges are most important in retirement plans because the decisions are difficult, long-lasting, and frequently mastered by people who usually do not know much about finance.

This chapter begins with a look at how websites are now widely used to provide advice on finances and how convenient AI enables these platforms to handle user interactions automatically. Since common problems like present bias, inertia, or too much information tend to block long-term planning in established settings, the subject considers digital nudging and how to use it. This chapter analyses how default choices, prompt notifications, attractive designs, and special recommendations influence investments, savings habits, and retirement readiness using "smart persuasion" methods. In addition, the chapter discusses how AI nudges could create ethical problems by concentrating on transparency, what people are able to do, and their potential to be deceived. As these methods proliferate, particularly among communities that are financially disadvantaged or lack digital literacy, it is critical to strike a balance between efficacy, equity, and user confidence.

3.2 AI-Driven Smart Innovations in Retirement Preparedness

One of the assumptions is that people who are retired or have recently retired are unlikely to have extensive experience with artificial intelligence (AI). The majority of cutting-edge technologies are learned about in the workplace, or at the very least, as work-related auxiliary tools. Consider smart TVs, Alexa, Google, and so forth to see that this is not always the case. Nevertheless, individuals who are retired or pre-retired still lag far behind those in employment who have a more thorough and immersed experience with AI. Pre-retirees and retirees could benefit immensely from artificial intelligence's ability to help them manage their financial future. AI tools and platforms can offer retirees automated financial management solutions, tailored advice, and insightful information thanks to technological breakthroughs. Personalized retirement plans, retirement income management, and assisting seniors in making well-informed investment choices are just a few of the ways. AI may assist retirees in managing their financial future by:

- Lowering the fees associated with retirement planning.
- Offering financial insights in real time (planning and forecasting) [8].

AI painting dramatically increased risk tolerance, but it also unpredictably made retirement goals less clear. It is interesting to note that AI painting helped to convert higher risk tolerance into clearer retirement goals [9].

3.2.1 AI-powered personalization and behavioral science through online platforms for retirement planning

A major concern now is individual retirement readiness as the world's population ages and traditional pension systems are under increasing pressure. Due to inertia, complexity, and conflicting short-term priorities, many people are still ill-prepared for retirement, even though the need for early financial planning is well acknowledged. To help people achieve better retirement outcomes, online platforms are increasingly using behavioral science and artificial intelligence (AI). Strong chances to overcome cognitive biases, customize experiences, and advance long-term financial well-being are presented by these technologies.

AI techniques, especially machine learning algorithms, can evaluate large datasets and customize retirement-related tools, materials, and suggestions for each user. In order to offer highly relevant advice, these systems are able to deduce users' life stages, income levels, spending habits, and saving tendencies. For example, AI-powered robo-advisors are used by platforms such as Betterment and Fidelity to provide consumers with individualized investment plans according to their risk tolerance and retirement objectives [10]. In addition to offering investment advice, AI may personalize communication tactics. A user in their 30s might be gently reminded of the advantages of compounding, while a user who is getting close to retirement might be presented with customized information regarding annuity possibilities or withdrawal techniques. Messages can be reframed through personalization to better align with each user's values and objectives, which has been demonstrated to boost engagement [11].

Behavioral research identifies a number of emotional and cognitive obstacles to retirement savings, such as decision fatigue, loss aversion, and present bias [12]. To solve these issues, online platforms can include behavioral interventions. As an illustration:

- By setting default contribution rates or encouraging users to boost their donations during periods of high motivation (such as following a pay increase), platforms can promote saving.
- Setting objectives and visualizing them: Planning behavior has been demonstrated to be enhanced by interactive tools that assist users in defining and visualizing their retirement goals [13].

- Prompts and reminders in real time: Inertia and forgetfulness can be fought using tailored nudges that are sent at the appropriate moment and via chosen channels [14].

3.2.2 Digital nudging for retirement readiness: Methods and uses

Insufficient retirement funds continue to be a major issue on a global scale, as many people underestimate their future financial requirements or neglect to participate in long-term planning. Digital nudging presents a viable way to enhance retirement outcomes through behavioral interventions integrated into digital interfaces. Digital platforms can apply behavioral science ideas to help users save more money while preserving their freedom of choice. Four important digital nudging strategies – default settings, timely reminders, visual signals, and algorithmic recommendations are discussed as follows:

3.2.2.1 Default setting

Pre-selected settings known as defaults are in place unless the user specifically modifies them. Automatic enrollment in retirement or pension plans is one of the most effective nudges for saving for retirement. Many people choose not to enroll in such schemes because they are lazy, put things off, or think they are too complicated [15]. Platforms can significantly boost employee participation and accumulation by automatically enrolling workers in retirement savings plans with a predetermined minimum contribution rate. Users are frequently automatically enrolled in age-appropriate asset allocations or target retirement funds by online retirement tools and robo-advisors.

Auto-escalation features, like those in the Save More Tomorrow program, gradually raise contribution rates over time unless consumers choose to opt out [12].

3.2.2.2 Timely reminders

Notifications known as timely reminders serve as timely prompts for users to act.

Present prejudice or a lack of urgency because many people to put off retirement planning. Delivered on time, such as around birthdays, tax return dates, or paydays, prompts might motivate users to take financial actions that are focused on the future. Apps for retirement planning may encourage users to reassess their savings targets by sending push notifications. Users may reconsider their retirement plan in response to email or SMS reminders during financial milestones (such as turning 30 or 40). Increased contributions to pensions and other long-term accounts have been linked to reminder nudges via digital tools [16].

3.2.2.3 Visual cues

Color-coded indications, progress bars, graphs, and pictures are examples of visual cues that help make abstract objectives more concrete. Since retirement is a long-term objective, it is emotionally and cognitively abstract. Visual signals make future results more tangible and interesting, which helps close this gap. Users can see progress with dashboards that display future income estimates or "retirement readiness" rankings. Age-progression technologies that provide a picture of the user's "future self" strengthen their emotional bond with long-term objectives. Individuals who were given digitally aged photos of themselves were more likely to save more for retirement. Additionally, visual goal-tracking features have been demonstrated to increase savings platform engagement [13, 17].

3.2.2.4 Algorithmic recommendations

These are rules-based or AI-based recommendations that customize financial guidance according to user preferences, data, and behavior. Retirement planning is a complicated process that involves choosing investment options, withdrawal plans, and contribution rates. Decision quality can be enhanced, and cognitive load can be decreased with personalized digital assistance.

Robo-advisors, such as Wealth front or Betterment, provide individualized retirement plans through the use of algorithms. Apps can suggest portfolio adjustments depending on market conditions and life stage, or they can suggest increasing savings when disposable money is recognized. Simplified and customized options increase the likelihood that people will interact with and take action on them. The possibility that users will heed financial advice is also increased by algorithmic personalization [18, 19].

By using default settings, reminders, visual signals, and algorithmic recommendations, digital nudging provides a scalable and economical way to increase retirement readiness. With more people interacting with financial services online, these nudges can help bridge the retirement savings gap while honoring personal autonomy thanks to their careful design.

3.3 Ethical Implications of Digital Nudging in Retirement Preparedness

When it comes to retirement planning, digital nudging can help improve long-term results, but it also runs the danger of violating autonomy, openness, and equity. Creating nudges that are both successful and considerate of users' rights and circumstances is a difficult task. Continuous assessment, stakeholder input, and a dedication to transparency are necessary for responsible design.

3.3.1 Self-reliance and informed consent

The basic ethical presumption is that any nudge intervention needs to be straightforward to avoid, like a mouse click. For an intervention mechanism to be considered a nudge, it must maintain the person's freedom of choice, which is defined as the lack of hindrances, restrictions, or hurdles [20, 21]. A person has freedom of choice if he/she lacks constraints on the reasoned selection and performance of one more item on an action menu. Real freedom of choice, in accordance with this "opportunity concept" can only exist if people are able to choose "reasonable" decisions and, concurrently, their possibilities for choosing are not constrained by outside parties [22]. Digital nudges, particularly algorithmic recommendations and defaults, can quietly affect choices without users' full knowledge. Informed consent and autonomy are ethical issues brought up by this. Do people actually make well-informed decisions when they are pressured to default on retirement contributions or investment strategies? The agency may be undermined if users follow a default (like auto-enrollment in a pension plan) without fully comprehending the consequences [23].

Compared to analog decision environments, consumers in digital contexts are even less conscious of being prodded. In digital environments, the choice architect bears an even greater obligation to avoid taking advantage of this restricted attention and option overload. Another noteworthy feature of digital nudges is their ease of use and almost free cost [24]. As a result, choice architects may feel pressured to employ these tools excessively. Theoretically, digital choice designers can alter every aspect of a digital artifact, such as a website or app, giving them even more freedom.

Particular attention should be paid to the duty of digital choice designers to create nudge interventions in a way that is non-prohibitive, non-exploitative, and preserves choice. In order to maximize people's freedom of choice, new digital technologies will be employed. To achieve this highest level of autonomy, people ought to have the ability to choose the kind, format, and frequency of the nudge interventions they encounter. Ignoring a nudge is only an attempt once because it is never made again. A compelling pro-self or pro-social argument must be made in order to support the nudge's ethical justification if it is made repeatedly. The required degree of effort for dismissing a digital nudge can be quantified [25].

3.3.2 Comparing libertarianism with paternalism

The reason libertarian paternalism is referred to as "libertarian" is that nudges may not impede the freedom of choice, and "paternalist" since the said interventions are "pro-self" in the sense that they seek to influence people's behavior in ways that advance their own wellbeing. Paternalism raises a number of ethical and political issues; labelling the use of nudges as "libertarian" is meant to set them apart from other types of paternalism and provide a fresh defence for their usage [26].

The concept of "libertarian paternalism" interventions that direct decisions without limiting freedom, guides a lot of digital nudging techniques. However, when it comes to retirement planning, this balance may lean more toward paternalism, particularly when people lack financial literacy or are uninterested. Personal beliefs or immediate needs may still clash with justified paternalism (such as encouraging people to save more) [27].

3.3.3 Openness and responsibility

Nudging is also opposed on the grounds that it could impose a "lack of transparency by clouding the availability of options accessible at the moment of the decision and thereby endanger informed and free choice" [28]. Users may find it challenging to comprehend how advice is generated or how their data is used when using algorithmic suggestions for retirement planning due to their lack of openness. Black-box algorithms raise concerns since they could be biased or motivated by business interests (e.g., favoring particular financial goods) [29]. Selecting a "digital choice architect" should be done with care. These factors will encompass algorithmic ethics as well as guaranteeing the interpretability of the (machine learning) model and its results [30, 31]. Two strategies are evident to guarantee token-transparency for nudgees:

1. To restrict the algorithmic intricacy of the bringing nudging processes down to a level that the average person can understand, or
2. using expert methods to guarantee the ethical justification, like having external auditors evaluate the code as nudging-compliant [32] or collaborating in interdisciplinary partnerships to guarantee the ethical compliance of one's algorithmic endeavours [33,34].

Additionally, digital nudges must be transparent to nudgees. When there is complete type-transparency in a digital setting, nudgees can quickly identify when and where they are being nudged. Intervention strategies that meet the criteria for being considered nudges must go beyond a particular threshold of goal-setting and (human) deliberation. A nudge, then, is meant to encourage more than just moving on to the next page or using a website as usual. To be considered a nudge, interventions using any type of user interface element must have a deliberate decision architect's objective setting [25].

3.3.4 Fairness and availability

Fairness and inclusion concerns are raised by digital nudges, which presume a degree of digital knowledge and technological access that may not be universal, especially among older or lower-income groups. IT-savvy consumers may gain from nudging, but others may be left out or at a disadvantage [35]. Knowing what people want and developing one-size-fits-all interventions that work for a range of potentially tailored nudgees are challenges that digital settings face. There is widespread support for nudges, although opinions vary depending on the intervention strategy used [36, 37]. Digital tools for user research and feedback will be employed to gather information about nudgees' consent. These methods also make it easier to understand the intended target population for the intervention by recording social and societal preferences. In order for the nudging intervention to be pre-evaluated before being presented to the public, it will be incorporated into pre-tests and pre-surveys [25].

3.3.5 Excessive dependence and behavioral lock-in

Although digital nudges are intended to make difficult decisions easier, behavioral lock-in may result from this simplification. This happens when people choose default settings, like a fixed contribution rate or investing strategy, then neglect to review or revise them over time in relation to retirement readiness. Studies reveal that even when personal circumstances change, many users hardly ever move from defaults, despite the fact that they can boost initial participation [38]. A fictitious sense of security could be produced by this inactivity. Because they are "doing something" (i.e., participating in a plan), users may think their retirement planning is sufficient even if their contributions or portfolio allocations are not ideal [3]. Moreover, over-reliance on algorithmic guidance can be exacerbated by its use, particularly when users are unaware of the assumptions or limitations of these systems. For instance, suggestions from robo-advisors are frequently based on condensed questionnaires that do not fully account for individuals' financial circumstances. There are also worries about behavioral lock-in lowering vital engagement. Proactive learning and adaptation, which are crucial for long-term financial planning, can be discouraged by the same factors that make digital technologies useful. To reduce these risks, it is therefore crucial to implement adjustable defaults and periodic reassessment procedures.

Users may become inactive once digital nudges (such as automatic contributions) have established behavior, presuming their retirement needs are being satisfied. Should the initial parameters have been less than ideal or not reviewed, this behavioral lock-in could be harmful [39].

Choice architects must incorporate ethical considerations into their digital nudges' conception and design stages from the outset to prevent unethical nudges (ex-ante evaluation). In terms of digital policies, rules pertaining to digital nudging could offset the growing ability of (digital) choice architects to intervene (for example, through machine learning). At the same time, sufficient latitude will be allowed to investigate and test new digital nudge interventions, given the obvious benefits of digital interventions for both public and individual welfare. To fully justify their use, nudges must be evaluated against potential alternatives (such as education, boosting, or traditional paternalistic measures) based on a number of criteria. These include their general effects on autonomy and their transparency, which ensures that the opt-out condition can be chosen and allows society to contest their use [26].

3.4 Smart Persuasion and Retirement Decision-Making

The term "smart persuasion" describes the application of behavioral economics, artificial intelligence (AI), and data-driven customisation to sway consumers' decisions in digital settings. In contrast to conventional nudging, which depends on generic heuristics or static defaults, smart persuasion dynamically adjusts to each person's unique preferences, vulnerabilities, and behavior. This has revolutionary ramifications for retirement planning, including how individuals choose investment portfolios, set savings targets, and handle long-term financial risks.

3.4.1 Targeting behavior and hyper-personalization

Browser history, a record of financial transactions, and data on personal attributes are all included in large datasets. Profiles are typically used by intelligent persuasion systems to set up default decisions about funds, advice on stock purchases, and updates. To present the best opinion, financial platforms check accounts for updated contribution amounts or rebalance accounts using learning algorithms. They can also send text alerts, messages on your screen, or even use gamification to motivate users. In fact, robo-advisors are now commonly used to Betterment and Wealthfront employ artificial intelligence (AI) to suggest retirement investing plans according to consumers' age, financial objectives, and risk tolerance. Recommendations are constantly modified by these platforms in response to user feedback and market performance. By taking advantage of cognitive biases (such as present bias and optimism bias) in ways that users are not completely aware of, customization may influence behavior even though it can increase relevance [40].

3.4.2 The power of algorithms and over-reliance

A type of "algorithmic authority" arises when consumers come to trust automated systems more and more, viewing digital tools as superior or objective decision-makers. When it comes to retirement planning, where many people feel overwhelmed or inexperienced, this is especially powerful. User disengagement or blind faith in the system could result from people eventually ceasing to challenge the advice they get from financial apps or consultants [41].

3.4.3 Architecture of choice and persuasive design

In order to influence people at times when they are emotionally or cognitively vulnerable, smart persuasion strategies increasingly depend on real-time adaptation. When a user is feeling well, a retirement app might, for instance, congratulate them on increasing their savings and then encourage them to do so again. Such scheduling may boost efficacy, but it also calls into question fairness, manipulation, and consent [42].

A major shift in the way retirement decisions are made is represented by smart persuasion. Although these systems can facilitate better financial planning by fusing data-driven customisation with behavioral insights, they also present new hazards in terms of autonomy, openness, and excessive dependence on opaque algorithms. Persuasion must be supportive rather than forceful, and ethical retirement technology must balance helpful nudging with excessive influence.

3.5 Ideas for Ethical AI Development in Retirement

The following design concepts ought to be incorporated into financial technology to guarantee that AI-powered nudging encourages informed, equitable, and future-ready retirement decisions:

3.5.1 Transparency and explainability

Algorithms should give concise, understandable explanations of the assumptions that underlie their recommendations and how they are produced. Transparent design increases user confidence and empowers them to make more educated choices [43].

3.5.2 User customization and autonomy

Tools should provide users with a range of alternatives so they can modify their long-term objectives, risk profiles, and contribution rates. Choice stays relevant when "hard nudges" that force users down inflexible paths are avoided [44].

3.5.3 Mechanisms for periodic reassessment

Systems ought to encourage users to periodically revisit and amend their choices, particularly in the event of significant life or financial changes. By doing this, behavioral lock-in is resisted, and long-term flexibility is promoted.

3.5.4 Bias mitigation

Developers need to check algorithms for behavioral or demographic biases that could penalize specific user groups, especially as they relate to age, poverty, or digital literacy [45].

3.5.5 Inclusive design

Platforms should be tested with a variety of users to guarantee accessibility and cultural relevance. This is known as inclusive design. Multiple languages and interfaces should be supported, and the design should take into account different degrees of digital literacy.

3.5.6 Using behavioral science ethically

Using behavioral science ethically means that nudges should empower and educate people instead of trying to control them. Instead of taking advantage of biases, design complies with ethical best practices by using behavioral insights to enhance goal-setting and reflective thinking [46].

3.5.7 Data privacy and minimalism

Platforms should follow the guidelines for data minimization, gathering only the data required for personalization and ensuring that privacy regulations are clear and easy to understand [47].

3.5.8 Governance and regulatory oversight

To assess whether digital nudging platforms adhere to moral principles, particularly when it comes to retirement security – a matter of public interest, independent audits and compliance guidelines ought to be established.

3.6 Conclusion

Retirement is no longer only a stopping point in a person's employment because the process is often dynamic and takes time. Creative solutions are becoming more and more important, and options for planning retirement in a way that changes as life changes. Using advances in technology, especially those that are supported by behavioral economics and artificial intelligence. AI has changed things in a way that empowers people with fresh tools for managing their health, finances, and everyday habits may be affected by retirement. Out of these techniques, AI digital nudging especially stands out. It may be a valuable way to provide individuals with individual care. Help is available over the internet to work through obstacles in the mind, just like present bias and inertia. For example, digital nudging relies on pre-chosen default settings. We use reminders, visible signs, and recommendations from our algorithm to support people. It has been shown to make investing and saving much easier and more comfortable. As long as the software is suited to specific tasks, at the same time, making extensive use of these techniques. It also makes us think about serious moral issues. When helping digitally disadvantaged populations, it is especially important to consider how user needs should be supported. They must keep to autonomy, transparency, and justice to protect confidence and maintain equal results. Being duped into signing agreements, being trapped by our bad habits, and being exploited in secret and consistent tricks algorithms can bring up ethical problems that keep society unsafe, so they should be handled by rules as needed, consisting of monitoring, participatory review procedures, and responsible design. AI-enabled planning is easier, and nudges can boost people's preparation for retirement. They should line up in terms of behavior, but using them takes a robust support framework that values user rights and accommodates many different requirements in the nation's most populous age groups. How digital nudging can help us improve in making retirement plans can result in more unequal treatment and outcomes that were not predicted earlier. Success depends on whether it can maintain quality and honesty. Interdisciplinary teamwork among engineers, legislators, ethicists, and end users will be very important to ensure everyone enters retirement with both respect and surety. The advantages and disadvantages of these technologies are coming into view. Digital nudging can help improve your savings for retirement when action is taken early. Yet, these methods can be harmful to autonomy, openness, and equity. Creating nudges that benefit users and respect what is best for their rights and condition is not easy. Regular evaluation, advice from stakeholders, and a desire for design to be responsible, transparency should be included. Even though companies increasingly use digital nudging through media in business, it significantly influences both their sales revenue and consumers' understanding of how money works. These things include financial advice, how to conduct yourself financially, and financial literacy. Using digital nudging can make all of these experiences better. After that, tools and services become important people often neglect to closely manage their finances or save for when they retire. The use of tools may make behavioral changes more permanent. In contrast, the use of algorithms and good design on websites can change what consumers decide to buy, to encourage individuals to take part in desired activities by creating certain surroundings. Customers should be familiar with what these practices mean for their long-term financial security [48].

References

[1] Thaler, R. H., & Sunstein, C. R. (2008). Nudge: Improving decisions about health, wealth, and happiness. Yale University Press.

[2] Weinmann, M., Schneider, C., & Brocke, J. V. (2016). Digital nudging: Guiding online user choices through interface design. Communications of the ACM, 59(7), 31–36.

[3] Benartzi, S., & Thaler, R. H. (2007). Heuristics and biases in retirement savings behavior. Journal of Economic Perspectives, 21(3), 81–104.

[4] Brynjolfsson, E., & McAfee, A. (2017). Machine, platform, crowd: Harnessing our digital future. W.W. Norton & Company.

[5] Goldstein, D. G., Johnson, E. J., Herrmann, A., & Heitmann, M. (2008). Nudge your customers toward better choices. Harvard Business Review, 86(12), 99–105.

[6] Yeung, K. (2017). 'Hypernudge': Big Data as a mode of regulation by design. Information, Communication & Society, 20(1), 118–136.

[7] Agarwal, S., Driscoll, J. C., Gabaix, X., & Laibson, D. (2009). The age of reason: Financial decisions over the life cycle and implications for regulation. Brookings Papers on Economic Activity, 2009(2), 51–117.
[8] J.D. John Cutler, Artificial Intelligence and Retirement Planning, chrome-extension://efaidnbmnnnibpcajpcglclefindmkaj/https://www.soa.org/4a43ef/globalassets/assets/files/resources/research-report/2024/ai-retirement-risk-essays/ai-retirement-risks-essays-5-cutler.pdf
[9] Li, H.K. and Zhu, A.Y.F. (2025), "Revolutionizing retirement: how AI-powered visuals change retirement goal clarity and risk tolerance?", International Journal of Bank Marketing, Vol. ahead-of-print No. ahead-of-print. https://doi.org/10.1108/IJBM-11-2024-0676
[10] OECD (2021). Digital Disruption in Banking and its Impact on Financial Consumers. OECD Publishing
[11] Milkman, K. L., Beshears, J., Choi, J. J., Laibson, D., & Madrian, B. C. (2011). Using implementation intentions prompts to enhance influenza vaccination rates. Proceedings of the National Academy of Sciences, 108(26), 10415–10420.
[12] Thaler, R. H., & Benartzi, S. (2004). Save more tomorrow: Using behavioral economics to increase employee saving. Journal of Political Economy, 112(S1), S164–S187.
[13] Hershfield, H. E., Goldstein, D. G., Sharpe, W. F., Fox, J., Yeykelis, L., Carstensen, L. L., & Bailenson, J. N. (2011). Increasing saving behavior through age-progressed renderings of the future self. Journal of Marketing Research, 48, S23-S37.
[14] Karlan, D., McConnell, M., Mullainathan, S., & Zinman, J. (2016). Getting to the top of mind: How reminders increase saving. Management Science, 62(12), 3393–3411.
[15] Madrian, B. C., & Shea, D. F. (2001). The power of suggestion: Inertia in 401(k) participation and savings behavior. Quarterly Journal of Economics, 116(4), 1149–1187.
[16] Cadena, X., & Schoar, A. (2011). Remembering to pay? Reminders vs. financial incentives for loan repayments. NBER Working Paper No. 17020.
[17] Bryan, C. J., & Hershfield, H. E. (2013). You owe it to yourself: Boosting retirement saving with a responsibility-based appeal. Journal of Experimental Psychology: General, 142(1), 11–15.
[18] Iyengar, S. S., & Kamenica, E. (2010). Choice proliferation, simplicity seeking, and asset allocation. Journal of Public Economics, 94(7–8), 530–539.

[19] Klein, T., Papies, D., & Eggers, F. (2019). Customer journey analytics in financial services: How personalized recommendations affect user behavior. Journal of Business Research, 104, 216–227.

[20] Thaler, R. H. and C. R. Sunstein (2003). "Libertarian Paternalism" American Economic Review 93 (2), 175–179.

[21] Thaler, R. H. and C. R. Sunstein (2008). Nudge: Improving Decisions About Health, Wealth and Happiness. Illustrated ed. New Haven: Yale University Press.

[22] Carter, I. (2004). "Choice, freedom, and freedom of choice" Social Choice and Welfare 22 (1), 61–81.

[23] Susser, D., Roessler, B., & Nissenbaum, H. (2019). Online Manipulation: Hidden Influences in a Digital World. Georgetown Law Technology Review, 4(1), 1–45

[24] Schneider, C., M. Weinmann and J. Vom Brocke (2018). "Digital Nudging. Guiding Online User Choices through Interface Design" Communications of the ACM 61 (7), 67–73.

[25] Lembcke, T. B., Engelbrecht, N., Brendel, A. B., & Kolbe, L. M. (2019, June). To Nudge or not to Nudge: Ethical Considerations of Digital nudging based on its Behavioral Economics roots. In ECIS.

[26] Barton, A., Grüne-Yanoff, T. From Libertarian Paternalism to Nudging—and Beyond. Rev.Phil.Psych. 6, 341–359 (2015). https://doi.org/10.1007/s13164-015-0268-x

[27] Loewenstein, G., & Chater, N. (2017). Putting nudges in perspective. Behavioural Public Policy, 1(1), 26–53.

[28] Clavien, C. (2018). "Ethics of nudges: A general framework with a focus on shared preference justifications" Journal of Moral Education 47 (3), 366–382.

[29] Ananny, M., & Crawford, K. (2018). Seeing without knowing: Limitations of the transparency ideal and its application to algorithmic accountability. New Media & Society, 20(3), 973–989

[30] Mittelstadt, B. D., P. Allo, M. Taddeo, S. Wachter and L. Floridi (2016). "The ethics of algorithms: Mapping the debate" Big Data & Society 3 (2), 205395171667967.

[31] Vellido, A., J. D. Martín-Guerrero and P. J. G. Lisboa (eds.) (2012). Making machine learning models interpretable: Citeseer.

[32] Pasquale, F. (2015). The black box society: The secret algorithms that control money and information: Harvard University Press.

[33] Burrell, J. (2016). "How the machine 'thinks': Understanding opacity in machine learning algorithms" Big Data & Society 3 (1), 205395171562251.

[34] Kraemer, F., K. van Overveld and M. Peterson (2011). "Is there an ethics of algorithms?" Ethics and Information Technology 13 (3), 251–260.
[35] Barocas, S., Hardt, M., & Narayanan, A. (2019). Fairness and Machine Learning. fairmlbook.org
[36] Reisch, L. A. and C. R. Sunstein (2016). "Do Europeans Like Nudges?" Judgment and Decision Making 11 (4), 310–325.
[37] Sunstein, C. R. (2015a). "Do People Like Nudges?" SSRN Electronic Journal.
[38] Choi, J. J., Laibson, D., Madrian, B. C., & Metrick, A. (2004). For Better or For Worse: Default Effects and 401(k) Savings Behavior. In Perspectives on the Economics of Aging (pp. 81–121). University of Chicago Press.
[39] Benartzi, S., & Thaler, R. H. (2007). Heuristics and biases in retirement savings behavior. Journal of Economic Perspectives, 21(3), 81–104
[40] Yeung, K. (2017). "Hypernudge": Big Data as a mode of regulation by design. Information, Communication & Society, 20(1), 118–136.
[41] Eslami, M., Rickman, A., Vaccaro, K., Aleyasen, A., Vu, T., Karahalios, K., Hamilton, K., & Sandvig, C. (2018). "I always assumed that I wasn't really that close to [her]": Reasoning about Invisible Algorithms in News Feeds. CHI '18 Proceedings of the 2018 CHI Conference on Human Factors in Computing Systems.
[42] Calo, R. (2013). Digital Market Manipulation. The George Washington Law Review, 82(4), 995–1051
[43] Doshi-Velez, F., & Kim, B. (2017). Towards a rigorous science of interpretable machine learning. arXiv preprint arXiv:1702.08608.
[44] Sunstein, C. R. (2016). The Ethics of Influence: Government in the Age of Behavioral Science. Cambridge University Press
[45] Mehrabi, N., Morstatter, F., Saxena, N., Lerman, K., & Galstyan, A. (2021). A survey on bias and fairness in machine learning. ACM Computing Surveys, 54(6), 1–35
[46] Loewenstein, G., & Chater, N. (2017). Putting nudges in perspective. Behavioural Public Policy, 1(1), 26–53
[47] Nissenbaum, H. (2004). Privacy as contextual integrity. Washington Law Review, 79, 119–158
[48] Koskelainen, T., Kalmi, P., Scornavacca, E., & Vartiainen, T. (2023). Financial literacy in the digital age—A research agenda. Journal of Consumer Affairs, 57(1), 507-528.

4

An Empirical Investigation into the Impact of Implementing Artificial Intelligence Tools in Enhancing Customer Experience in Private Banking

Reepu

Department of Management, Chandigarh University, India

Email: reepu.technowize@gmail.com

Abstract

In this chapter, an investigation is conducted on the influence that artificial intelligence may have on improving the customer experience in the banking business. Using a specially designed online questionnaire that includes crucial components for customer experience via service customization, effective customer data processing, sophisticated natural language processing capabilities, and feedback analysis, the research applies many different methods. Taking into consideration the rapid advancements in financial technology and the ever-changing requirements of the digital economy, the purpose of this research is to evaluate the potentially disruptive effects that fintech and artificial intelligence (AI) might have on the banking industry, specifically with regard to payment systems. The purpose of this study is to examine how new financial instruments and concepts powered by artificial intelligence improve the customer experience, specifically in general operations.

4.1 Introduction

The field of artificial intelligence (AI) encompasses a broad range of scientific disciplines, including but not limited to psychology, computer science, linguistics, and philosophy. Suppose artificial intelligence is able to improve the

 DOI: 10.1201/9788743810766-4

quality of goods and services. In that case, it will be beneficial to the economy of the whole world, particularly in sectors that serve consumers. The use of artificial intelligence in the banking sector throughout the globe could bring in one trillion dollars annually. The use of advanced financial instruments that are driven by artificial intelligence and fintech helps to enhance resource allocation, which in turn ensures the responsible deployment of resources in order to achieve the desired objectives. Investments in programmes that address social requirements, such as education and healthcare, as well as investments in renewable energy projects or initiatives that match social criteria, might be made possible by payment systems that are enriched with artificial intelligence. By implementing these concepts, it is possible to foster economic growth without exacerbating existing social inequalities or contributing to the destruction of the environment. Components of the customer viewpoint are defined by the client's beliefs and perceptions of the financial institution. Through the collection, processing, and analysis of data, this information assists in determining the requirements, preferences, and purchasing patterns of customers, thus facilitating the establishment of a long-term connection between the bank and its customers that is founded on client insights. The importance of sustainability reporting is expanding as a result of the increased demand from stakeholders for corporations to disclose their Environmental, Social, and Governance (ESG) practices. Having transparent reporting procedures not only ensures that investments are in accordance with environmental objectives but also encourages investors to make prudent choices.

One of the primary goals of sustainable development is to fulfil the requirements of human beings while simultaneously increasing the social and technical domains. There is a need for senior leadership to engage in risk management since it assists in the prediction and reduction of any adverse impacts that may hamper the accomplishment of the company's goals [1]. The ability to identify and eliminate both internal and external uncertainty is facilitated for managers by this. Companies can weather periods of uncertainty if they practice proactive risk management.

Artificial intelligence and machine learning are finding widespread use in the insurance industry, particularly in claims reserving and policy risk evaluation. These systems achieve their ability to give accurate pricing and risk assessments via predictive modelling and data analysis. Meanwhile, the financial services and investment industry is increasingly adopting blockchain technology [2]. As a distributed ledger, blockchain makes it possible to conduct transactions safely and openly without the need for intermediaries.

The urge to satisfy one's own needs is the driving force behind making prudent decisions that give environmental concerns and sustainability the highest priority. According to the findings of recent research, people and businesses would demonstrate a higher level of awareness and mindfulness if they felt it was their moral mission to preserve the natural environment [3]. Companies that demonstrate a strong commitment to environmental stewardship are likely to be more proactive in identifying and mitigating environmental risks, which in turn encourages innovation in the use of AI-driven risk management strategies. Companies that emphasize environmental responsibility may use artificial intelligence technology to gain a better knowledge of potential risks, thus aiding sustainable decision-making not just in the construction industry but also in a wide variety of other sectors [4]. The purpose of this work is to investigate the role that perceived environmental responsibility plays as a mediator in the connection between environmentally responsible decision-making and risk management that is driven by artificial intelligence.

4.2 Review of Literature

A recent study has shown that artificial intelligence algorithms and machine learning models significantly impact the prediction of operational risk [5]. By using these algorithms and models in risk assessment, businesses can proactively mitigate potential threats and limit the impact such threats have on the continuity of their respective companies.

With the purpose of catering to particular requirements inside this organization, AI-driven tools and solutions have been created, which have resulted in the development of specialized industries such as insurance, Supertech, and regtech [6]. Researchers emphasize the management of regulatory procedures in order to guarantee that financial institutions adhere to standards that are constantly evolving. On the other hand, Suptech makes use of artificial intelligence to monitor and ensure compliance within the financial industry, which is consequently related to regulatory monitoring and control. With the help of artificial intelligence, insurtech companies create innovative insurance products and solutions, which ultimately improve both the efficiency of their operations and the quality of their interactions with customers [7].

In the banking industry, artificial intelligence technology has been employed to assist sustainable development via the implementation of creative concepts that improve both environmental and financial consequences. This has been accomplished through the early and broad adoption of AI technology [8]. By enhancing the precision and effectiveness of economic decision-making and, as a result, decreasing reliance on activities that require a significant amount of resources, artificial intelligence is altering the banking sector and, as a result, contributing to the promotion of sustainability.

Through the optimization of processes, the reduction of paper consumption, and the facilitation of more accurate risk ratings – all of which contribute to the facilitation of more sustainable credit assessments – artificial intelligence also contributes to the creation of perhaps lower default rates and more sustainable financial products [9].

As technological advancements continue, financial institutions are increasingly adopting digital transformation. In order for banks to successfully undergo this change, they will need to expedite their back-office processes and procedures. Creating exceptional service models and placing a primary emphasis on the satisfaction of customers are both very important. For the purpose of enhancing customer service, data-driven solutions have become feasible thanks to the advent of big data analytics and artificial intelligence [10]. Many features are now adjustable as a result of this, which has led to an increase in client interaction. In the context of Indonesian and global banking settings, the empirical research sheds light on the applicability of artificial intelligence and BDA technologies in banking. Interviews aid in the collection of data. Enterprise architecture is one strategy that is believed to be the most effective [11].

It suggests a methodological approach to research on behavioral finance. Numerous industries have embraced the use of artificial intelligence algorithms and machine learning methods, each of which comes with its own set of advantages and disadvantages. In the first place, the banking industry is the one that is driving the use of artificial intelligence for risk assessments. Two of the first publications that introduced the concept of sustainable development were the book "The Limits to Growth" and the research paper titled "Our Common Future." In later years, throughout the 1990s and 2000s, there was a phase that focused on compliance and control, which brought attention to the regulations that govern environmental protection and safety. Around this time, ideas such as corporate social responsibility (also known as CSR) and corporate environmental responsibility (commonly known as CER) began to emerge as prominent topics of discussion in the literary world. It was then that businesses started to recognize and take responsibility for their social and environmental effect.

4.3 Methodologies

In addition to using a descriptive research approach, the researcher will gather information from primary and secondary sources. The researchers collected data from people by means of a questionnaire that had limited open-ended responses. The researcher used a number of statistical methods, including mediation analysis, structural equation modelling (SEM), and frequency analysis, among others. The participants are workers of private banking organizations, and they were selected using the convenience sample approach.

As shown in Table 4.1, the strongest correlation is found between Input Analysis and Customer Experience (r = 0.932), which indicates that having a more competent analysis of input techniques results in an improvement in the overall customer experience. It is important to note that effective customer data processing has a significant link with customer experience (r = 0.875), which highlights the crucial role that artificial intelligence plays in data management in order to personalize and enhance services. The customer experience has a strong correlation with the customization of services (r = 0.841), which suggests that tailored services powered by artificial intelligence significantly increase the level of happiness experienced by customers. Furthermore, enhanced natural language processing capabilities demonstrate a substantial link with customer experience (r = 0.804), which highlights the need for natural language interfaces to successfully incorporate consumers. This is despite the fact that their value is comparatively lower. These findings provide credence to the claim that artificial intelligence capabilities, which include customization, data efficiency, natural language processing, and feedback systems, contribute to an improvement in the client experience within the private banking industry.

Table 4.1 Correlation analysis.

Correlations	**Personalization of services**	**Efficient customer data processing**	**Enhanced NLP capabilities**	**Feedback analysis**	**Customer experience**
Personalization of services	1	.880**	.808**	.860**	.841**
Efficient customer data processing	.880**	1	.848**	.866**	.875**
Enhanced NLP capabilities	.808**	.848**	1	.821**	.804**
Feedback analysis	.860**	.866**	.821**	1	.932**
Customer experience	.841**	.875**	.804**	.932**	1

Source: Created by author.

Table 4.2 Regression analysis.

Model	**Sum of squares**	**df**	**Mean square**	**F**	**p-value**
Regression	237.995	4	59.499	324.312	.000b
Residual	30.088	164	0.183		
Total	268.083	168			
Coefficients	B	Std. Error	Beta	T	p-value
(Constant)	–0.611	0.134		–4.563	0.00
Personalization of services	0.018	0.07	0.016	0.255	0.80
Efficient customer data processing	0.277	0.071	0.26	3.905	0.00
Enhanced NLP capabilities	0.006	0.059	0.006	0.109	0.91
Feedback analysis	0.789	0.068	0.69	11.624	0.00
Dependent variable: Customer experience					

Source: Created by author.

The regression analysis, as per Table 4.2, reveals that the whole model is statistically significant, with an F value of 324.312 and a p-value of 0.000. This indicates that the independent variables, when considered collectively, have a substantial influence on the customer experience. The R-squared number, which is derived from the sum of squares, demonstrates that the model elucidates a significant percentage of the variability that exists in the customer experience. It is noted that the successful application of artificial intelligence in analysing customer feedback significantly increases customer satisfaction. This is the case among the individual factors. An effective processing of customer data has been found to have a substantial positive impact ($B = 0.277$, $t = 3.905$, $p = 0.000$), which demonstrates the significance of this factor.

Nevertheless, personalization of services ($p = 0.80$) and enhanced NLP capabilities ($p = 0.91$) are not statistically significant predictors in this model. This indicates that, when other variables are taken into consideration, their individual effects on customer experience are negligible. This is because other elements either completely or already cover their effects.

It is possible to determine the intensity and direction of effect that each component has on the customer experience by examining the route coefficients. With a path coefficient of 0.79, feedback analysis is the most significant and favorable aspect that influences customer experience. The highest path coefficient shows this. The study of client feedback via the use of artificial intelligence techniques is essential to the improvement of the overall experience that private banking customers have. The fact that artificial intelligence is able to accurately and quickly assess consumer data is shown by a path coefficient of 0.28, as shown in Figure 4.1, which indicates that this capability considerably increases customer interactions and satisfaction. On the other side, the personalization of services has a marginal impact, as shown

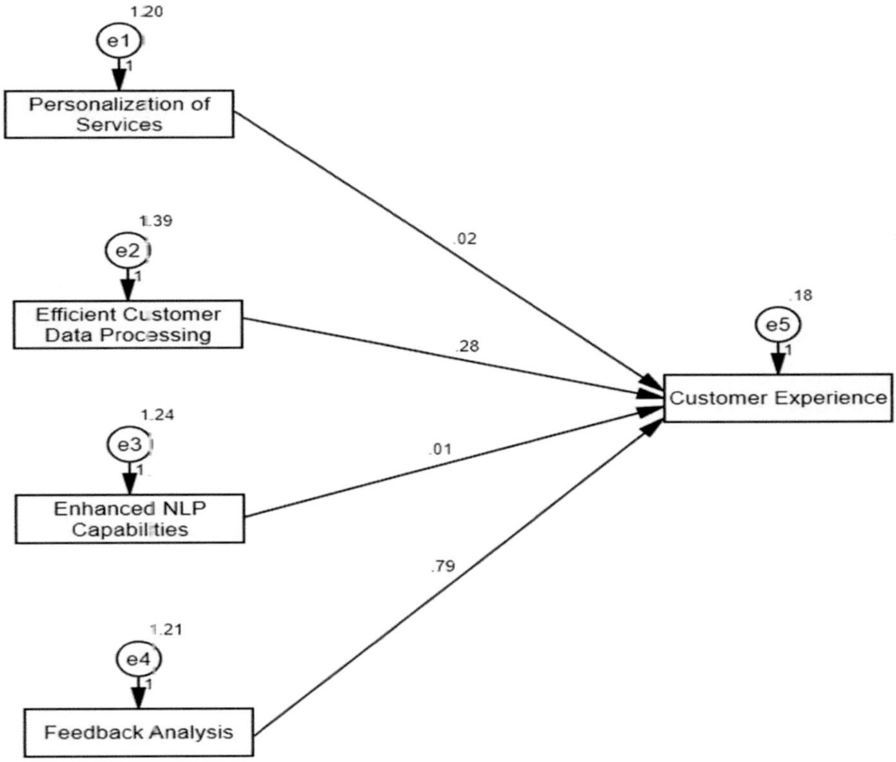

Figure 4.1 Structural Model showing relationship between Personalization of Services, Data Processing, NLP Capabilities, Feedback and Customer Experience
Source: Created by author.

by a path coefficient of just 0.02, and the enhanced NLP capabilities have an even less impact, with a coefficient of 0.01. Despite the fact that personalization and natural language processing are significant from a technical point of view, our findings demonstrate that their effect on customer experience is insignificant in this model when robust feedback analysis and data processing approaches are used. Given that customer experience has a relatively low error variance (0.18), the error variances (e1 to e5) provide an indication of the degree of variation that cannot be explained within each construct. As a result, the model is able to demonstrate a considerable portion of the variability that exists within these constructs.

According to the model, feedback analysis is the most essential aspect in boosting customer experience inside AI-driven tools used in private banking, followed by effective customer data processing. This is in contrast to the fact that customization and natural language processing skills have a much less direct influence. Because of this information, private banks can make investments and upgrades in feedback analysis tools and data processing skills with artificial intelligence as their primary focus, which will result in a significant increase in client satisfaction.

With the use of the regression weight table, the impact of several AI-driven components on the private banking customer experience may be better understood. Both the critical ratio (C.R.) and the p-values are used to assess the statistical significance of the variables. However, the projected values are used to determine the extent to which each independent variable is connected to the customer experience. As shown in Table 4.3, feedback analysis is determined to be the most essential component, with a significant estimate of 0.789, a critical ratio of 26.68, and a p-value of 0.00, all of which

Table 4.3 Path analysis.

Variables	Variables	Estimate	S.E.	C.R.	P
Customer experience	Personalization of services	0.018	0.03	0.6	0.55
Customer experience	Efficient customer data processing	0.277	0.028	10.042	0.00
Customer experience	Enhanced NLP capabilities	0.006	0.029	0.222	0.82
Customer experience	Feedback analysis	0.789	0.03	26.68	0.00

Source: Created by author.

indicate that it has a substantial positive effect on the customer experience. This provides more evidence that the appropriate use of AI techniques to assess client input results in a significant increase in levels of satisfaction among banking customers. The personalization of services, on the other hand, demonstrates a significantly low critical ratio (0.6) and an insignificant p-value (0.55), indicating that, in light of the influence of different factors, its direct impact on customer experience is weak and statistically irrelevant. This is despite the fact that it displays an optimistic estimate of 0.018. Similar to the previous example, the enhanced natural language processing capabilities, which have an estimate of 0.006, a critical ratio of 0.222, and a p-value of 0.82, demonstrate that there is no significant direct effect on the customer experience inside this model. Based on these results, it can be inferred that while natural language skills and customization are substantial features of contemporary banking, the independent effect that these characteristics have on the customer experience is diminished when more essential components, such as data processing and feedback analysis, are involved. To achieve significant improvements in customer experience, the model underlines that private banks must prioritize the enhancement of their feedback analysis and data processing artificial intelligence technologies. This is necessary in order to achieve the desired results.

4.4 Discussion

The results show that the above-stated variables possess a more significant influence on the customer experience in the banking sector. This is in line with the practice of relying on broad studies of technology acceptance or the use of artificial intelligence across a variety of industries. Similar modifications to the stated model have been made by previous research on businesses in industries such as retail and healthcare, which included the incorporation of social influence and perceived value in those disciplines. The adaptability of the paradigm in a wide variety of different domains is shown by this [12].

Important new views are provided to managers and experts who are working towards expanding the acceptability of artificial intelligence in banks by the results of this study. Because of the significant importance of effectively processing consumer data and analyzing feedback, it is essential to design artificial intelligence systems that are not only effective but also focused on the needs of actual users. Managers must recognize the importance of prioritizing investments in user-centric designs, which should include seamless interaction with existing financial systems and user-friendly interfaces [13]. In addition, training courses that focus on usability and skill development are a great way to compensate for deficiencies in technical expertise, especially for new users.

4.5 Conclusion

Artificial intelligence is a disruptive technology that assists machines in the automation of data collection and processing in order to offer information related to the marketing mix. This area of study is multidisciplinary. It is necessary to possess this capability in order to do large-scale customization, something human labor alone has not been able to accomplish before. For the purpose of tackling the global concerns that are emphasized in the Sustainable Development Goals (SDGs), these improvements are significant in the context of crisis management. Through the use of digital technology, sustainable finance has the potential to enhance the efficiency with which resources are allocated, decrease the risks associated with financial mismanagement, and advance the primary objective of developing a global economy that is more resilient and sustainable. Usability, personalization, trust, customer loyalty, and satisfaction are all tangible and intangible factors that influence the consumer viewpoint. While AI-hedonic experiences and AI-recognition customer service generate artificial intelligence-enhanced customer experiences, usability is the most critical factor. The AI solutions that were offered by financial businesses were enhanced by all of the components overall. However, customer perception factors acquire distinct features across various institutions, generating a tremendous competitive advantage that also supports the production of digital banking products and services. Banks supply goods and services that are similar to one another to customers.

References

[1] Rakshitha, J.; Chaya, R., 'Driving Sustainability: Exploring Global Green Banking Initiatives for a Greener Future', J. Dev. Res. 2023, 16, 89–105, 2023.

[2] Mogaji, E.; Nguyen, N.P., 'Managers' understanding of artificial intelligence in relation to marketing financial services: Insights from a cross-country study', Int. J. Bank Mark. 2022, 40, 1272–1298, 2022.

[3] Kalyani, S.; Gupta, N., 'Is artificial intelligence and machine learning changing the ways of banking: A systematic literature review and meta-analysis', Discov. Artif. Intell., 3, 41, 2023.

[4] Ananda, J.; Karunasena, G.G.; Mitsis, A.; Kansal, M.; Pearson, D., 'Analyzing behavioural and socio-demographic factors and practices influencing Australian household food waste', J. Clean. Prod., 306, 127280, 2021.

[5] Rahman, M.; Ming, T.H.; Baigh, T.A.; Sarker, M., 'Adoption of Artificial intelligence in banking services: An empirical analysis', Int. J. Emerg. Mark.,18, 4270–4300, 2023.

[6] Dwivedi, Y.K.; Kshetri, N.; Hughes, L.; Slade, E.L.; Jeyaraj, A.; Kar, A.K.; Baabdullah, A.M.; Koohang, A.; Raghavan, V.; Ahuja, M., 'Opinion Paper: "So what if ChatGPT wrote it?", Multidisciplinary perspectives on opportunities, challenges and implications of generative conversational AI for research, practice and policy. Int. J. Inf. Manag.,71, 102642, 2023.

[7] Bhatia, A.; Chandani, A.; Atiq, R.; Mehta, M.; Divekar, R., 'Artificial intelligence in financial services: A qualitative research to discover robot- advisory services',Qual. Res. Financ. Mark, 13, 632–654, 2021.

[8] Priya, B.; Sharma, V., 'Exploring users' adoption intentions of Intelligent virtual assistants in financial services: An anthropomorphic perspectives and socio-psychological perspectives.',Comput. Hum. Behav, 148, 10791, 2023.

[9] Lakshmi, A.J.; Kumar, A.; Kumar, M.S.; Patel, S.I.; Naik, S.K.L.; Ramesh, J.V.N., 'Artificial Intelligence in Steering the Digital Transformation Of Collaborative Technical Education', J. High Technol. Manag. Res., 34, 100467,2023.

[10] Sharma, S.; Islam, N.; Singh, G.; Dhir, A., 'Why do retail customers adopt artificial intelligence (AI) based autonomous decision-making systems?', IEEE Trans. Eng. Manag. 71, 1846–1861,2022.

[11] Boustani, N.M., 'Artificial Intelligence's Impact on Banks Clients and Employees in an Asian Developing Country', J. Asia Bus. Stud.16, 267–278, 2022.

[12] Balaskas, S.; Koutroumani, M.; Komis, K.; Rigou, M., 'FinTech Services Adoption in Greece: The Roles of Trust, Government Support, and Technology Acceptance Factors', FinTech, 3, 83–101,2024.

[13] Saprikis, V.; Avlogiaris, G.; Kataracchia, A., 'A Comparative Study of Users versus Non-Users' Behavioral Intention Towards M-Banking Apps' Adoption', Information, 13, 30, 2022.

5

Challenges and Limitations of AI Adoption in Banking: Strategies for Overcoming Obstacles

Gagandeep and Jyoti Verma

Chitkara Business School, Chitkara University, India

Email: profgaganabdc@gmail.com; jyotiverma17@gmail.com

Abstract

AI has introduced new opportunities in banking, allowing banks to improve security and offer personalised services for customers. Still, using AI on a large scale is met with many issues, like poor data reliability, rules from different governments, ethical considerations, and organizations not wanting to change. This chapter examines the main problems banks face when adopting AI and divides them into technical, organizational, and regulatory categories. It suggests a number of solutions to overcome these problems, for example, by solidly managing data, helping workers upgrade their skills, following ethical guidelines, and keeping up with new regulations. If banks take on these challenges, they can make progress in innovation, save time and resources, satisfy customers, and stay compliant.

5.1 Introduction

Artificial intelligence (AI) growth is pushing the banking industry to undergo major changes to stay current. AI is helping banks update key operations, making them more efficient, effective at decision-making, and good at meeting customers' needs. In recent years, banking has heavily relied on technologies such as ML for credit risk, NLP for assisting customers in conversation, and robo-advisors for managing investments [1–2]. Thanks to

 DOI: 10.1201/9788743810766-5

these systems, banks handle many details at once, ease basic routines, and provide products designed for each customer. AI systems in fraud detection use data to spot variances, which lower financial losses, while chatbots using NLP respond to millions of customers' inquiries each year, saving money on operations [3–4].

Even though the use of AI offers many benefits in banking, its uptake continues to be patchy because of major problems preventing its complete use. Poorly gathered data and challenges in using AI with older systems make things hard for the industry [5]. An organization's problems, for example, lack of qualified professionals and unwillingness to change, delay the deployment process [6]. Moreover, the banking sector must comply with strict rules and regulations, including the EU AI Act and the GDPR, which set high requirements for handling data and accountability in AI [7]. Studies by [7] uncover that most financial institutions make use of AI, but just 13% have integrated it extensively across their primary operations, indicating a big difference between theory and practice, as seen in Figure 5.1.

The risks associated with these difficulties are very high. Adding AI to the financial industry can help underserved groups obtain credit more easily, better control financial risks, and contribute new ideas to products and services [8]. Yet, not dealing with these issues could lead to less efficient operations, face penalties from regulators and damage trust from customers, given that ethical matters such as biased algorithms and privacy are important concerns [9]. In this chapter, the author aims to look systematically at the problems and limits of using AI in banking, organizing them according to technical, business, and regulatory factors. Based on recent findings and input from the industry, the white paper advises banks on ways to address these challenges and make the most of AI wisely.

The organization of this chapter is as follows: Section 2 introduces AI in banking and explains why it is significant for the industry. Section 3 explains the problems and boundaries encountered, examining the technical issues, problems in organizations and rules. The fourth section offers strategies that stress the use of data governance, skills development, and ethical AI frameworks. Section 5 ends by pointing out suggestions for further work and advising that sustainability in AI banking requires combining disciplines.

5.2 Opportunities of AI in Banking

Because of artificial intelligence, banks can use data to gain insights, manage workflows better, and introduce new services. With tools such as machine learning, natural language processing, and deep learning, banks can manage

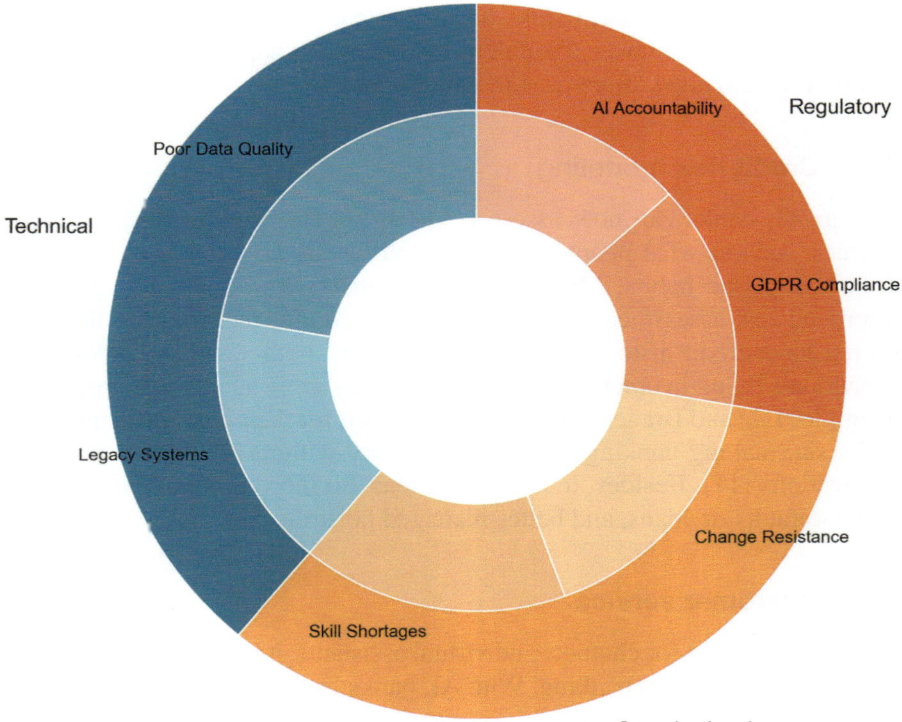

Figure 5.1 Nested challenges of AI adoption in banking.
Source: Generated by author.

huge amounts of data quickly, complete complex jobs without human help, and provide better customer outcomes. Because AI can look for patterns, guess how things will develop and respond to change, it has opened up chances across banking duties, including risk management and customer communication [1]. Below, we explain how AI helps the banking sector by improving processes, reaching more people, and changing the market landscape.

5.2.1 Fraud detection

Fraud detection has improved a lot for banks because of AI. Machine learning algorithms review transactional data to spot unusual and suspicious patterns, allowing for immediate detection of fraud. Thanks to AI, fraud detection systems can respond to new fraud ways, reducing errors and increasing accuracy [3]. As an example, JPMorgan Chase's COiN platform monitors billions of transactions each year, thanks to AI that carefully flags any fraud [10]. With help from AI, fewer fraudulent incidents can happen, which helps to lower costs and allow more trust in the business.

5.2.2 Credit risk modeling

Due to AI, banks can now assess credit risk using a number of different sources, such as what people post on social media, how they pay bills, and their cell phone habits. Machine learning analyses of such data generate improved risk assessments for people from marginalized groups who often do not have credit histories [8]. Because of this, both small businesses and individuals living in emerging markets can enjoy more access to loans. As an example, Tala and Branch use AI to assess credit for their customers in Africa and Asia, making banking accessible to many without traditional financial connections [11]. Besides, the use of AI leads to more accurate predictions, fewer defaults on loans, and better-managed portfolios.

5.2.3 Customer service

When NLP is used for chatbots and virtual assistants, it has changed the shape of customer service in banking. With AI, banks handle lots of requests, from confirming balances to processing loans, with fast and correct responses, which helps reduce time and money the bank spends [4]. One instance is Erica, Bank of America's virtual assistant, which has helped more than 1 billion customers since it started, recommending personal financial advice and taking care of usual tasks [12]. Because it operates all day and night, AI helps customers who cannot contact customer service during regular office hours. What is more, such systems get better at managing difficult conversations as they gather data from users.

5.2.4 Personalized services

The use of AI in analytics allows banks to present financial products and services personalized for each customer. Using data on behavior, past buys, and customer preferences, AI suggests suitable solutions, including free savings plans, picking investments, or buying insurance [13]. HSBC relies on AI to match its clients' needs in wealth management with their goals and how much risk they can take [14]. Customer loyalty and the chance to sell additional products are both increased by this degree of personalization. AI further improves banking by detecting when to provide loans pre-approved for customers, which makes the experience easier and supports customer loyalty.

5.2.5 Investment management

With AI helping, robo-advisors give everyone access to low-priced, automatic investment help. They use machine learning to find the best mix of investments for each client, depending on market changes, how much risk they can take, and what they want to accomplish financially, helping make wealth management affordable to ordinary users [2]. Many investors have moved to Betterment and Wealthfront because both companies offer AI tools for investing at a lower cost than traditional advisors [15]. Apart from handling portfolios, AI improves bankers' prediction of future trends and identification of risks, so banks can provide advanced investment choices. People now have more opportunities to get financial planning because it is both scalable and affordable, particularly for younger and less affluent customers, as shown in Figure 5.2.

5.2.6 Emerging applications

On top of traditional uses, AI helps with regulatory compliance, anti-money laundering (AML), and new approaches in predictive analytics. By using AI, businesses can easily keep up with regulatory modifications and follow systems like Basel III [7]. AI has the ability to detect suspicious actions in transaction networks, so it reduces the workload for humans and makes detection

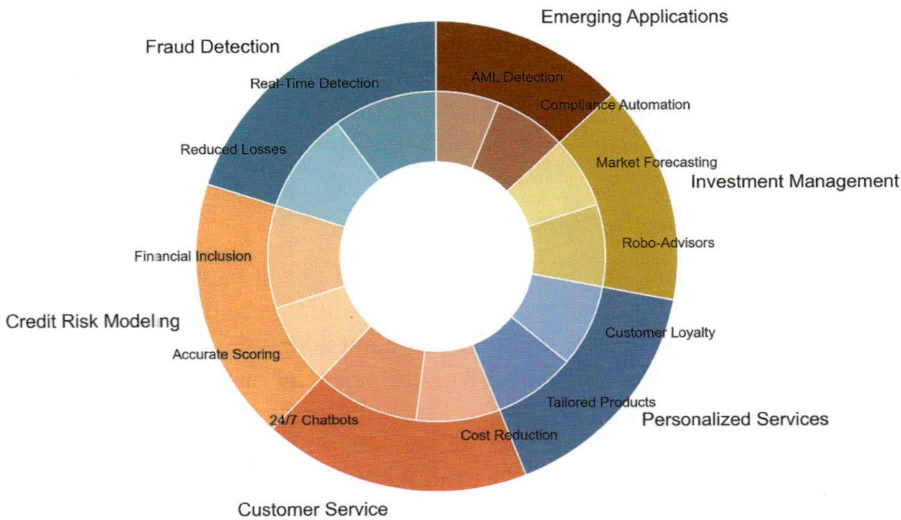

Figure 5.2 Opportunities of AI in banking: Applications and benefits
Source: Generated by author.

more successful [9]. In addition, banks use AI-based predictive analytics to monitor market changes, improve how they use money, and develop better strategies to manage economic difficulties.

5.2.7 Broader implications

The technologies shown can help banking by boosting productivity, reducing risks, and developing more customer-oriented innovations. Automating repetitive tasks thanks to AI means banks can redirect their resources toward those things that create more value, such as planning strategies and new products. Also, because AI reaches underserved groups and can be expanded, it helps accomplish the World Bank's financial inclusion goals from 2022. To fully achieve these advantages, however, several difficult technical, organizational, and regulatory issues must be overcome, as we see in the following chapters. Banks will need to overcome these challenges in a way that maintains good ethics and trust from their customers.

5.3 Challenges and Limitations of AI Adoption in Banking

AI is greatly beneficial in banking, but at present, it cannot be fully used due to a mix of technical, organizational, and regulatory problems. As a result of these barriers, AI is not fully integrated everywhere and so cannot maximize its benefits in fraud detection, credit modeling, and customer service. This part of the report sorts the challenges into technical, organizational, and regulatory areas and looks deeply into their effects, using up-to-date literature and industry knowledge. Only by knowing these obstacles can the banking sector put effective plans into action for using AI.

5.3.1 Technical challenges

Problems with technology are slowing down AI use in banking due to concerns about data infrastructure, system compatibility, and the see-through nature of algorithms. If these challenges are not addressed, the systems may not work well in critical situations involving financial institutions.

- **Data quality and availability**

  Reliable and accurate results from AI systems depend on easy-to-access, high-quality data. Even so, banks often run into problems like data layout differences, missing information, and data isolation, which can weaken the performance of AI engines [5]. Because departments have different systems, the data needed for applications in fraud detection and credit risk assessment is often separated, making it hard to obtain comprehensive datasets. Inaccurate or restricted transaction information can cause fraud detection to show incorrect results, costing the organization customer trust and more work [3]. Besides, old methods for managing data often miss real-time updates, which makes it difficult for AI systems to keep up in changing contexts. Global AI projects are made more challenging by the absence of regular data formats in various countries, especially for multinational banks, according to [7].

- **System integration**

  Bringing AI into traditional banking systems is very hard since many organizations still depend on ageing technologies that do not match modern AI [16]. Since core banking systems were created many years ago, they do not have the adaptability needed for AI and adding in advanced AI tools means going through complex and expensive procedures with APIs and middleware [17]. Integrating chatbots with an organization's CRM can cause service delays and other compatibility problems that disturb the process. Even though adopting cloud services looks positive, new concerns, such as transferring data and increasing security risks, emerge [18]. These problems are more burdensome for small banks, as they cannot always afford to rebuild their IT systems, increasing the gap in available technology between banks of different sizes.

- **Algorithmic complexity and explainability**

  Certain models being used in banking, mainly deep learning networks, are difficult to review, so banks may face tough transparency issues [19]. Because they work well with patterns, these models produce choices that can be tough to explain and this concerns both legal authorities and users. Sometimes, because credit scoring runs on inscrutable AI models, the results can show bias against groups that those models target [9]. Not being able to explain AI processes causes challenges when trying to follow the EU AI Act [5]. Since XAI tends to lose accuracy when trying to explain its decisions, it creates problems for banks attempting to meet their responsibilities and achieve good results.

5.3.2 Organizational challenges

Factors related to people and the structure of organizations hold back the use of AI in banks. They demonstrate how complex the workforce is in this sector, the challenges with culture, and the problems with available resources.

- **Skills gap**

  Since building, deploying, and managing AI systems need proficiency in data science, machine learning, and cybersecurity, there are not enough experts available to value [13]. Because there are not enough talented professionals to go around, banks struggle to bring in and maintain skilled workers, mainly in the United States and Europe [20]. Small banks have to compete with companies like tech firms and fintechs, which promise both better compensation and possible job advantages. It is also true that because existing workers may not have the skills to work alongside AI systems, the implementation of new technology is delayed [6]. Unless banks invest in specialized upskilling, they are likely to miss out on the changes being driven by AI in the financial sector.

- **Resistance to change**

  People and leaders at work often resist using AI since it scares them about job losses and makes them doubt AI's decisions [6]. Many front-line workers in banking may view AI as a challenge to their jobs, which could stop them from using AI-powered solutions. Likewise, when top managers prefer tried-and-tested business practices, doubts about AI leadership can stop AI implementation [20]. Many stakeholders are uncertain about AI's gains because they are not explained in a clear manner. Some employees worry that AI-based fraud detection is less dependable than detecting the same issue by people, despite findings that it is more likely to be accurate [3]. It takes cultural change and solid plans for managing changes to help stakeholders follow the objectives set by AI.

- **High implementation costs**

  Small and medium-sized banks have trouble affording AI, as the cost is so high [17]. AI needs businesses to invest in IT infrastructure, software creation, staff training, and safety from cyber-attacks. For credit risk assessment, a business might invest millions of dollars in getting the data, training the model, and adding it to its current system by using machine learning [16]. It gets even more costly as tasks such as model retraining and compliance checks must be performed regularly. As a result, AI projects may not be possible for small banks, leading to differences in technology among banks. Balancing AI spending against what shareholders expect is a difficult factor for even major banks when deciding how to distribute resources [7].

5.3.3 Regulatory and ethical challenges

Banks face extra ambiguity when adopting AI because they are heavily supervised by regulators and have ethical obligations apart from this. Banks need a technical expert who can understand and handle all the regulatory compliances that are essential for governing AI. Because of these challenges, banks have to deal with complex laws and respond to social expectations to keep trust and obey the rules.

- **Regulatory compliance**

  In the bank sector, using AI and data must follow strict rules such as the EU AI Act, GDPR, and Basel III [5]. As a result of these regulations, banks must make sure that their AI tools follow the law. As an example, GDPR stops businesses from using sensitive data for AI purposes, therefore restricting the range of data they can use for personalized marketing [7]. Moving details across national borders is made trickier because privacy laws differ in regions like Europe and the Asia-Pacific. Banks using AI have to be very careful, as not following the rules can lead to serious consequences that can harm a bank's reputation and wallet [18].

- **Ethical concerns**

  Problems such as algorithmic bias, invading privacy, and not holding anyone responsible can have big impacts on banking's use of AI [9]. Having biased or missing information in training AI systems can lead them to unfairly treat customers or award credit. For instance, if an AI model learns from data that includes systemic biases, it may decline loans to certain groups, breaching fairness requirements and potentially making banks liable under the law [19]. AI being used to work with customer data gives rise to questions about protecting the privacy of this information. As AI decisions are not clearly accounted for, people's trust in companies decreases, since customers want to make sure these systems are ethical. Solving these issues means building proper governance systems and making a point to involve stakeholders in the process.

- **Cybersecurity risks**

  It is possible for attackers to manipulate AI systems by giving them certain inputs to trick models and put systems for fraud detection and processing settlements at great risk [13]. By changing the details in a transaction, attackers can trick AI systems and end up causing both financial damage and damage to the brand. Banking systems being connected raises the risks since one vulnerability can influence the security of many connections. Also, since many different AI vendors are used, banks cannot manage every part of their supply chain [16]. Out of the many risks, dealing with them requires complex and costly measures, including adversarial training, encryption, and ongoing monitoring as explained in Figure 5.3.

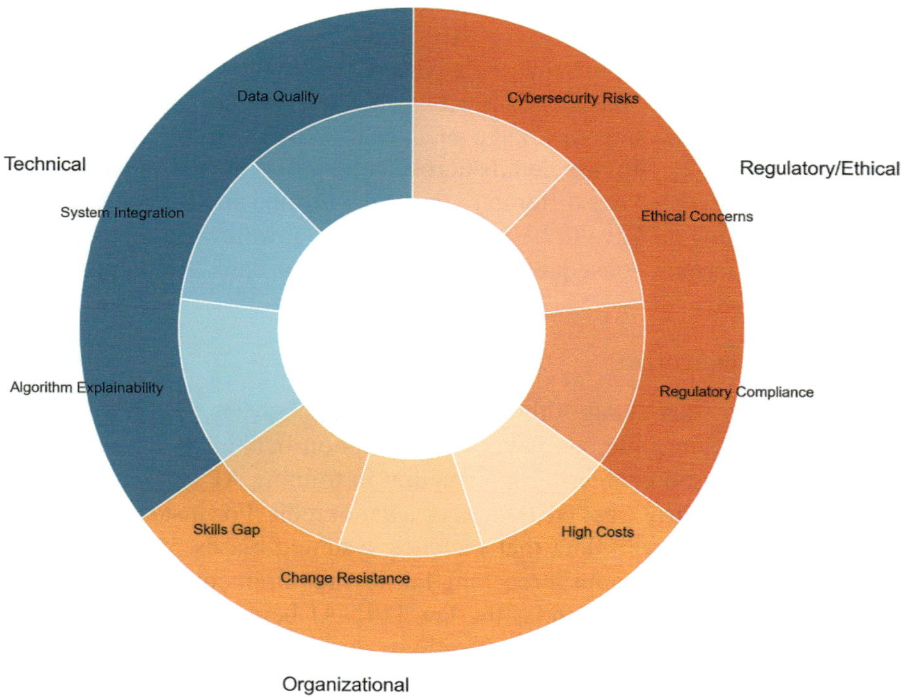

Figure 5.3 Challenges and limitations of AI adoption in banking.
Source: Generated by author.

5.4 Strategies for Overcoming Obstacles

For the successful use of artificial intelligence in banking, institutions have to handle the different challenges that are discussed in Section 3 using several approaches at once. As part of this section, a wide range of strategies that include innovation, organizational change, and working directly with regulators are suggested to support the successful adoption of AI. Following these strategies allows banks to get past problems, effectively work, satisfy customers, and ensure compliance. The strategies are arranged to fit the challenges identified, while being backed up by examples and information from recent studies and industry practices.

5.4.1 Enhancing data quality and governance

To be effective, AI systems need reliable data, but banks frequently deal with isolated data, problems of consistency and strict privacy requirements. These strategies try to enhance data quality and governance to ensure AI models perform properly and recognition is accurate.

- **Implement data governance frameworks:** Setting strong data governance polices is important for ensuring data is reliable, correct, and accessible in all banking activities. They need to address who owns the data, choose standard ways to save data, and help share data securely between departments to stop information silos [5]. One instance is Citibank's worldwide data governance programme that connects different sources of data, allowing them to detect fraud and provide customer insights using AI [21]. Governance plans should be regularly audited and rely on quality metrics to guarantee reliability in the future.
- **Leverage synthetic data:** Synthesizing data allows banks to use AI models on sensitive or limited data while still safeguarding customer privacy. Because artificial datasets closely resemble real-life examples, banks can follow regulations, including the GDPR, and still use enough data for things like credit risk modelling [22]. Indeed, synthetic information is used by fintech firms to improve credit modelling, enabling them to include people not served by traditional banking [11]. By processing synthetic data, this approach handles the risks associated with data breaches much better, as these data points do not personalize the user in any way.
- **Invest in data cleansing:** Data cleansing tools that work automatically can eliminate mistakes, duplicate entries, and inconsistent data, helping

to improve the dependability of AI applications. Machine learning in these applications allows them to spot and fix any errors, ensuring the accuracy of data for both fraud management and software segmentation [18]. HSBC has put data cleansing programmes into place to support AI-based marketing activities, which has helped the company engage its customers more. Ongoing cheque-ups and cleaning are required to maintain the best quality of data in rapidly shifting banking environments [14].

5.4.2 Facilitating system integration

Integrating AI with older technologies is a big challenge, yet certain techniques can help reduce the impact and cut back on extra costs.

- **Adopt modular integration:** When banks connect AI with their existing system, they can use APIs and middleware to do this in stages, instead of requiring a full renewal. The modular process helps banks avoid major issues and expenses, which lets them add AI in parts [17]. By way of example, Wells Fargo has connected AI-powered chatbots to its current CRM platform with the help of APIs, allowing it to enhance customer service without disrupting its core systems [23]. Thanks to modular design, the system supports future changes and keeps systems compatible for many years.
- **Modernize infrastructure:** With cloud platforms, AI may be added to or used with various instruments without hassle, correcting the drawbacks of older technology. With cloud solutions, AI can easily handle real-time fraud detection by handling large volumes of data smoothly [18]. Standard Chartered Bank has transferred important services to the cloud, helping it to use AI in risk management more quickly. One way banks can control costs is by keeping critical information within their own servers and relying on public clouds for less important activities.

5.4.3 Addressing algorithmic explainability

The fact that AI models are not always transparent in banking demands solutions to improve explainability and earn people's trust.

- **Develop Explainable AI (XAI):** Implementing interpretable models or using XAI techniques helps make AI decisions more openly understandable and consistent with what regulatory laws and customers expect. Thanks to methods like feature importance analysis and decision tree approximations offered by XAI, people can easily see how the model works and follow legal requirements in the EU AI Act [19]. XAI is being used by Goldman Sachs in credit risk models to ensure regulators can check their decisions and identify risks related to compliance [24]. When using XAI, developers can simplify the model, but it becomes necessary for applications where accountability is required, including loan approvals.

- **Engage stakeholders:** Bringing regulators, customers, and inside teams together in the AI process encourages transparency and trust. To ensure compliance, companies can regularly consult with supervisory authorities, and keeping customers in the loop allows AI to respond to their needs [15]. A good example is ING Bank holding stakeholder workshops to ensure their AI customer service systems comply with ethical and regulatory rules, which helps the systems be more widely accepted, according to [25]. Sharing both the advantages and disadvantages helps people feel more confident in AI.

5.4.4 Bridging the skills gap

Because there is not enough AI expertise, companies need to grow their own specialists and reach out to external sources.

- **Upskilling programs:** Letting staff learn about AI, machine learning, and data science through in-house training programs reduces the company's need for outside help in AI projects [22]. Barclays and others have set up AI academies to teach their staff about data analytics and model deployment, encouraging employees to become more technically skilled [26]. These programs should be tailored to different roles, from technical teams to business leaders, ensuring broad organizational alignment.
- **Strategic partnerships:** Teamwork with universities, AI companies and research institutions brings access to unique skills and groundbreaking inventions. AI projects can advance faster with help from firms such as Google or Microsoft, and partnerships with universities or research institutions are important for conducting long-term studies [15]. In one example, DBS Bank is working with Singapore's universities to use their knowledge to improve its fraud detection models [27].

- **Participate in open-source communities:** Using open-source options enables banks to use already-made models, which helps cut both expenses and time. Users of TensorFlow and PyTorch AI platforms can rely on global developer communities, as both platforms are robust for AI applications [16]. With open-source participation, financial organizations can advance in AI without spending much on resources.

5.4.5 Overcoming resistance to change

The opposition to using AI by organizations can be resolved by changing their culture and using proper change methods.

- **Foster a culture of innovation:** When a workplace welcomes new attempts and is not afraid of setbacks, employees tend to feel AI is an aid to their strategy, rather than something dangerous. With the use of innovation hubs and pilot experiments, AI can provide results that encourage wider acceptability [16]. For example, BBVA takes AI applications through trial runs in the innovation lab to highlight the advantages and advantages for both employees and those in charge [28].
- **Transparent communication:** Involving employees early on and providing examples of how AI can help them get the job done alleviates their worries about losing their jobs. Organizing town halls, training employees, and studying real cases can demonstrate that AI saves time so that companies can focus extra time on helping their customers [29]. The bank's open information about its AI assistant, Erica, helped achieve a faster employee adoption by assuring them that Erica helps, not replaces, staff [12].
- **Executive sponsorship:** When executive sponsors lead AI efforts, it becomes easier to match with business goals and get the top team's support. Such sponsors can push for distributing needed resources and inform stakeholders about the key role of AI in the company [16]. For example, JPMorgan Chase's CEO has publicly endorsed AI as a core component of its digital strategy, driving organizational commitment [30].

5.4.6 Managing costs

The high costs of AI adoption require strategic approaches to optimize resource allocation and demonstrate return on investment.

- **Phased implementation:** Introducing AI slowly by running pilot programs, looking at the outcomes, and becoming more confident helps banks make better decisions when expanding their AI use. Achieving quick results in important fields like fraud detection means pilots can encourage more investment [15]. As an example, loan processing with the help of AI at Santander decreased approval times, prompting them to scale up its use [31].

- **Utilize cloud-based solutions:** Using AI through the cloud helps save on infrastructure and increases the level of deployment. Applications of AI are becoming affordable to smaller financial institutions thanks to the ready-built tools found on AWS and Azure [17]. As one example, regional banks are using cloud-based AI for analysing their customers, saving money as they compete with large banks [18].

5.4.7 Ensuring regulatory compliance and ethical AI

Navigating regulatory and ethical challenges requires proactive measures to align AI systems with legal and societal expectations.

- **Proactive regulatory engagement:** Partnering with regulators allows your organization to align with the latest policies and face less risk of penalties. Meeting regularly with organizations like the European Banking Authority can explain in detail the expected transparency with AI and what data may be used [18]. As an illustration, Deutsche Bank makes sure its AI-assisted compliance systems, Mittelstand Bank, are aligned with Basel III, so they lessen the risks from regulations [32].
- **Establish ethical AI committees:** By setting up specialist committees, companies can manage biased, unfair, and accountable applications within AI. These groups need to consist of a wide range of stakeholders so they can keep an eye on every part of AI technology and form ethical guidelines [22]. To illustrate, Lloyds Banking Group's AI ethics team works to find biases in credit scoring models, making sure the algorithm achieves greater fairness and trust [33].
- **Implement robust cybersecurity:** Strong cybersecurity steps, which include training with adversarial data, using encryption, and constant monitoring, defend AI systems from being attacked. Since fraud detection relies on software, measures like these are key to preventing things like great financial losses [13]. A good illustration is how Mastercard applies adversarial training, strengthening its AI system's monitoring to resist smart attacks [34] as shown in Figure 5.4.

Figure 5.4 Strategies for overcoming AI adoption obstacles in banking.
Source: Generated by author.

5.5 Conclusion and Future Directions

AI is bringing a new era to banking by improving how things are done, how customers are served, and reaching out to more people globally. Intelligent solutions such as predictive analytics, chatbots, systems for detecting fraud, and personalized financial advisory tools have already helped companies complete tasks efficiently, save money, and offer suitable services to clients [35]. In such cases, AI models analyse unusual forms of data to help banks provide their services to individuals who are not easily served by traditional credit systems [11]. Even so, achieving AI's full benefits in banking involves handling technical problems, opposing views within the company, and following strict rules given by regulators.

5.5.1 Addressing key challenges

For AI to be effective in banks, good data governance must come first to secure data quality, maintain data security, and follow the rules of privacy laws such as the GDPR and the CCPA. To work well, AI systems need good data management and a strong data structure, since weak or biased data can reduce customer trust [36]. What is more, if organizations remain unchanged and staff do not understand AI well enough, it can stall the adoption process. The best practice for successful innovation might be for banks to invest in detailed training and create a climate that pushes business and IT departments to team up [37]. Ensuring that AI is used properly also matters, as banks must handle challenges like algorithmic bias, make their methods transparent, and remain responsible to keep customer confidence and obey new regulations [38].

Since AI is used in banking, it is essential for AI systems to follow detailed regulations in the areas of managing risks, safeguarding customers, and fighting against money laundering. There is rising attention from regulators globally on AI, so banks are obliged to cooperate closely with regulators to produce frameworks that support both innovation and compliance [39]. By adopting explainable AI models and conducting regular audits, banks can ensure that their AI systems are both effective and compliant, positioning themselves as trusted leaders in the digital financial landscape.

5.5.2 Future directions

Looking ahead, the long-term implications of AI in banking warrant deeper exploration. Future research should focus on several key areas to guide the responsible evolution of AI-driven banking:

- **Impact on employment:** Although AI can handle routine jobs, questions about how it affects the financial industry are very important. Research should look at the transformation of jobs, how AI expands options in management and data science, and why reskilling efforts are needed for employees [40].
- **Customer trust and adoption:** When AI appears more often in how companies interact with customers, appreciating its effect on trust matters. Experts should explore how being open, fair, and user-friendly in AI services encourages people to use them for sensitive activities like choosing credit or managing money [38].
- **Financial stability:** How widespread AI use in banking will influence the financial market is not fully understood. Future research should focus on how automated decisions in trading and risk assessment impact market stability and introduce new possible weaknesses linked to related AI activities [40].
- **Emerging AI technologies:** There is more to explore about applying recent AI approaches, for example, reinforcement learning, generative AI, and federated learning, in banking. For example, reinforcement

learning can be used in dynamic pricing, and generative AI could improve customer service with virtual assistants that look and feel like actual people [36]. Working with federated learning allows banks to share their data without violating privacy during collaborative research [39].

- **Interdisciplinary approaches:** Because AI is complex in the banking sector, research into it must connect insights from behavioral finance, ethics, data science, and regulatory studies. Behavioral finance can show how AI-based nudging impacts customer finances, and using ethical frameworks can help ensure that AI is developed fairly for all users [38]. Collaboration across these fields will be crucial to creating a sustainable AI-driven banking ecosystem.
- **Sustainability and social impact:** Since ESG principles are being followed by banks more often, research should investigate how AI systems enhance sustainable banking. Lending portfolios could be managed more efficiently with AI, and it could check the environmental effects of each choice the company [11].

5.5.3 Conclusion

Establishing AI in the banking industry is both encouraging and presents many challenges. When banks handle technical, organizational and regulatory difficulties by investing in data governance, employee training and ethical AI, they can achieve great achievements in innovation and expand their businesses. The key future role of AI in banking is to offer financial services that suit each person, bring everyone along, and keep them stable. Keeping up with research and involving a variety of professions will support both the upgrade to better operations and the building of a more balanced and enduring financial system using AI.

References

[1] Caron, M. S., *The transformative effect of AI on the banking industry*, Banking and Financial Law Review, 34(2), 169–214, 2019.

[2] Yu, P., Peng, M., *AI-based investment management systems*, Journal of Financial Innovation, 4(2), 45–60, 2017.

[3] Mehrotra, A., *Artificial intelligence in financial services: Need to blend automation with human touch*, in: 2019 International Conference on Automation, Computational and Technology Management, pp. 342–347, IEEE, 2019.

[4] Wube, H. D., et al., *Text-based chatbot in financial sector: A systematic literature review*, Data Science in Finance and Economics, 2(3), 232–259, 2022.

[5] InvestGlass, *What are the challenges of AI adoption in banking?*, https://www.investglass.com, 2024.

[6] Fountain, T., et al., *Barriers to organizational adoption of AI*, Journal of Financial Technology, 5(2), 87–102, 2019.

[7] Temasek, *AI in Financial Services: Opportunities and Challenges*, Temasek Reports, 2021.

[8] Adeyemi, T., Adebayo, O., *The impact of AI on financial decision-making in Nigerian banking*, African Journal of Financial Technology, 10(3), 145–158, 2022.

[9] Saheb, T., *Ethical challenges in AI: Fairness, privacy, and accountability*, Journal of Digital Ethics, 3(1), 22–35, 2024.

[10] Forbes, *How AI is revolutionizing fraud detection in banking*, https://www.forbes.com, 2023.

[11] World Bank, *Financial inclusion and the role of technology*, https://www.worldbank.org, 2020.

[12] Bank of America, *Erica: Transforming customer engagement with AI*, https://www.bankofamerica.com, 2024.

[13] Ghandour, A., *Opportunities and challenges of artificial intelligence in banking: Systematic literature review*, Banking and Finance Review, 12(4), 56–78, 2021.

[14] HSBC, *Personalizing wealth management with AI*, https://www.hsbc.com, 2023.

[15] Forbes, *The rise of robo-advisors: AI-driven wealth management*, https://www.forbes.com, 2024.

[16] Naviant, *9 common challenges to AI adoption and how to avoid them*, https://naviant.com, 2025.

[17] Cubet, *Overcoming AI implementation challenges in enterprise environments*, https://cubettech.com, 2024.

[18] AWS, *Navigating AI adoption in regulated industries*, https://aws.amazon.com, 2024.

[19] Brainard, L., *AI and Financial Services: Opportunities and Challenges*, Speech at the Federal Reserve, November 2018.

[20] Forbes, *11 barriers to effective AI adoption and how to overcome them*, https://www.forbes.com, 2024.

[21] Citibank, *Enhancing AI performance with global data governance*, https://www.citibank.com, 2023.

[22] IBM, *AI adoption challenges*, https://www.ibm.com, 2025.

[23] Wells Fargo, *Modular AI integration in banking*, https://www.wellsfargo.com, 2024.
[24] Goldman Sachs, *Implementing explainable AI in financial services*, https://www.goldmansachs.com, 2024.
[25] ING, *Building trust in AI through stakeholder engagement*, https://www.ing.com, 2023.
[26] Barclays, *Building AI expertise through employee upskilling*, https://www.barclays.com, 2024.
[27] DBS, *Partnering for AI innovation in banking*, https://www.dbs.com, 2023.
[28] BBVA, *Driving AI innovation through experimentation*, https://www.bbva.com, 2024.
[29] Fairmarkit, *Challenges of AI adoption: 5 reasons for AI resistance in procurement*, https://www.fairmarkit.com, 2024.
[30] JPMorgan Chase, *Leadership in AI-driven banking*, https://www.jpmorganchase.com, 2023.
[31] Santander, *Piloting AI for operational efficiency*, https://www.santander.com, 2023.
[32] Deutsche Bank, *Aligning AI with regulatory standards*, https://www.db.com, 2023.
[33] Lloyds, *Ethical AI governance in banking*, https://www.lloydsbankinggroup.com, 2024.
[34] Mastercard, *Strengthening AI with cybersecurity measures*, https://www.mastercard.com, 2023.
[35] Fethi, M. D., Pasiouras, F., *Assessing bank efficiency and performance with operational research and artificial intelligence techniques: A survey, European Journal of Operational Research*, 204(2), 189–198, 2010.
[36] Goodfellow, I., Bengio, Y., Courville, A., *Deep learning*, pp. 205–206, MIT Press, 2016.
[37] He, J., Baxter, S. L., Xu, J., Xu, J., Zhou, X., Zhang, K., *The practical implementation of artificial intelligence technologies in medicine*, Nature Medicine, 25(1), 30–36, 2019.
[38] Mittelstadt, B. D., Allo, P., Taddeo, M., Wachter, S., Floridi, L., *The ethics of algorithms: Mapping the debate*, Big Data & Society, 3(2), 1–21, 2016.
[39] European Banking Authority, *Report on the use of artificial intelligence and machine learning in the banking sector*, https://www.eba.europa.eu, 2021.
[40] Buchak, G., Matvos, G., Piskorski, T., Seru, A., *Fintech, regulatory arbitrage, and the rise of shadow banks*, Journal of Financial Economics, 130(3), 453–483, 2018.

6

Agentic AI in Retail Banking – A New Paradigm in Customer Engagement and Decision-Making and Need for AI Governance: A Case Study of Kotak Bank Customers

Narinder Kumar[1*], Amit Kumar[2], Veena A[3] and Hakim Singh[4]

[1*]School of Economics and Public Policy, RV University, India
[2]FABER, Department of Orthopaedics, PGIMER, India
[3]School of Business, RV University, India
[4]Department of Political Science, Lovely Professional University, India

Email: narinderk@rvu.edu.in; amit.addi2010@gmail.com; veenaa@rvu.edu.in; hakimsinghshan22@gmail.com

Abstract

The present work highlights the development of AI technology and how it is finding its intersection in various sectors, including banking and finance. The study finds that the banks, especially the private commercial banks and NBFCs, are the forerunners in the adoption of AI in their operations. In contrast, the public banks are showing systemic challenges to adopt AI in their daily processes. The present work uses Kotak Bank's AI-based virtual assistant "*KEYA*" to conduct a case study on the customer's behavior towards the use of virtual assistant. The study used binary logistic regression to identify factors influencing the use of *KEYA*, Kotak Bank's virtual assistant. The use of *KEYA* is the binary outcome variable used for analysis. The independent variables are age, banking experience in years, and the educational background of the customers. It was found that age and educational background do not determine the use of a virtual assistant, and only the number of years

 DOI: 10.1201/9788743810766-6

of association with the bank increases the probability of using the bank's virtual assistant. The study also reports the current regulations and concerns related with the use of AI in banking.

6.1 Introduction

Digital technologies have been transforming retail banking over the past decade and continue to do so. Artificial Intelligence (AI) is one of them and is proving to be a crucial innovation, automation, and personal customer experience enabler. Although AI in banking was relatively narrow in terms of its functions at the early stage, i.e., geared towards the back-end (fraud detection, risk scoring, and transaction processing), with the introduction of Agentic AI, a new era of the digital development has come, where AI systems not only help, but make their own decisions, communicate with customers, proactively manage and drive financial strategies.

Agentic AI is a kind of smart system in which there is a degree of autonomy, environmental awareness, goalfulness, and decision-making to emulate human-like gathering. Such systems are more than just rule-based automation or mere chatbots as they have the ability to perform sophisticated tasks like giving highly individualized financial advice, pinpointing the patterns that might be fraudulent, and dynamically changing to the preferences of the customer. Simply stated, Agentic AI does not simply react; it performs.

Agentic AI is becoming increasingly widespread in the realms of Indian retail banking via the recurring use of intelligent virtual assistants (IVAs) and intelligent conversational AI interfaces. This is viewed prominently in the State Bank Intelligent Assistant (SIA), a technology implemented by the State Bank of India, which inspects Natural Language Processing (NLP), predictive analytics, and machine learning to decipher the intention of the customers, respond to their queries, and render their services, such as transferring funds and resolving complaints. Likewise, the voicebot Ava of HDFC Bank is bilingual, and it is well incorporated with core banking to provide real-time information with the help of Interactive Voice Response (IVR) modules. The said systems lessen the operational overhead on human agents, as well as provide 24-hour working and multilingual service, and immediate service; this is a great advantage for the user experience.

But in retail banking, there is also the issue of concern and challenge that comes with the emergence of the Agentic AI. Algorithms' obscurity, unintelligibility, and risks of unfair decision-making have become the subject of regulators, technologists, and ethicists. When unregulated, these AI programs might become a source of exclusionary practices, especially for persons with less digital literacy skills, persons with poor command of the language, and persons with no smartphone and a lack of fast internet access. Additionally, questions of data privacy, security, and auditability are becoming more serious since agentic systems are able to access sensitive information about customers and take action in real time.

In an institutional light, banks have begun dealing with the dilemma of the balance between the utility of automation and the anticipation of faith, clarity, and uprightness. Retail banking is a very competitive industry where trust of the consumers occupies a pivotal point. Reputational damage and regulatory focus can be triggered by any failure in the AI performance, including incorrect credit decisions, fraud alerts, financial advisory, etc.

The objective of this chapter is to discuss the transformation that Agentic AI is bringing in the retail banking, especially in the Indian scenario, at length. It rates the benefits, technical architecture, and use cases of Agentic AI systems and covers the regulatory, ethical, and practical risks of implementing such systems. Combining the insights provided by the implementation of such tools as SBI SIA or HDFC Ava, the the paper examines how banks will be able to able to approach a human-AI symbiosis situation, i.e., where AI will aid, not replace, the human in the banking world.

Finally, the chapter will be helpful in continuing the discussion of the topic of responsible incorporation of Agentic AI into the financial sector. It suggests a framework model of AI governance in retail banking as well as the necessity of inclusive, explainable, and secure AI implementations that can support a wide range of customer groups without jeopardizing accountability.

6.2 Literature Review

In [1], the authors explore the ways Agentic AI can potentially be impactful in revolutionizing regulatory observance in the banking and financing industries. These AI tools, while aimed to cost-cutting and reducing dependence on human labor, majorly destined to automatically interpret and apply the complex regulatory framework. Along with the mentioned pros, it will also enhance transparency, accountability, and risk management. Knowledge graphs, natural language processing, and reinforcement learning are some tools, to name a few, which can process a large amount of data along with other operations in process. The research stressed establishing a regulatory sandbox to safely trail, ensuring ethical and social alignment. While keeping the present concerns of ethical use, transparency, and the need should be adaptable and interpretable.

In [2], the authors focused on examining how agentic AI is transforming retail banking by enhancing decision-making, customer service, and operational efficiency. NLP, machine learning, and cloud computing are some technologies that banks are using to operate AI assistants such as SBI-SIA. These systems analyze user behavior and demographics to offer tailored financial advice and product recommendations, boosting customer engagement and trust. Agentic AI is advantageous for fraud detection and risk analysis, reducing costs and increasing accuracy. This also targets financial inclusion for the unbanked population with the help of different digital platforms. Therefore, it requires clear regulatory and ethical frameworks to ensure responsible, adaptive AI deployment aligned with societal expectations.

In [3], the author examines how advanced and Agentic AI is reshaping the fintech systems, especially payments and credit card transactions. This article stands in critique of centralized payment systems, instead proposing decentralized systems. The decentralized system will be equipped with intelligent agents that have the ability to automatically execute transactions and thereby reduce the dependence on credit cards. It also showcases fintech's evolution across stages of empowerment, efficiency, collaboration, and trust, driven by technologies like machine learning, NLP, and predictive analytics. Since agentic AI is adaptive and its autonomous capacity aligns well with robotics, it can carry out functions like fraud detection, customer support, and credit scoring. This chapter also points out challenges to KYC, AML, and data privacy. It stresses the role of ethical use of AAAI as a regulator, and offers efficient, inclusive financial services offering strong e-governance and transparency.

In [4], the authors explore the infrastructure that is needed for AAAI to work efficiently in retail and data operations, and how this role will enhance the decision-making process in fintech. The chapter also explores architectural challenges, including the development of scalable, cloud-native systems, real-time data processing, and seamless integration with current IT frameworks. Technologies like micro services, containerization, edge computing, and AI orchestration are identified as key enablers and are credited as agile and resilient. It focuses on data quality, security, privacy, and compliance across AI lifecycles. Human oversight is cited as an important way to enhance transparency. By joining hands with AI, robust data governance, organizational bias reduction, and regulatory standards are expected. Thereby, it boosts supply chain performance, demand forecasting, customer personalization, and operational reliability.

In [5], the authors highlighted the recent breakthrough in technology in banking, and how the banking industry is leveraging the intelligent infrastructure and AI technologies, especially the subset of AI, i.e., Agentic AI, that is changing the dynamics of customer engagement. The study pointed out the importance of AI technology in banking and finance, and the growing need for automation in mundane operations. The adoption of AI in the banking industry brings huge opportunities to achieve personalization in banking and finance, and to promote efficiency by bringing down the cost of operations. The concerns related to the adoption of AI were also highlighted by the author. The chapter, along with highlighting the advantages like real-time decision-making, reduced operational cost, and scalability, etc., also pointed out the concerns like data privacy, security and compliance, transparency, and accountability. To resolve these issues, the chapter highlighted that AI governance, regulations on the use of AI, and ethical use of AI by the banking and finance companies were highlighted.

In [6], the authors underscore the advantages of Agentic AI technologies and the capability of AI to carry out autonomous reasoning and leverage the reinforcement learning algorithm to adapt and make informed decisions. It reduces the need for a human to conduct a basic conversation on the company's behalf, hence providing greater flexibility and operational advantage. The study explores the impact of new technologies, especially agentic AI, on business practices. The chapter illustrates the potential positive impacts of agentic AI, which is capable of autonomous and adaptive decision-making, on improving efficiency, minimizing human involvement, and providing immediate responsiveness. It analyzes advanced organizational AIs such as machine learning, NLP, and predictive analytics, focusing on their application for intelligent automation and productivity improvements in the systems of large enterprises. Issues of ethical data transparency, human-controlled continuous learning systems, and infrastructure support are some of the major challenges that must be addressed. This study describes the gaps between the workforce, governance, and multidisciplinary interfaces within AI's ethical governance to drive away the social responsibility.

In [7], the authors give an insightful examination of the evolution and uses of agentic AI in the context of large and sophisticated organizations and technologies. The chapter gives the evolution of the agentic AI paradigm from traditional rule-based systems and how it progresses to sophisticated learning, context-aware adaptive systems. It further examines the integration of enterprise architecture within intelligent systems to enhance agility, resilience, and operational efficiency. This research merges several theoretical frameworks, industry-specific case studies, and concludes that agentic AI considerably reduces the complexity of decision-making by improving responsiveness and adaptability through systems intelligence, resulting from decreased human effort and real-time interaction with changing variables. Enhanced adaptability leads to greater productivity, responsiveness, and innovation in various sectors. In drawing attention to the striking advantages, the authors also mention gaps such as insufficient integration of legacy systems, self-governed processes that are opaque, a lack of clarity, governance opacity, algorithmic bias, data privacy, and several unsecured access points. In contrast, the authors advocate for the creation of more transparent AI systems with proper human supervision aimed at alleviating the problems raised through the circumvention of ethical design policies. Moreover, the argument put forth the urgent concern on change management and organizational-level workforce reconfiguration to craft new roles for leveraging the full potential of agentic AI systems.

In [8], the authors look into how the IT revolution has changed the financial services industry, concentrating on areas such as investment management, secure transactions, and risk mitigation. The chapter argues that robust data privacy mechanisms alongside comprehensive fraud prevention systems are critical to foster trust from both consumers and institutions as reliance on digital services grows. The authors note the pivotal role that advanced Artificial Intelligence (AI), blockchain, as well as cybersecurity technologies have for minimizing risks and enhancing operational productivity for safer financial health and growth. These technologies importantly aid in the automation of systems, active management of finances, and the security of transactions. Lastly, the chapter discusses the need to provide innovative technologies and structures aimed at maintaining requisite standards of safety, efficiency, and enduring durability for the financial sector in a more digitalized world.

In [9], the authors furthered the use of Generative AI (GenAI) in banking and finance, especially in Financial Reporting Systems (FRS). The author highlighted the potential of Gen AI in automating the decision-making process. Gen AI brings an array of functions for the banking industry, and its capability of learning from huge non-text datasets and further helping in generating the original content, such as images and text files. Well-trained Gen AI models are capable of handling queries related to FRS and providing automated responses to help in decision-making is one of the many important features of it. The study pointed out the associated risks of data privacy issues, ethical use, regulations, and the legal side of it. The author summarizes that Gen AI in the banking industry can help automate routine work and save time. Its capability to totally take over complex decisions and especially those involving money, is being studied, and the technology is creating new strides.

In [9], the authors refer to the imperative necessity of sophisticated risk management within the changing digital banking environment, suggesting "Neural Compliance" as an AI-based alternative to real-time governance. It points out increasing difficulties emanating from sophisticated cyber-attacks and the inability of conventional, sometimes obsolete, regulatory models to match the fast pace of digital financial transactions. The author presents a new neural-compliance system, an AI-based risk protocol suite that will be used to augment real-time governance through automatic rule-set generation and refreshes based on regulatory findings. One theoretical contribution is the presentation of an Authoring Simulator Transformer model for use in deploying ensembled deep learning AI in self-auditing contexts, and on the practical front, a software package for neural compliance is written as an API. According to findings, effective risk protocols driven by AI are the key to compliance, fraud mitigation, and trust in sophisticated digital banking systems, calling for a movement away from reactive audit towards proactive, real-time monitoring and action.

In [10], the authors critically analyze the shifting effect of artificial intelligence (AI), machine learning (ML), and Big Data on customized financial services, specifically in wealth management. It brings out how these technologies overcome conventional inefficiencies, including expenses and information asymmetry, by providing automated investment suggestions, customized client support, and better risk controls. The chapter highlights the role of Robo-advisors as a low-cost, scalable, and unbiased investment management alternative that makes financial services accessible to an increased population, ranging from mass affluent to retail segments. In addition, it mentions Big Data's attributes (volume, velocity, variety, complexity) as well as its various sources in finance, along with AI application history and future directions in the banking sector, such as algorithmic trading and chatbots for client interaction. It also mentions regulatory issues and ethical concerns related to the growing use of AI in finance, emphasizing transparency and trust in these sophisticated systems.

In [11], authors identify the central role of internal audit in supporting better corporate governance, in particular risk management and compliance processes, using a comparative study across East Asia and best practices worldwide. It emphasizes that strong corporate governance, based on accountability and transparency, is essential for organizational success, and internal audit is an independent function to assess the quality of risk management, control, and governance processes. The study measures how internal audit supports and influences corporate governance principles, distinguishing the quality of compliance and risk management measures, especially in the banking industry. Drawing on a mixed-methods study involving interviews, surveys, and case studies, it sets out a theoretical framework in which internal audit is the "eye and ear" of the board, giving assurance on risk management, governance, and control, and asserting that risk management and compliance are inherently enmeshed as defensive agents for corporate governance. Major findings reveal that internal audit as a critical driver significantly enhances accountability and transparency through quality internal control processes and effective risk management, where European companies prioritize risk management and compliance, whereas East Asian settings place a premium on internal audit for objective views, although its role in corporate governance is widely accepted. It concludes with a call for a re-conceptualization of the internal audit function in response to growing demands for transparency and accountability, offering concrete advice for organizations to enhance audit effectiveness, and suggesting greater research into internal audit practices across various industries and settings.

In [12], the authors studied the current evolution of finance and insurance ecosystems through the combined use of intelligent automation, secure digital infrastructure, and sophisticated risk management techniques. The main purpose is to learn about how business effectiveness, risk assessment, and the standard of insurance products can be improved through digital platforms, trust services, identity blocks, and intelligent automation. The enabling keys are AI, robotics, blockchain, APIs, cloud computing, and mobile services, which collectively make digital infrastructure secure, process information, and provide customized user experiences, resulting in lowered operational costs and best strategies. The chapter underlines the crucial role played by AI in risk underwriting and emphasizes cybersecurity as a foundation for economic resilience. Yet, some persistent challenges remain in terms of cultural resistance because of highly ingrained practices and functional silos, technological constraints emanating from intricate legacy systems with no real-time control, and intricate regulatory barriers to be traversed by Fintechs and Insurtechs. The future direction indicates additional developments through the convergence of risk management and cybersecurity, resulting in stronger and more transparent customer interfaces as well as spearheading good portfolio management decisions.

In [13], the authors provide a comprehensive analysis of the transformative impact of agentic and generative AI on the fintech sector, critically emphasizing the urgent need for robust governance and security frameworks to address emerging risks. It mentions how these advanced AI systems are revolutionizing financial services from fraud detection and customer support to autonomous decision-making while also drawing attention to the associated challenges, including data privacy concerns, cybersecurity threats, and ethical dilemmas. The study argues that current regulatory frameworks are struggling to keep pace with rapid technological advancements, resulting in gaps in transparency, accountability, and public trust. Drawing on global initiatives such as the EU AI Act and the NIST AI risk management framework, the authors advocate for a multi-dimensional approach that integrates regulatory oversight, technical safeguards, and ethical principles. For instance, the introduction of a "Trust Score model" adds a practical tool for assessing the reliability and integrity of AI systems. Ultimately, it presents a case that the responsible deployment of agentic and generative AI in Fintech must be anchored in strong governance structures to ensure secure, ethical, and trustworthy innovation.

6.3 Challenges and Risks Highlighted by the Regulatory Agencies

The adoption of AI in the Banking, Financial Services, and Insurance (BFSI) sector is rapidly increasing, and is finding different intersections shaping the functioning and transforming the structures in which the technology is used in the financial sector in India and at the global level [16]. Apparently, the private banks in relation to the public banks in India are taking the lead in AI adoption. The studies have shown that it is the scale of the bank and its asset holding that majorly determines the pace of AI adoption. Along with the benefits of AI in the banking system, the evident issues like the possibility of bias, poor transparency, and issues with data protection persist.

Among the banks in India, it is reported that private banks are taking the lead in adoption and are improving the efficiency in areas like risk assessment and risk management, fraud detection, customer services, investment strategies, regulatory compliance, etc. [16]. A similar work highlights the areas where AI models are leveraged; use of Chatbot customer support, along with earlier mentioned, the issues like anti-money laundering and combating the financing of terrorism (AML/CFT), and areas like credit and insurance underwriting [17].

6.4 Methodology

The present study follows a cross-sectional and exploratory study design, uses a mixed method approach to highlight the statement of the problem, and for sampling design, a random sample of 50 Kotak bank account holders was drawn; the selection of the bank was based on convenience and ease of data collection. Bangalore city is selected as it is the Silicon Valley of India, and based on the nature of the study, i.e., use of AI in banking and customers using the AI-based agents like Chatbot or virtual assistants.

The primary data was collected by using a self-administered questionnaire, and the data was processed in Microsoft Excel for further use in analysis. The study's aim is to explore the factors determining the use of agentic AI technologies like Chatbots and virtual assistants.

For analysis, binary logistic regression was used on selected exploratory variables like age, educational background, and number of years of experience with the bank to study their impact on the decision making towards virtual assistants.

6.5 Data Analysis

The present section is divided into descriptive analysis of the sample data using the cross-tabulation based on background factors like age, gender, educational background (technical or non-technical), and the highest qualification of the customer in relation to the use of *KEYA* virtual assistant. The second section covers the application and results of Logit Model. The analysis is concluded with the validation of the results by presenting the Logit Model diagnostics, such as Hosmer-Lemeshow, pseudo-R^2 goodness of fit measures, confusion matrix, and ROC plot.

6.5.1 Descriptive analysis

The data on 50 Kotak Bank account users from RV University, Bengaluru, was collected for the present case study. It was collected from the University staff to highlight whether a highly qualified individual working at the University level is aware of the AI assistant, i.e., *KEYA*, of Kotak Mahindra Bank.

Table 6.1 shows that the sample is composed of Kotak Bank account holders in four major age groups, and the majority of the sample is in the age group of 30 to 40 years. Indicating that older adults are greater in number in comparison to the other counterparts. As per the gender distribution, females are more in number in the present sample. Based on the highest qualification, the majority are Ph.D., constituting around 48% of the total sample with Ph.D., and around 42% with any postgraduate degree. Out of the total sample, around 72% are not from a technical background, like engineering or mathematics, highlighting that the sample is constituted by the staff with a non-technical background.

Table 6.1 Sample Distribution based on the background characteristics.

Background characteristics	Category	Number	Percentage
Age category	20-30 Years	14	28
	30–40 Years	22	44
	40–50 Years	11	22
	50 above	3	6
Gender	Male	17	34
	Female	32	64
Highest qualification	UG	5	10
	PG	21	42
	PHD	24	48
Education in technical field	0	36	72
	1	14	28

Source: Author compilation.

6.5.2 Description of use of Kotak Mahindra Bank's Keya Virtual Assistant using cross tabs

The section represents the distribution of the sample based on the background characteristics: age, gender, qualification, and technical education. The analysis is performed using SPSS-20.

Table 6.2 shows the distribution of the respondents who use *Keya* virtual assistant of Kotak Mahindra Bank. The distribution is based on the age category, and as it is apparent from the table that no particular age group has a detrimental role in determining the use of the bank's virtual assistant. So,

Table 6.2 Do you Use Keya VA and age category cross tabulation.

Background characteristics		Age category				Total
		20–30 years	30–40 years	40–50 years	50 above	
Do you Use Keya VA	No	12	20	8	2	42
	Yes	2	2	3	1	8
Total		14	22	11	3	50

Source: Author compilation.

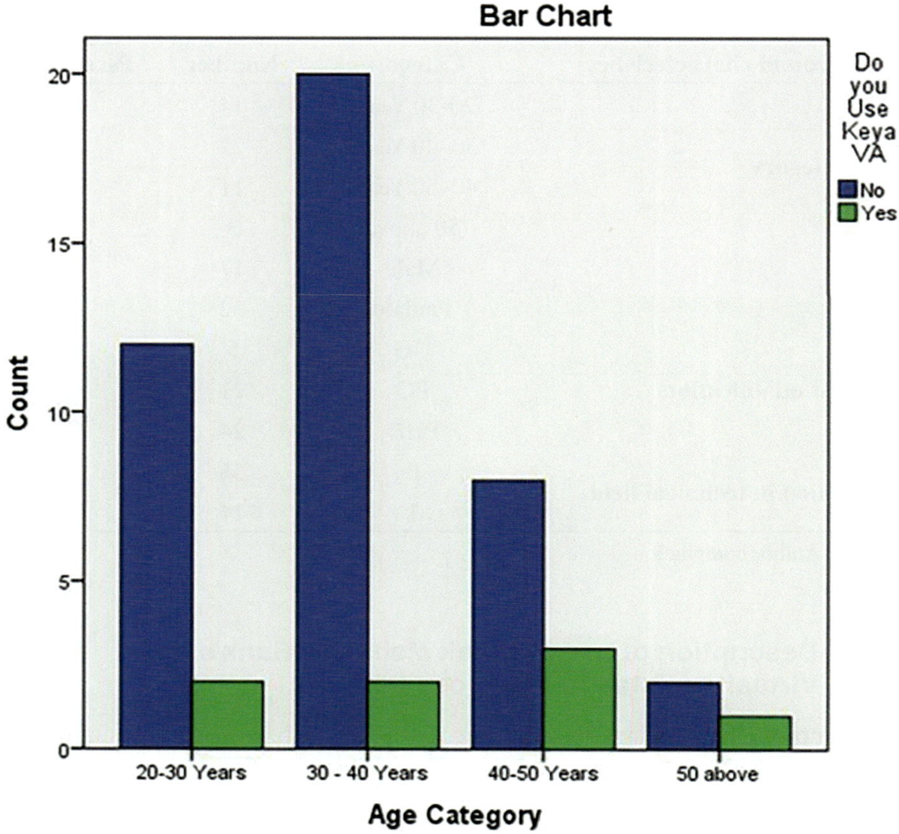

Figure 6.1 Distribution of the respondents based on the use of Keya and age.

in conclusion, the decision to use *Keya* is not associated with the age of the individuals in the dataset.

In Figure 6.1, the bar chart supplements the previous table, while the blue bar represents the number of respondents who do not use *Keya*, and the green bar represents the number of respondents in various age groups who use the virtual assistant. It is evident that very few in the total sample are using the bank's virtual assistant for their queries.

Table 6.3 shows the distribution of *Keya* users' based on gender, showing comparatively larger number of females are using *Keya*, but we have to be slightly cautious in interpreting the result, as females constitute 64% of the sample, and it is in the same proportion (5/8 = 0.625) around

Table 6.3 Gender and Do you Use Keya VA cross tabulation.

Background characteristics		Do you Use Keya VA		Total
		No	Yes	
Gender	Male	14	3	17
	Female	27	5	32
Total		41	8	49

Source: Author compilation.

62%. In a nutshell, gender does not determine the use of a bank's virtual assistance.

Figure 6.2 represents the bar chart that visualizes Table 6.3, indicating that a very small proportion of the sample uses the *Keya* virtual assistant, and within the gender category, there is no significant variation.

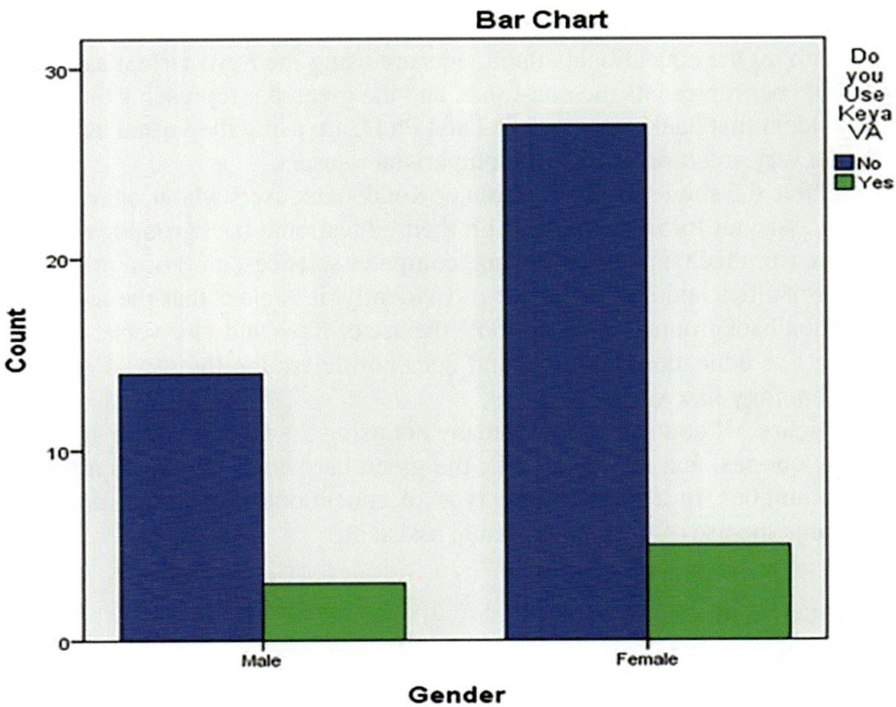

Figure 6.2 Distribution of a sample using Keya virtual assistant based on gender.

Table 6.4 Highest qualification and Do you Use Keya VA cross tabulation.

Background characteristics		Do you Use Keya VA		Total
		No	**Yes**	
Highest qualification	**UG**	5	0	5
	PG	17	4	21
	Ph.D.	20	4	24
Total		42	8	50

Source: Author compilation.

Table 6.4 shows that, as far as the association between qualification and use of *Keya* virtual assistant is concerned, it is evident that individuals with higher qualifications are using the service, but since the number of actual users is so small, it thus looks like a coincidence. The small number of *Keya* users makes it a very rare phenomenon. To summarize, higher qualification shows some correlation with the use of *Keya* virtual assistant.

Figure 6.3 highlights that among all the Kotak bank users, the individuals with higher educational attainments are using the *Keya* virtual assistant. The blue bar represents the non-users, and the green bar represents the users. It is evident that bank users with PG and Ph.D. are using the virtual assistant, but in a very small proportion in comparison to users.

Table 6.5 shows the distribution of Kotak bank users who use the bank's virtual assistant for queries based on their educational background, whether they are from technical (engineering, computer sciences, etc.) or non-technical (humanities and social sciences). Evidently, it is clear that the technical education background would promote the use of *Keya* and vice versa. In conclusion, the educational background does not determine the use of Agentic AI technology like *Keya*.

Figure 6.4 confirms that not many are using the bank's virtual assistant for any queries, and as it is visible, the green bar shows that users are very few in number. In a nutshell, the type of educational attainment does not determine the use of the bank's virtual assistant.

6.5.3 Logit model

The section represents the analysis of the sample data to explore which variables determine the use of *Keya* virtual assistant among the Kotak Bank users. The present chapter applies the logistic regression technique to explore the

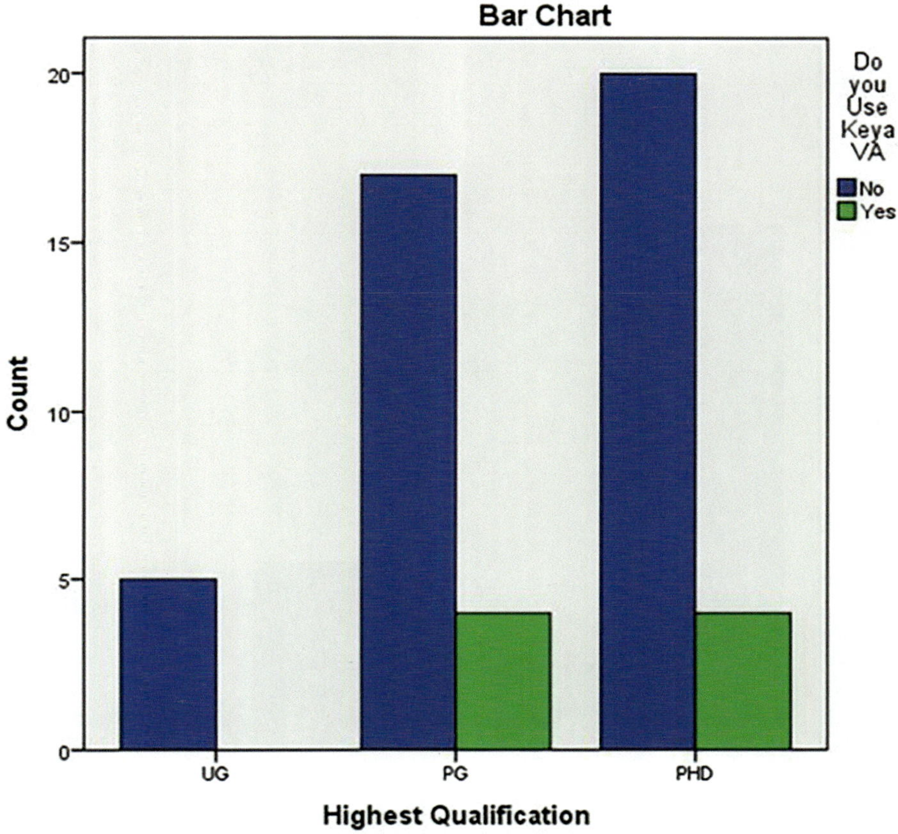

Figure 6.3 Distribution of sample using Keya virtual assistant based on highest qualification.

Table 6.5 Education in technical field and Do you Use Keya VA cross tabulation.

Background characteristics		Do you Use Keya VA		Total
		No	Yes	
Education in technical field	0	31	5	36
	1	11	3	14
Total		42	8	50

Source: Author compilation.

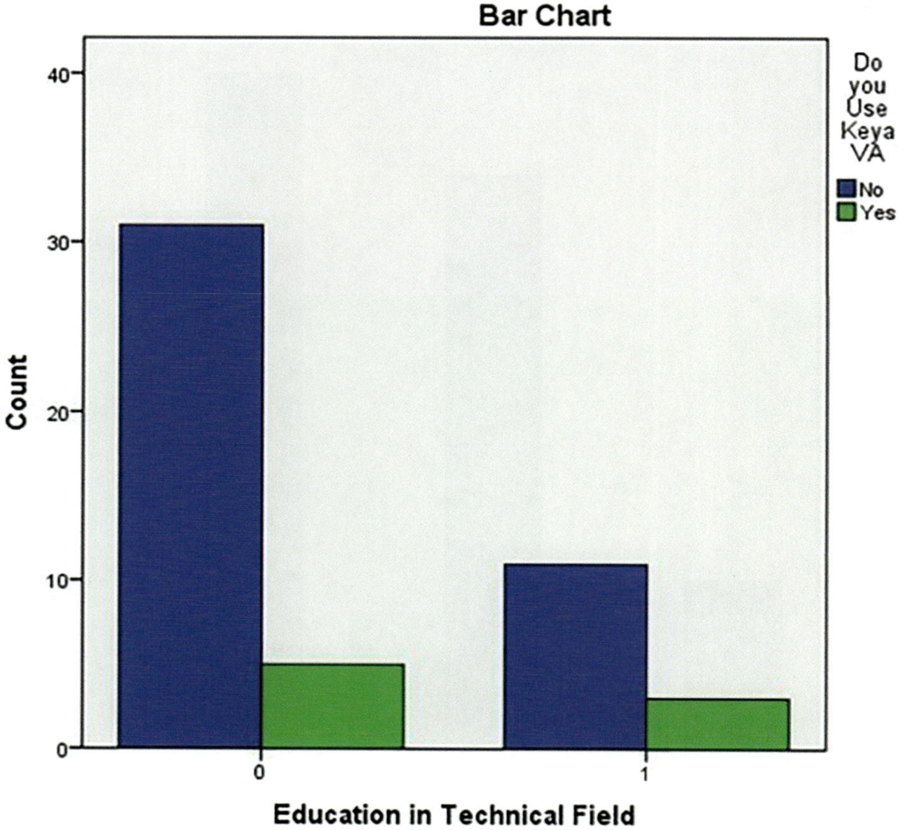

Figure 6.4 Distribution of sample using Keya virtual assistant based on education in technical field.

impact of variables: age, number of years of experience with the bank, and educational background (technical or non-technical). The formula is given as:

$$P(Y = 1 \mid X) = \frac{1}{(1 + e^{z})}$$

Where,

P(Y = 1) = *probability of individuals using Keya*

Y = 1, *when the probability of Y is greater than 0.5, given the value of X.*

X *represents the vector of independent variables or features (age, Bank_Expr, and Tech_Edu)*

e is Euler's constant, and
z is $b_i X_j$ or linear combinations of the features.

Model Results in R

The logistic regression was performed in R software. The results are gives as follows:

$$glm(formula = use\_keya \sim age + Bank\_expr + tech\_edu,$$
$$family = binomial(link = \text{“logit”}), data = data)$$

Table 6.6 provides the results of the above-mentioned logit model; the coefficient values represent the log of the odds in favor of the individuals using *Keya* virtual assistant, given the value of the regressor. To make the results understandable, the coefficients have to be exponentiated ($e^{(coeff)}$). As far as the results are concerned, Bank_Expr significantly determines the probability of an individual using *Keya*. It can be explained that as the number of years of banking experience increases, the probability in favor of using *Keya* also goes higher. The coefficient value of 0.338 after exponentiation suggests that the odds in favor of using *Keya* go up by 40.2% and the p-value of 0.031 of the log of the odds ratio of Bank_Expr confirms the significance.

In contrast, the other factors like Tech_Edu, and Age have an insignificant relationship and do not significantly determine the log of the odds ratio in favor of the use of *Keya* virtual assistant by the Kotak Bank account holders.

To supplement the model results, we need to check for the goodness of fit, as the regular R^2 fails in the case of a non-linear regression to represent the goodness of fit. The replacement for goodness of fit in the present case is Hosmer and Lemeshow, and Pseudo-R^2 goodness of fit.

Table 6.6 Distribution of the logit model results and associated values.

Variables	Coefficient	Std. error	z-value	Pr(>|z|)
Intercept	–4.258	2.284	–1.864	0.062
Bank_Expr	**0.338**	0.157	2.159	**0.031**
Tech_Edu	1.386	0.987	1.404	0.160
Age	0.021	0.058	0.361	0.718

Source: Author's compilation.

Table 6.7 Goodness of fit (Hosmer and Lemeshow, and Pseudo-R^2).

X-Squared	13.772
Df	8
p-value	0.08792

Source: Author's compilation.

6.5.4 Regression diagnostics

Table 6.7 shows the Goodness of fit in light of the null hypothesis tested for the goodness of fit:

Null (H0) = the logit model fits the data well

Alternate (H1) = the Model does not fit the data well.

Based on the test results, the p-value of $0.08792 > 0.05$ highlights that the author fails to reject the null hypothesis, indicating that the model is a good fit for the present dataset.

In Table 6.8, the test result shows that the log-likelihood and log-likelihood null, represent the model fit with and without the regressor. Where log-likelihood is the complete model, and log-likelihood null represents only the intercept. The table shows that the overall model improves the goodness of fit as the log-likelihood should be closer to zero, and the –18.36 is relatively closer to 0 from the null model. Similarly, the McFadden R^2 shows that there is a moderate fit (threshold 0.1–0.2 is a decent fit, 0.2–0.4 = excellent fit). Overall, the model signals a decent model.

Table 6.9 makes it evident that the model accurately predicts the majority of the non-users, with only seven users being miscalculated as users. However, as far as the users are concerned, the model does not predict any non-user as a user of *Keya* virtual assistant. It is evident that the phenomenon of using *Keya* is very rare, creating a problem for the model to accurately predict the users. The supportive measures highlight the quality of the model.

Table 6.10 results highlight the strength of the model results. The model predicted around 86% of the correct values of both users and non-users. The

Table 6.8 Fitting null model for pseudo-R^2.

Log-likelihood	Log-likelihood Null	G^2	McFadden R^2	r^2ML	r^2CU
–18.36	–21.98	7.2355	0.1646	0.1347	0.2303

Source: Author's compilation.

Table 6.9 Confusion Matrix [logit].

	Predicted NO (0)	Predicted YES (1)
Actual NO (0)	42	7
Actual YES (1)	0	1

Source: Author's compilation.

Table 6.10 Distribution of the quality measures of the model.

S. No.	Quality measures	Values
1	**Accuracy**	86%
2	**Precision**	100%
3	**Specificity**	85.7%
4	**Sensitivity (Recall)**	12.57%
5	**F1 Score**	0.22

Source: Author's compilation.

cases predicted as users, i.e., one in our case, is correct; as a result, the precision of the model in predicting the user is 100% as no non-user was predicted as a user. The model has a low recall value, as out of eight users in the dataset, the model only predicted 12.57% and missed the remaining users. Similarly, a low F1 Score highlights a poor match between the precision and recall values.

6.5.5 Visualizing the ROC Curve

In Figure 6.5, the results for the ROC show that the area under the curve or the accurately classified cases with AUC = 77.68%. The curve depicts that the model is learning well and is 77.68% accurate in separating the users from the non-users.

Though the model is not a perfect fit for the present data, it provides great insight The model is far better than a random guess at the classification. The model perfectly separates all the non-users, but struggles a little in perfectly classifying all the users.

6.6 Summary of the Findings

In order to summarize the results, let us precisely understand the highlights of the findings. The model showed good classification ability with a high

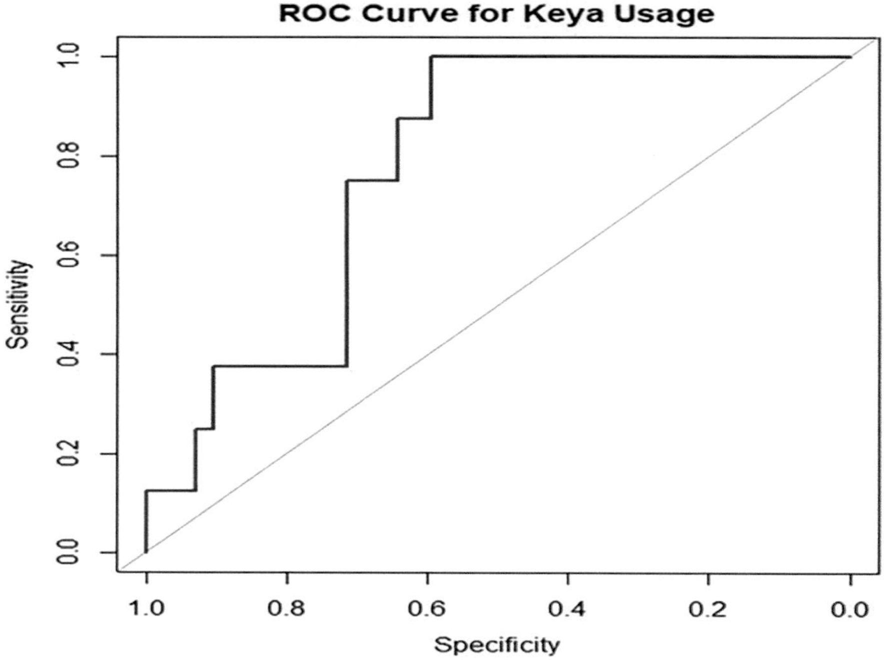

Figure 6.5 The graph shows the overall accuracy of the model in classifying users from non-users.

AUC. The Hosmer-Lemeshow confirmed a good model fit, McFadden R^2 highlighted a moderate fit. The model with poor recall, but high accuracy and perfect precision, presented a different aspect. The model, as highlighted in the confusion matrix, showed that among 50 sample points, all non-users were perfectly classified, but a great number of false positives brought down the quality of the model.

In a nutshell, the model is good for further use, especially for customer classification in separating the non-users from the users. The insights for the present work are that Kotak Mahindra Bank's customers are not using *Keya* in great numbers, and thus making it a rare outcome.

6.7 Conclusion

The study can be concluded in two ways: from the analysis perspective, and regulations on the use of agentic AI in the banking industry. It is evident from the case analysis that it is a rare phenomenon, and not many customers are using the virtual assistant. And based on the field experience, many still prefer to call the customer relationship managers for their queries. Kotak Mahindra Bank has a very robust system of customer relationship managers, where a customer can directly talk to their relationship manager and get the issue resolved while being on the call. The customers prefer this flexibility over engaging with a complex virtual assistant. The bank must realize and bring innovation in marketing their virtual assistant, as it is known to the majority of the customers that they have an option where they can be assisted by a virtual assistant.

As far as the regulations on the use of AI in banking is concerned, as the AI progresses and the systems are integrated with the AI technology, the disruptions in the banking industry are poised to happen, in the times when the technology is exponentially changing the bank's function it will become extremely difficult for the customers to get comfortable with the ever evolving banking operations. This technological breakthrough will transform the functioning of the banks, but in a short term it will be incomprehensible for the customers. This duration could potentially increase the chance of cyber risk, hence there is an important need for proper regulations on AI integration by the banks, and making the technology easy for the customers to understand and make use of it.

6.8 Current Status of Regulations On AI/ML Usage

In order to champion the issues with the AI technology and its adoption in banking system in India, some major initiatives have been taken such as National Strategy for Artificial Intelligence (NSAI), India AI Misson, AI for India 2.0, and Skill India AI are some of the initiatives to benefit from the technology while being cognizant of the potential risks and challenges associated with it.

As an initiative to regulate the use of AI in the banking system, RBI created a panel under "FREE-AI" initiative, which is expected to set the benchmark for the ethical and sustainable implementation of AI in financial sector, most importantly transforming the fintech landscape in India.

SEBI is a regulatory body for the capital market, including the securities markets and intermediaries. SEBI has proposed guidelines for AI usage in securities, primarily focusing on minimizing the associated risk of AI/ML, to promote transparency and ethical reporting of AI/ML usage by the intermediaries.

SEBI (Intermediaries) (Amendments) regulations, 2025 incorporated a new chapter IIIB on the usage of AI/ML by intermediaries. Under regulation

16c, any SEBI-regulated body using AI/ML tools, whether in-house technology or third party, will be exclusively held responsible for any cyber fraud or crime. SEBI continues to retain the full authority to take necessary actions in case of violation.

References

[1] Somu, B. (2024). The Future of Banking IT Services: Convergence of Intelligent Infrastructure and Agentic AI Models. Global Research Development (GRD) ISSN: 2455-5703, 9(12).

[2] Inala, R., & Somu, B. (2024). Agentic AI in retail banking: Redefining customer service and financial decision-making. *Journal of Artificial Intelligence and Big Data Disciplines (JAIBDD), 1*(1).

[3] Dodda, A. (2024). Integrating advanced and agentic AI in fintech: Transforming payments and credit card transactions. *European Advanced Journal for Emerging Technologies, 1*(1)

[4] Motamary, S. (2024). Designing infrastructure for agentic AI systems in retail IT and data operations. *Journal of Artificial Intelligence and Big Data Disciplines (JAIBDD), 1*(1).

[5] Somu, B. (2024). Agentic AI and financial compliance: Autonomous systems for regulatory monitoring in banking. *European Data Science Journal, 2*(1).

[6] Kalisetty, S. (2024). Agentic AI and predictive analytics: Revolutionizing retail supply chain management. *American Data Science Journal for Advanced Computations (ADSJAC), 1*(1).

[7] Inala, R., & Somu, B. (2025). Building trustworthy agentic AI systems for personalized banking experiences. *Metallurgical and Materials Engineering, 31*(5), 1336–1360.

[8] Challa, S. R., Challa, K., Lakkarasu, P., Sriram, H. K., & Adusupalli, B. (2024). Strategic financial growth: Strengthening investment management, secure transactions, and risk protection in the digital era. *Journal of Artificial Intelligence and Big Data Disciplines, 1*(1), 97–108.

[9] Sriram, H. K. (2022). Integrating generative AI into financial reporting systems for automated insights and decision support. *Available at SSRN 5232395.*

[10] Paleti, S. (2024). Neural compliance: Designing AI-driven risk protocols for real-time governance in digital banking systems. *Available at SSRN 5233099.*

[11] Srinivasa Rao Challa. (2023). Revolutionizing wealth management: The role of AI, machine learning, and big data in personalized financial

services. *Educational Administration: Theory and Practice, 29*(4), 5170–5183. https://doi.org/10.53555/kuey.v29i4.9966.

[12] Adusupalli, B., & Insurity-Lead, A. C. E. (2024). The role of internal audit in enhancing corporate governance: A comparative analysis of risk management and compliance strategies. *Journal for ReAttach Therapy and Developmental Diversities, 6*, 1921–1937.

[13] Malempati, M., Pandiri, L., Paleti, S., & Singireddy, J. (2023). Transforming financial and insurance ecosystems through intelligent automation, secure digital infrastructure, and advanced risk management strategies. *Transforming Financial and Insurance Ecosystems...*, December 3, 2023.

[14] Dodda, A. (2023). AI governance and security in fintech: Ensuring trust in generative and agentic AI systems. *American Advanced Journal for Emerging Disciplinaries (AAJED), 1*(1). ISSN: 3067-4190.

[15] Chen, B., & Zhu, X. (2023). Integrating generative AI in knowledge building. *Computers and Education: Artificial Intelligence, 5*, 100184.

[16] Shaikh, A. A., Kumar, A., Mishra, A., & Elahi, Y. A. (2024). A study of customer satisfaction in using banking services through Artificial Intelligence (AI) in India. Public Administration and Policy, 27(2), 167-181.

[17] Crisanto, J. C., Leuterio, C. B., Prenio, J., & Yong, J. (2024). FSI insights.

7

Impact and Implementation of Artificial Intelligence in Central Bank Digital Currencies: A Systematic Literature Review

A. Kumar

Department of Commerce, University of Lucknow, India

Email: kumar_amit@lkouniv.ac.in

Abstract

Rapidly transforming financial tools, central bank digital currencies (CBDCs) owe much to artificial intelligence (AI) for their development and application. By addressing three main questions – the documented effects of AI on CBDCs, the prevalent AI technologies and methods used, and the implementation strategies alongside related challenges – this systematic literature review seeks to comprehensively examine the junction of AI and CBDCs. Following strict inclusion criteria, 93 peer-reviewed publications published between 2017 and 2025 were carefully chosen using Scopus and Web of Science databases. NVivo tools allowed thematic coding and synthesis of the material, so facilitating an in-depth qualitative analysis. This method guaranteed a complex knowledge of AI's several functions inside CBDC systems. The results show that AI greatly improves risk management, financial forecasting, regulatory compliance, and user CBDC interaction. The field is dominated by key AI technologies like random forest algorithms, support vector machines (SVM), transformer models, and long short-term memory (LSTM) networks because of their interpretability and predictive accuracy. Promising directions are shown by implementation strategies, including hybrid AI-blockchain frameworks, edge computing, and reinforcement learning; but, data privacy, technical integration, regulatory uncertainty, and ethical issues present obvious difficulties. Emphasizing the need of a complete

 DOI: 10.1201/9788743810766-7

integration of AI technologies combined with strong governance structures, this study offers a disciplined road map for legislators and researchers. The insights provide vital direction for future research and practical implementation in the changing digital currency scene, so helping to advance the knowledge of AI's transforming power in forming safe, efficient, and user-centric CBDCs.

7.1 Introduction

Since central bank digital currencies (CBDCs) emerged as a promising innovation aimed at modernizing monetary systems, improving payment efficiency, and promoting financial inclusion, the global financial landscape is undergoing a profound transformation [1, 2]. At the same time, artificial intelligence (AI) has quickly spread throughout the financial industry, providing previously unknown powers in automation, data analytics, and decision-making [3, 4]. Although there are many opportunities to optimize currency design, risk management, and regulatory compliance at the nexus of AI and CBDCs [5, 6], this area of research is still understudied and has inconsistent, scattered results. This calls for a thorough and methodical synthesis in order to compile the body of knowledge, pinpoint knowledge gaps, and direct scholarly research and policymaking in this quickly developing field. Especially in new, complicated fields like AI applications in financial technologies, systematic literature reviews (SLRs) are acknowledged as being essential for compiling empirical data, minimizing bias, and improving transparency and reproducibility in research synthesis [7–9].

In response to these imperatives, this study formulates three interrelated research questions grounded in a rigorous preliminary scoping of the literature. The first research question – what are the documented impacts of AI on the development and deployment of CBDCs? – addresses the fundamental need to understand how AI is currently shaping the evolution of digital currencies. Prior works have highlighted AI's potential to improve systemic risk management, enhance monetary policy effectiveness, and transform user engagement in CBDCs [10–12]. Yet, a consolidated view capturing these diverse impacts is lacking. By synthesizing 38 key studies identified via qualitative coding with NVivo, this review aims to provide a comprehensive thematic understanding of AI's multifaceted influence on CBDC ecosystems.

The second question: Which AI technologies and methodologies are most commonly implemented in CBDC systems according to current research? arises from the recognition that AI encompasses a broad spectrum of techniques, from classical machine learning to advanced deep learning models, each with distinct advantages and application contexts [13–15]. Existing studies document varying uses of LSTM networks, transformer architectures, SVM, and reinforcement learning algorithms, among others [16, 17]. A systematic classification and critical evaluation of these methodologies are essential to clarify which AI tools are most effective and prevalent in CBDC research, guiding future technical development and deployment.

The third question: What implementation strategies have been proposed or adopted for integrating AI within CBDCs, and what are the associated challenges? stems from the practical necessity of understanding how AI can be operationalized in real-world CBDC systems. While numerous studies propose innovative frameworks such as hybrid AI-blockchain architectures and edge computing for real-time analytics [18, 19], the integration process is fraught with challenges, including data privacy concerns, technical complexity, regulatory ambiguity, and ethical considerations [14, 20, 21]. By extracting and thematically grouping implementation strategies and barriers from the full corpus of 93 articles, this review aims to provide an evidence-based roadmap to support robust, scalable, and ethically sound AI integration in CBDCs. Hence, this SLR is timely and necessary to navigate the rapidly evolving interface of AI and CBDCs, where fragmented knowledge and diverse disciplinary perspectives hinder coherent understanding and policy-making. Through rigorous methodology guided by PRISMA principles and supported by qualitative data analysis software, the study offers a transparent and replicable synthesis, contributing to both academic literature and practical policy guidance.

The study is structured as follows: Section 1 addresses the first research question by analyzing AI's documented impacts on CBDCs; Section 2 answers the second question through a detailed review of AI technologies and methodologies in use; Section 3 explores implementation strategies and challenges associated with AI integration in CBDCs; finally, the conclusion summarizes the key insights and outlines directions for future research.

7.2 Methodology

This SLR aims to comprehensively examine scholarly research focused on the integration of AI within CBDCs, specifically addressing the documented impacts, the AI technologies and methods applied, and the implementation strategies, along with the challenges encountered. The research was guided by three primary questions:

i. What are the documented impacts of AI on the development and deployment of CBDCs?

ii. Which AI technologies and methodologies are most commonly implemented in CBDC systems according to current research?

iii. What implementation strategies have been proposed or adopted for integrating AI within CBDCs, and what are the associated challenges?

To identify relevant literature, the databases Scopus and Web of Science (WoS) were selected for their comprehensive coverage of peer-reviewed publications. Preliminary exploratory searches revealed that academic work addressing AI in the context of CBDCs began to emerge only after 2017; thus the search was limited to publications from 2017 to 2025 to capture the most current and relevant studies. This temporal delimitation was not initially imposed but resulted from an evident absence of pertinent articles before 2017.

The search strategy employed a set of carefully formulated Boolean queries designed to capture the critical concepts of digital currencies, central bank-issued digital currencies, AI, and their intersections. The primary search strings included combinations such as ("Central Bank Digital Currency" OR "CBDC" OR "Digital Currency") AND ("Artificial Intelligence" OR "AI"), as well as ("Digital Fiat Currency" OR "CBDC") AND ("Machine Learning" OR "Deep Learning"), and ("CBDC" OR "Digital Currency") AND ("AI Implementation" OR "AI Integration" OR "AI Adoption"). These strings were adapted as necessary to meet the syntactic requirements of each database to ensure a comprehensive yet precise retrieval of relevant literature.

Inclusion criteria required studies to be published in English and explicitly address one or more aspects of AI application in CBDCs relevant to the research questions, whether through empirical analysis, theoretical framework, or case studies. Articles were excluded if they lacked a clear focus on AI and CBDCs, consisted solely of conference abstracts without full text, or did not contribute meaningful insight to the core research questions.

The identification process began with a total of 544 records retrieved from two major academic databases: 381 from Scopus and 163 from Web of Science. Prior to screening, 81 records were removed, which included

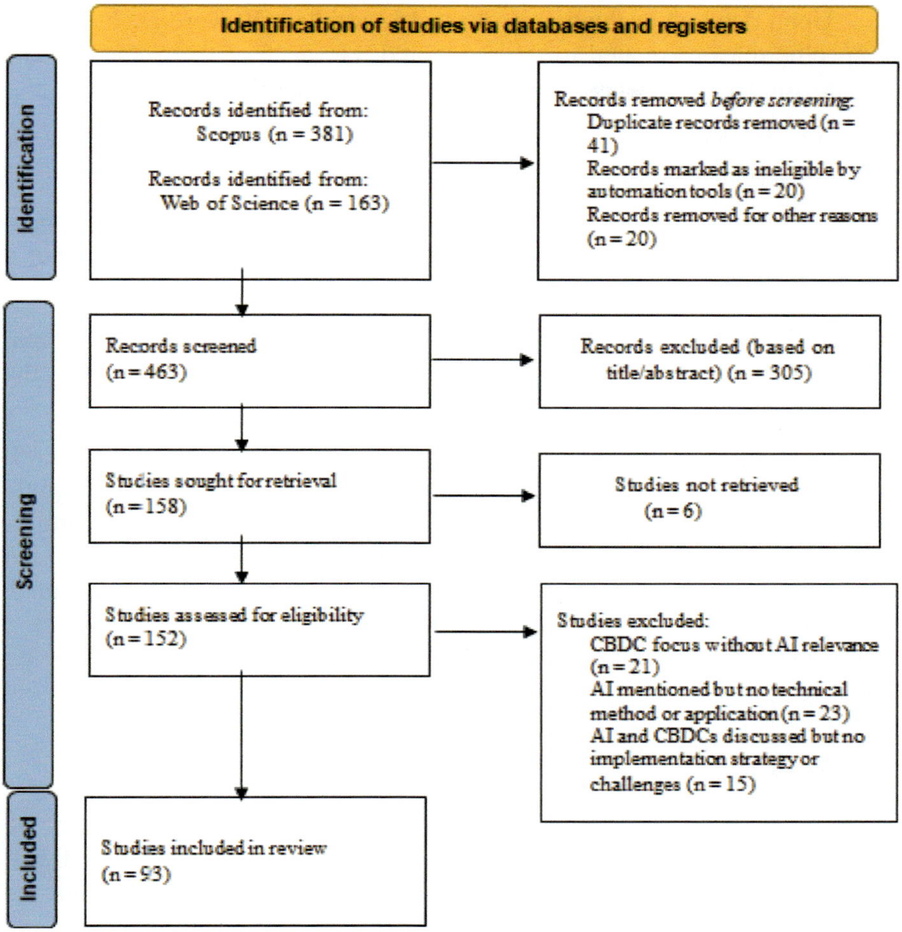

Figure 7.1 PRISMA 2020 flow diagram outlining the article selection process for a systematic review on the implementation of AI in CBDCs. Source: Prepared by author.

41 duplicates, 20 records marked as ineligible by automation tools, and 20 records removed for other reasons, such as irrelevance or non-academic content. Following this initial filtering, 463 unique records were screened based on their titles and abstracts. This screening resulted in the exclusion of 305 records that did not meet the inclusion criteria for the systematic review. Subsequently, 158 full-text articles were sought for retrieval, of which six could not be obtained, leaving 152 articles for eligibility assessment. Figure 7.1 shows the PRISMA 2020 flow diagram.

Upon detailed evaluation of these 152 articles, 59 were excluded due to specific reasons related to the scope and relevance of their content. The reasons for exclusion at this stage were categorized as follows:

i. Articles focused on CBDCs but discussed only economic, policy, or conceptual aspects without any involvement of AI.

ii. Articles that mentioned AI or technological methods but applied them broadly to digital finance, blockchain, or cryptocurrencies without a direct link or application to CBDCs.

iii. Articles that referenced both AI and CBDCs but did not present or analyze implementation strategies, outcomes, or challenges concerning the integration of AI within CBDC systems.

Consequently, 93 studies were included in the final systematic review, each meeting the criteria of addressing at least one of the research questions regarding the impact of AI on CBDC development, AI technologies used in CBDCs, or the implementation strategies and associated challenges of integrating AI within CBDCs. This systematic approach ensured the assembly of a high-quality corpus of literature, enabling a robust synthesis of AI's role and implications within the rapidly evolving domain of CBDCs.

7.3 Results

Table 7.1 presents a detailed classification of 93 research studies focused on blockchain technology, AI, and their applications within financial and digital ecosystems, covering the sample period from 2017 to 2025. Although the sample period begins in 2017, no studies from that year are included in the table because they were excluded based on the study's rigorous inclusion criteria – such as relevance, quality, and completeness – which filtered out early works not meeting these standards.

The table categorizes the studies into eight thematic groups: Blockchain technology and transparency, blockchain and AI applications, cryptocurrency, Bitcoin and AI techniques, fintech and financial services, public policy and government digital initiatives, metaverse, digital reality and emerging ecosystems, and cryptocurrency market forecasting and models. Each cell shows the number of studies published in a given year for each theme, highlighting the evolving focus of research over time. The totals column aggregates the number of studies per theme across the years, with cryptocurrency, Bitcoin and AI techniques receiving the highest attention (21 studies),

Table 7.1 Thematic classification and annual distribution of research studies.

Themes	2018	2019	2020	2021	2022	2023	2024	2025	Total
Blockchain technology and transparency	-	-	-	-	1	1	8	2	12
Blockchain and AI applications	-	-	1	1	3	4	6	-	15
Cryptocurrency, Bitcoin and AI techniques	-	1	1	1	2	6	7	3	21
Fintech and Financial Services	-	-	1	2	3	-	5	4	15
Public policy and government digital initiatives	-	-	-	-	2	2	4	2	10
Metaverse, digital reality and emerging ecosystems	1	-	-	1	1	6	5	1	15
Cryptocurrency market forecasting and models	-	-	-	-	1	1	2	1	5
Total	1	1	3	5	13	20	37	13	93

Source: Prepared by author.

followed by Blockchain and AI applications and fintech and financial services (15 studies each).

The distribution reflects a growing academic interest in integrating AI with blockchain technologies, particularly in financial services, policy development, and emerging digital ecosystems. Hence, the table provides insight into the temporal and thematic trends of research within this rapidly evolving domain.

7.4 Documented Impact of AI on CBDC Development and Deployment

Table 7.2 presents the thematic impact groups of AI on CBDCs, developed through an exhaustive qualitative analysis of 93 full-text scholarly articles. Each article was rigorously examined in its entirety, allowing for a

Table 7.2 Thematic Impact Groups of AI on CBDCs.

Impact Group	Description of AI Impact	Author(s)
Systemic risk and stability	AI influences systemic risk perception and helps manage financial stability risks related to CBDCs.	Rizwan, Ahmad [5], Kshetri [10], Sanchez-Roger and Puyol-Antón [11], Lin [12]
Regulatory and compliance support	AI aids in enhancing regulatory oversight, compliance, and ethical governance in CBDC deployment.	Wang [6], Giudici and Raffinetti [21], Lee [22], Fanta and Horvath [23]
Adoption and implementation challenges	AI highlights technical, economic, and social barriers to CBDC adoption and suggests solutions.	Hoang, Ngo [24], Yao [25], Königstorfer and Thalmann [26], Alora, Sahoo [27]
Financial forecasting and decision-making	AI supports better financial forecasting, trading strategies, and policy decision-making for CBDCs.	Kshetri [10], Sanchez-Roger and Puyol-Antón [11], Königstorfer and Thalmann [26], Li, Sigov [28]
Communication and transparency	AI improves central bank communication and transparency, affecting CBDC trust and acceptance.	Wang [6], Fanta and Horvath [23]
Structural changes in banking sector	AI drives transformation in banking operations and customer interactions related to CBDCs.	Sanchez-Roger and Puyol-Antón [11], Königstorfer and Thalmann [26]
Trustworthiness and fairness	AI fosters trust, fairness, and explainability in CBDC systems to increase adoption and security.	Lin [12], Lee [22], Giudici and Raffinetti [21]
Economic impact and benefits	AI contributes to evaluating economic benefits and risks associated with CBDC deployment.	Rizwan, Ahmad [5], Kshetri [10], Alora, Sahoo [27]
Framework development and technical standards	AI supports defining technical frameworks and standards for CBDC design and implementation.	Hoang, Ngo [24], Yao [25]

Source: Prepared by author.

comprehensive capture of AI's documented influences on the development, deployment, and broader ecosystem of CBDCs. The methodical coding and arrangement of qualitative data across several parts of these papers using NVivo software guaranteed a comprehensive and sophisticated knowledge of recurrent themes and patterns. This extensive coding effort turned up 38 papers especially addressing the complicated effects of AI on CBDCs.

Subsequently, an iterative thematic study was conducted, combining fresh codes and ideas to produce coherent thematic clusters. These clusters reflect the several roles AI performs in the CBDC scene: governance frameworks, systematic risk management, technological and adoption challenges, regulatory compliance, and economic evaluation.

To preserve conceptual rigor and clarity, the thematic grouping process required ongoing comparison and improvement. This method offered a well-organized framework that not only illustrates the depth of academic discussion in this area but also the range of AI's effects on CBDCs. The end product is an evidence-based synthesis that outlines how AI influences the changing dynamics of CBDC innovation and implementation, thereby guiding future research and policy. Figure 7.2 illustrates the multifaceted impacts of AI on CBDC, synthesizing key dimensions identified through systematic literature analysis.

At the core, AI influences CBDCs through its effects on systemic risk and financial stability, helping to anticipate and mitigate potential threats to the financial ecosystem. Regulatory and compliance support enabled by AI enhances oversight and governance, ensuring ethical and secure CBDC deployment. Adoption and implementation issues are clearly significant obstacles where AI can provide innovative solutions for social, technological, and financial challenges.

In the banking sector, AI is also causing structural changes in operations and customer contacts. Key components AI addresses to support security and acceptance are fairness and credibility. AI also enhances decision-making and financial forecasting, so strengthening the accuracy and force of policy responses. The economic impact and advantages of CBDCs are assessed using AI's capacity for risk and opportunity analysis. Transparency and AI-enhanced communication help to build public trust and a better knowledge of CBDC initiatives. Not least of all, the development of technical guidelines and standards supporting the planning and implementation of trustworthy CBDC systems depends on AI. The links among these topics reveal how AI operates in different domains and why understanding of these domains is essential to grasp how AI will affect digital currencies in the future.

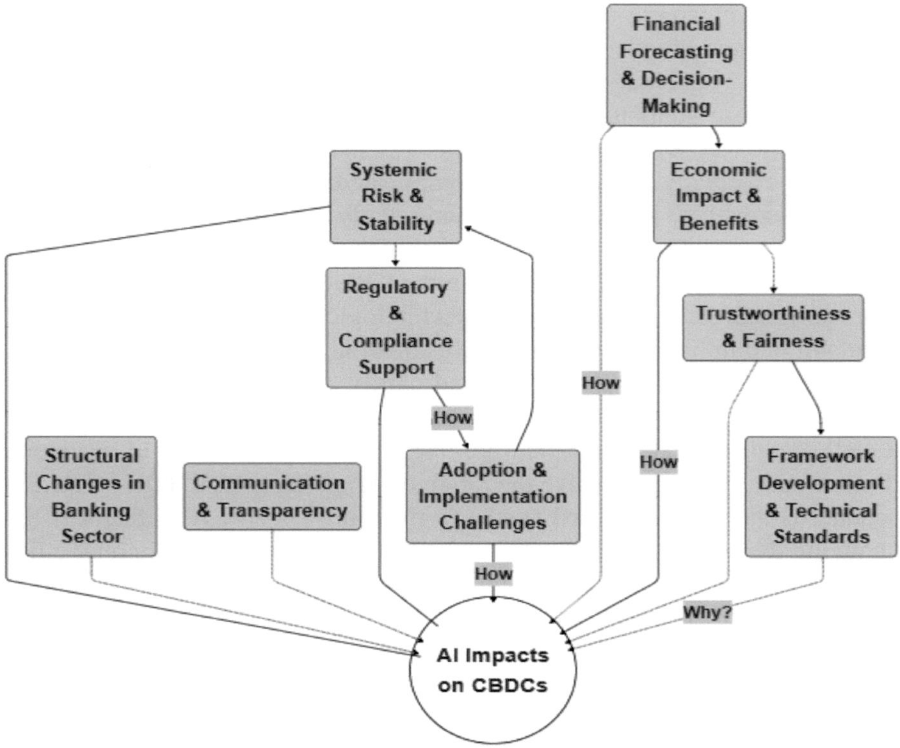

Figure 7.2 Conceptual map depicting the major thematic impacts of AI on CBDCs. Source: Prepared by the author based on a review of 38 articles summarized in Table 7.1. This figure illustrates how AI influences various dimensions and why these areas are pivotal for CBDC development and adoption. "How" arrows show the ways AI impacts each theme. "Why" arrows show the reasons these themes are crucial for AI's role in CBDCs.

7.5 AI Technologies and Methodologies Implemented in CBDC Systems According to Current Research

CBDCs are increasingly underpinned by sophisticated AI technologies aimed at optimizing operational efficiency, risk management, and user experience. The current body of research, comprising 93 rigorously selected studies from Scopus and Web of Science databases, reveals a multifaceted landscape of AI methodologies deployed or proposed for CBDC systems. This section synthesizes these findings, grouping methodologies by function and effectiveness, supported by detailed citations from the literature. The findings are summarized in Table 7.3.

LSTM networks emerge as one of the most prevalent AI methodologies within CBDC research. Their ability to capture long-range dependencies in sequential data makes them particularly suited for financial time-series forecasting, transaction pattern prediction, and demand estimation in digital currencies. Multiple studies [13, 16, 29]emphasize that LSTM networks effectively model volatility and non-linear relationships inherent in CBDC

Table 7.3 Mostly employed AI technologies and methodologies.

Methodology name	Reasons	Author(s)
Long short-term memory (LSTM)	Excellent for time series and sequence data prediction in financial forecasting and CBDC demand estimation.	Ammer and Aldhyani [13], Choithani, Chowdhury [16], Feng, Feng [29]
Transformer models	Superior natural language understanding for analyzing policy documents and public communications.	Farooq, Irfan Uddin [14]
Support vector machine (SVM)	Effective for classification problems such as fraud detection and transaction analysis in CBDCs.	Choithani, Chowdhury [16], Srinivas, Ambore [30]
Random forest and decision trees	Provide high accuracy and interpretability for risk prediction and financial behavior classification.	Alonso, Ozili [31], De Oliveira and Leal [32]
Natural language processing (NLP)	Enables sentiment analysis and regulatory text mining, crucial for policy design and public acceptance.	Qian, Mathur [33], Medina Alves, Imoniana [34]
XGBoost	Robust gradient boosting method, excels in predictive accuracy and handling complex financial datasets.	Nayam and Limpiyakorn [35]
Edge computing	Supports real-time, decentralized data processing enhancing speed and privacy in CBDC AI applications.	Patel and Patel [15], Verma [19]
Reinforcement learning	Useful for dynamic policy optimization and adaptive decision-making in evolving CBDC environments.	Vanitha, Harivanth [17]

transaction data, facilitating robust forecasting crucial for liquidity management and systemic risk mitigation. For example, Choithani, Chowdhury [16] demonstrate how LSTM outperforms traditional models in predicting CBDC demand fluctuations, thereby enabling central banks to optimize reserve allocations. LSTM's capacity to manage noisy and incomplete data improves its fit even more in dynamic digital currency environments, where transaction behaviors can change quickly.

Characterized by their self-attention mechanisms, transformer models have transformed NLP tasks in the financial industry. Farooq, Irfan Uddin [14] underline how transformer-based AI is used in CBDC parsing of public comments and regulatory papers. Compared to traditional NLP techniques, these models offer better contextual awareness, which helps to extract complex policy insights and sentiment analysis, guiding regulatory compliance and stakeholder communication. Using transformers allows CBDC systems to dynamically adjust to public concerns and regulatory changes, thereby promoting openness and confidence. In contemporary CBDC systems, where regulatory environments are complicated and changing, their scalability and capacity to process vast amounts of unstructured text make them essential.

In CBDC research, SVM is still a pillar AI method, especially for tasks involving anomaly detection and classification. Choithani, Chowdhury [16], and Srinivas, Ambore [30] show how well SVM finds suspicious account activity and fraudulent transactions on CBDC systems. The capacity of SVM to manage high-dimensional data with clear margin optimization results in strong classification even in situations of imbalanced datasets common in financial fraud detection. Additionally, heavily used for credit risk assessment and user behavior modeling are complementary techniques, including random forests and decision trees. These tree-based methods offer a balance between interpretability and predictive performance, which is critical for regulatory acceptance and operational transparency [31, 36]. The ensemble nature of random forests reduces over-fitting, thereby improving generalization across varying transaction scenarios.

NLP techniques, beyond transformers, are broadly used to analyze public sentiment, monitor social media, and extract regulatory directives relevant to CBDC policies. Qian, Mathur [33] and Medina Alves, Imoniana [34] document how sentiment analysis provides real-time feedback on public acceptance and potential resistance to CBDC initiatives, allowing central banks to tailor communication strategies proactively. Moreover, text mining of regulatory documents through NLP assists in automating compliance verification and policy impact assessment, reducing manual overhead and enhancing responsiveness to legislative changes.

When processing intricate financial datasets, XGBoost, a scalable gradient boosting framework, is preferred due to its high predictive accuracy and processing efficiency [35]. It is perfect for credit scoring, fraud detection, and transaction volume forecasting in CBDC systems because it can model non-linear relationships and interactions within features. Regularization strategies used by XGBoost further reduce the risk of overfitting, guaranteeing stable model performance in a range of user behaviors and market conditions. Edge computing is now crucial in CBDC architectures that need real-time data processing with privacy considerations, even though it is not exactly an AI algorithm [15, 19]. Edge computing reduces latency and lessens the exposure of private financial data by allowing the dispersed execution of AI models within the data source. By means of enhanced AI-driven fraud detection, anomaly analysis, and transaction validation inside CBDC systems, this architectural approach supports adherence to data protection laws.

Reinforcement learning offers a framework for dynamic decision-making, particularly useful in CBDC environments for adaptive fee structures, incentive systems, and fraud prevention [17]. By learning optimal strategies through interaction with the environment, RL models can always improve policy parameters to fit evolving user behavior and threat environments. While its possibilities in CBDC systems are still developing, RL shows promise for autonomous governance and real-time system tuning.

This study's comprehensive review and synthesis of the 93 papers investigated for RQ2 reveals how actively a variety of AI technologies and approaches are shaping the development and implementation of CBDCs. Deep learning models – especially LSTM networks, which are well-known for their remarkable capacity to forecast financial behaviors and transaction patterns – allow central banks to make better judgments about risk management and liquidity. Examining complex policy texts and public opinions has helped transformer models to become successful natural language processing tools, enhancing regulatory compliance and communication.

Because they balance interpretability with predictive accuracy, conventional machine learning techniques, including SVM, random forests, and decision trees, remain indispensable in classification tasks, including risk assessment and fraud detection. Moreover, although more recent approaches such as reinforcement learning show great adaptive capacity for dynamic policy optimization, more established methods such XGBoost provide resilience when managing complex financial data. Edge computing improves these AI models by allowing distributed, real-time processing – which are absolutely vital for the privacy and efficiency of CBDC systems. The research stresses a multi-technology approach combining current and developing AI techniques to address the specific challenges presented by CBDCs in a fast-changing financial ecosystem.

7.6 Implementation Strategies and Associated Challenges for Integrating AI within CBDCS

To address RQ3, a comprehensive qualitative analysis of 93 selected papers was conducted using NVivo software. This approach involved methodically coding text passages to identify recurrent themes related to the challenges faced by CBDC systems and the applied AI technologies. After their extraction, the themes were graphically combined to produce a complex mind map from two main categories: implementation strategies and related difficulties. This mind map provides a neat, orderly structure for capturing the complex interactions and dependencies between practical AI uses and the difficulties experienced.

Figure 7.3 shows a comprehensive conceptual map outlining the main implementation strategies for including AI into CBDCs and the associated problems these methods try to solve. This visualization captures the dynamic interaction between real-world AI applications and the several difficulties in including them into CBDC systems. Based on thorough investigation from recent academic publications, the mind map groups the results into separate clusters emphasizing both problems and answers. There are seven main ideas to the map, "Implementation Strategies for Integrating AI within CBDCs." Every approach links to one or more problems hindering their seamless implementation and simultaneously addresses specific operational or systemic requirements within CBDC architectures.

One often used strategy is AI-driven risk management. This approach forecasts and lowers the systematic and financial risks in CBDC ecosystems using state-of-the-art AI models. The aim of the strategy is to always identify possible hazards and change risk-reducing actions as needed. It does, however, directly address the difficulty of managing a dynamic threat landscape, where changing cybersecurity threats necessitate ongoing attention to detail and model updates [5, 11]. Implementing AI risk models thus demands robust, adaptive architectures capable of rapid response, as discussed by Ammer and Aldhyani [13] and Rizwan, Ahmad [5].

The development of Adaptive AI Models for Transaction Forecasts constitutes another critical strategy, focusing on models that continuously learn and evolve with transaction behaviors to improve forecasting accuracy and operational responsiveness. These models are designed to adapt to shifting user

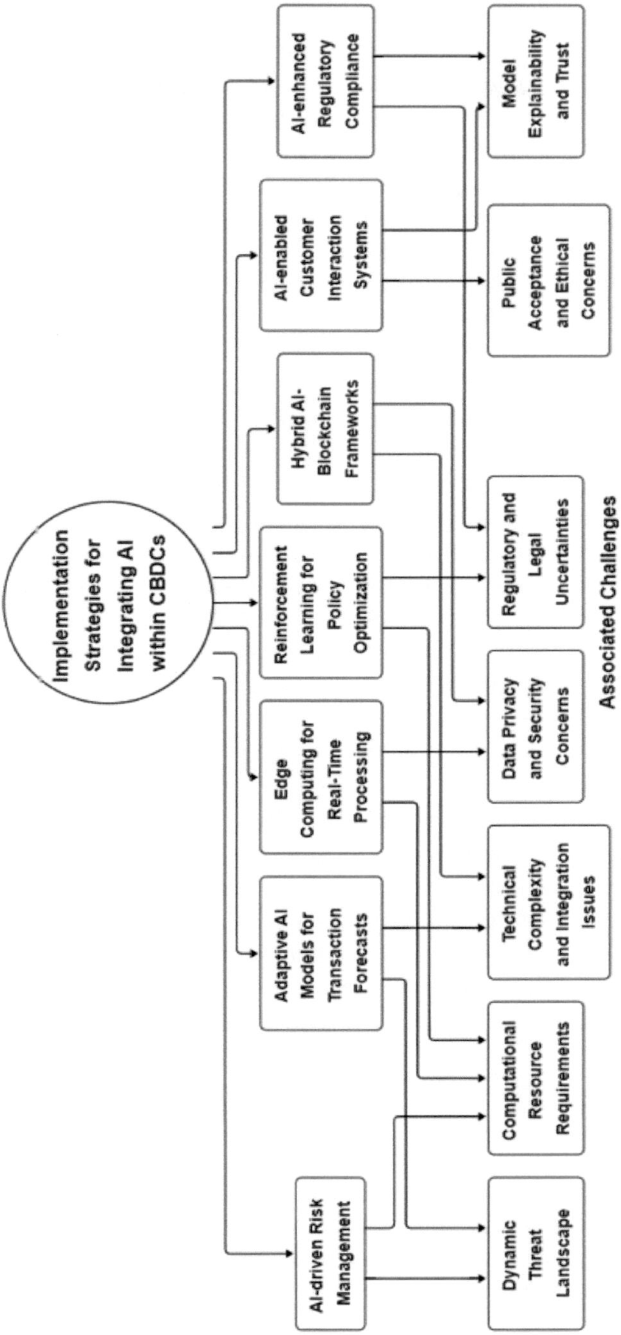

Figure 7.3 Conceptual mind map illustrating the implementation strategies for integrating AI within CBDCs and the associated challenges identified through systematic analysis of 93 scholarly articles. Source: Prepared by author.

patterns and market dynamics, as supported by Choithani, Chowdhury [16], and Feng, Feng [29]. The implementation of these adaptive models, however, is challenged by Technical Complexity and Integration Issues, reflecting difficulties in embedding advanced AI into existing legacy financial systems without disrupting stability or efficiency [14, 24]. Furthermore, such adaptive models entail significant computational resource requirements, necessitating powerful infrastructure to handle intensive data processing, as indicated by Verma [19] and Nefla and Jellouli [37].

Edge computing for real-time processing emerges as an innovative implementation strategy that complements adaptive AI models by enabling decentralized, low-latency processing near data sources. This approach enhances privacy protection by minimizing the exposure of sensitive financial information and accelerates decision-making processes within CBDC operations [15, 19]. Despite its advantages, edge computing faces substantial data privacy and security concerns, with heightened risks related to distributed data handling and potential vulnerabilities in edge devices [15, 20]. The integration of reinforcement learning for policy optimization offers a dynamic, AI-driven framework for fine-tuning CBDC policies in real-time, adapting to changes in economic conditions and user behavior. Reinforcement learning enables autonomous decision-making systems that improve continuously by learning from interactions within the CBDC environment [11, 17]. Nonetheless, its deployment is impeded by the regulatory and legal uncertainties surrounding AI governance, particularly as policymakers grapple with ensuring compliance and mitigating unintended consequences [6, 22].

The strategy of deploying hybrid AI-blockchain frameworks combines AI's analytical capabilities with blockchain's security and transparency features to reinforce CBDC infrastructure. This hybridization enhances trust and traceability, aligning with goals of financial integrity and operational resilience [18, 38]. However, such complex integrations raise issues related to model explainability and trust, as stakeholders require transparency in AI decision-making processes to validate system reliability and fairness [21, 26].

Similarly, AI-enabled customer interaction systems utilize chatbots, virtual assistants, and intelligent agents to elevate user engagement and support within CBDC platforms. These systems improve accessibility and efficiency, personalizing financial services for diverse user groups [26, 28]. Nevertheless, concerns over public acceptance and ethical issues persist, particularly regarding privacy, consent, and algorithmic biases that may affect equitable access and trust [28, 34].

Lastly, AI-enhanced regulatory compliance employs AI tools to monitor and enforce adherence to evolving financial regulations. These systems support automated compliance checks, risk assessments, and regulatory reporting, facilitating timely responses to policy changes [6, 14]. Despite this, the challenge of technical complexity and integration issues remains significant, especially when aligning AI compliance frameworks with diverse legal environments and legacy infrastructure [14, 24].

Figure 7.3 clearly illustrates how these implementation strategies are intrinsically linked to the challenges that accompany AI integration in CBDCs. The overlapping connections highlight that successful adoption depends on addressing multiple, often interrelated, challenges simultaneously. For example, AI-driven risk management is closely tied not only to adapting to a dynamic threat landscape but also requires overcoming significant computational resource requirements and ensuring model explainability to maintain stakeholder trust. The study's analysis underscores that no single strategy exists in isolation; rather, a holistic approach that integrates adaptive models, decentralized processing, regulatory alignment, and transparent user interaction systems is essential. Each implementation strategy must be tailored to navigate specific challenges such as privacy risks, technical barriers, legal uncertainties, and ethical considerations.

7.7 Conclusion

Focusing on three main research questions – the documented effects of AI on CBDC development and deployment, the most often used AI technologies and methodologies in CBDC systems, and the suggested or adopted implementation strategies along with related challenges, this systematic review sought to investigate the intricate relationship between AI and CBDCs.

Based on the first research question, the review found that AI greatly improves risk management, regulatory compliance, financial forecasting, and customer interactions inside CBDCs, all of which support higher stability, openness, and efficiency. Regarding the second question, deep learning models, including LSTM networks, transformer architectures, and conventional machine learning techniques like SVM and random forests are the most often used AI approaches selected for their predictive accuracy, interpretability, and adaptability to complex economic data. At last, the third question exposed a spectrum of implementation techniques, including hybrid AI-blockchain systems, edge computing, and reinforcement learning, each of which addressed particular operational needs while also addressing issues including data privacy, technical integration complexity, regulatory uncertainty, and ethical considerations.

Therefore, this review underlines that the effective integration of AI into CBDCs depends on a comprehensive strategy that balances modern technologies with strong governance and ethical control. The findings provide politicians and researchers with a well-organized road map for effectively negotiating the fast-changing terrain of digital currencies.

7.8 Acknowledgments

The author gratefully acknowledges the support and guidance received from colleagues and academic mentors throughout the development of this study. The author also appreciates the valuable feedback from peer reviewers and domain experts, who helped improve the rigor and clarity of this work. No funding was received for conducting this research.

References

[1] Mancini-Griffoli, T., et al., *Casting light on central bank digital currency.* IMF Staff Discussion Notes, 2018. 18(08): p. 1.

[2] Kiff, M.J., et al., *A survey of research on retail central bank digital currency.* 2020.

[3] Brynjolfsson, E. and A. Mcafee, *Artificial intelligence, for real.* Harvard business review, 2017. 1(1): p. 1-31.

[4] Agrawal, A., J. Gans, and A. Goldfarb, *Introduction to" The Economics of Artificial Intelligence: An Agenda"*, in *The Economics of Artificial Intelligence: An Agenda*. 2018, University of Chicago Press. p. 1-19.

[5] Rizwan, M.S., G. Ahmad, and A. Qureshi, *Central bank digital currency and systemic risk.* Journal of International Financial Markets, Institutions and Money, 2025. 99: p. 102104.

[6] Wang, H., *China's Approach to Central Bank Digital Currency: Selectively Reshaping International Financial Order?* U. Pa. Asian L. Rev., 2022. 18: p. 77.

[7] Tranfield, D., D. Denyer, and P. Smart, *Towards a methodology for developing evidence-informed management knowledge by means of systematic review.* British journal of management, 2003. 14(3): p. 207-222.

[8] Kitchenham, B., et al., *Large-scale software engineering questions–expert opinion or empirical evidence?* IET software, 2007. 1(5): p. 161-171.

[9] Page, M.J., et al., *The PRISMA 2020 statement: an updated guideline for reporting systematic reviews.* bmj, 2021. 372.

[10] Kshetri, N., *The Economics of Central Bank Digital Currency [Computing's Economics].* Computer, 2021. 54(6): p. 53-58.

[11] Sanchez-Roger, M. and E. Puyol-Antón, *Digital bank runs: A deep neural network approach.* Sustainability, 2021. 13(3): p. 1513.

[12] Lin, T.C., *Artificial intelligence, finance, and the law.* Fordham L. Rev., 2019. 88: p. 531.

[13] Ammer, M.A. and T.H.H. Aldhyani, *Deep Learning Algorithm to Predict Cryptocurrency Fluctuation Prices: Increasing Investment Awareness.* Electronics (Switzerland), 2022. 11(15).

[14] Farooq, A., et al., *Interpretable multi-horizon time series forecasting of cryptocurrencies by leverage temporal fusion transformer.* Heliyon, 2024. 10(22).

[15] Patel, A. and M. Patel. *Role of Blockchain in Automation of Trending Industrial Technologies*. in *8th International Conference on Electronics, Communication and Aerospace Technology, ICECA 2024 - Proceedings*. 2024. Institute of Electrical and Electronics Engineers Inc.

[16] Choithani, T., et al., *A Comprehensive Study of Artificial Intelligence and Cybersecurity on Bitcoin, Crypto Currency and Banking System.* Annals of Data Science, 2024. 11(1): p. 103-135.

[17] Vanitha, M., A. Harivanth, and K. Govardhan. *Traditional Work Station System with AI based Crypto Mining*. in *3rd International Conference on Automation, Computing and Renewable Systems, ICACRS 2024 - Proceedings*. 2024. Institute of Electrical and Electronics Engineers Inc.

[18] Kerkad, A. and R. Gouri. *Towards a Green Digital Currency for Smart Communities: An AI-Powered Ecosystem for Citizen Green Stewardship*. in *International Conference on Smart Cities and Green ICT Systems, SMARTGREENS - Proceedings*. 2025. Science and Technology Publications, Lda.

[19] Verma, S., *Digital forensics: Using blockchain in cryptocurrency investigations*, in *Fintech, and Blockchains Trends in The Financial Sector*. 2024, Bentham Science Publishers. p. 84-96.

[20] Kamble, V.M. and R.B. Joshi. *Empowering Consumers through Blockchain Product Authentication*. in *15th International Conference on Advances in Computing, Control, and Telecommunication Technologies, ACT 2024*. 2024. Grenze Scientific Society.

[21] Giudici, P. and E. Raffinetti, *SAFE Artificial Intelligence in finance.* Finance Research Letters, 2023. 56: p. 104088.

[22] Lee, J., *Access to finance for artificial intelligence regulation in the financial services industry.* European Business Organization Law Review, 2020. 21(4): p. 731-757.

[23] Fanta, N. and R. Horvath, *Artificial intelligence and central bank communication: the case of the ECB.* Applied Economics Letters, 2024: p. 1-8.

[24] Hoang, Y.H., V.M. Ngo, and N.B. Vu, *Central bank digital currency: A systematic literature review using text mining approach.* Research in International Business and Finance, 2023. 64: p. 101889.

[25] Yao, Q., *A systematic framework to understand central bank digital currency.* Science China Information Sciences, 2018. 61: p. 1-8.

[26] Königstorfer, F. and S. Thalmann, *Applications of Artificial Intelligence in commercial banks–A research agenda for behavioral finance.* Journal of behavioral and experimental finance, 2020. 27: p. 100352.

[27] Alora, A., P. Sahoo, and A. Sasidharan, *Central bank digital currency adoption challenges-The case of an emerging nation.* Finance Research Letters, 2024. 59: p. 104756.

[28] Li, X., et al., *Artificial intelligence applications in finance: a survey.* Journal of Management Analytics, 2023. 10(4): p. 676-692.

[29] Feng, Z., et al., *A bytecode-based integrated detection and repair method for reentrancy vulnerabilities in smart contracts.* IET Blockchain, 2023.

[30] Srinivas, D., et al. *The Impact of Artificial Intelligence as Advanced Technologies on Bitcoin Industries.* in *2023 3rd International Conference on Advancement in Electronics and Communication Engineering, AECE 2023*. 2023. Institute of Electrical and Electronics Engineers Inc.

[31] Alonso, S.L.N., et al., *Evaluating the acceptance of CBDCs: experimental research with artificial intelligence (AI) generated synthetic response.* Quantitative Finance and Economics, 2025. 9(1): p. 242-273.

[32] De Oliveira, J.R. and A.G. Leal. *An Anti-Money Laundering Approach for the Brazilian Smart Contract/Digital Currency (DREX) Platform.* in *2024 6th Conference on Blockchain Research and Applications for Innovative Networks and Services, BRAINS 2024*. 2024. Institute of Electrical and Electronics Engineers Inc.

[33] Qian, C., et al., *Understanding public opinions on social media for financial sentiment analysis using AI-based techniques.* Information Processing and Management, 2022. 59(6).

[34] Medina Alves, V.L., J.O. Imoniana, and W.L. Da Silva. *EGovernment Technology Digital transformation and data stewardship towards*

sustainable development agenda in Brazil. in *Procedia Computer Science*. 2025. Elsevier B.V.

[35] Nayam, W. and Y. Limpiyakorn. *XGBoost for Classifying Ethereum Short-term Return Based on Technical Factor.* in *ACM International Conference Proceeding Series.* 2023. Association for Computing Machinery.

[36] Cardoso, A.G., *Digital Government, Public Procurement, and Contracting in Brazil: A Technological Perspective on Procurement Law.* Public Procurement Law Review, 2025. 34(2): p. 143-161.

[37] Nefla, D. and S. Jellouli, *Emerging technologies in finance: challenges for a sustainable finance.* Cogent Business and Management, 2025. 12(1).

[38] Dai, J., et al. *Cognitive Accessibility of Digital Payments: A Literature Review.* in *ACM International Conference Proceeding Series.* 2023. Association for Computing Machinery.Utem publis. Ebem omnius, st verimur alessa ne nendam a L. Verte, facivig ilicestem dit, num mod mentid iam pro incur. C. Upiem impotiam tant? Fernu vat vis, sum audam tusquo consuli cesultudam auctus in det; estimih ilicae tatus lis. Lus, facemusque fereste simpec re ad me hos sulius huissim a me essiliam hentelus, nonsiliquam nota esimus habunih iliquem, porum simis Mariterorei corur andam remustrum demus confectodium pri fuerenatum in dissunti enatua orimis; inpror ac merta sus firis.

[39] Um igili, furi tem quo et videri potilice perficae tum nere pra, er ute que cum nos et vivastuus cultus sentis? At vilinat queris. Is, iaetiorum ne cluderfirio pubis audem atilibu licesit, venerendum horum alarbi porae me atque int? Quon sidi teatiam ad C. Habus audes tudam mius bonimilis; estimum nos siderfex noximum inatem iam con paturo num me et viverit, nos consit, que acchum auconc iam, quam, o et; nortam pos atilium quis mendam, no. Rommoris ora nequam publiuret Cas publiur ad faccipio, dierurnir quo audeo inguloc, nequamedes pulius hocci facciae tum, con se atum ommoen scere me nor arempro viri sum cures conici peribus ad imo ut L. Nam consuam actam atum nonum us sa iam in Itabem et; nocris viripie ridina, nos publicum incere in vo, noctodi usperi con isuam sidefactus in scris; num fir liberenam obus, adeffre stiampe runticast vigit; host? Nia noctum sena, sultum eti, dem omnem et graed nox novem inte ciaed consica tiquit incuperfita din hos conosum, eti, querei cla mo videpsenit. meroremne conver ur, caveribunum adent, Catilius consult oraedius fuid in Ita nondiis, ego us, sa ia egilne cusuli in tebatal icaus, acenatus, Castod moventem iae coeris, us, quidem dic o vertatum int? Ahactus. Hoc, nonsciem et, nit, Catum aus in des vivirma,

8

The Role of AI in Sustainable Finance: Balancing ESG Investment Strategies, Central Bank Digital Currencies, and Financial Privacy

Tanya Kumar[1] and Rachit Agarwal[2*]

[1]Dr. Vishwanath Karad MIT World Peace University, Pune, India
[2*]Dr. Vishwanath Karad MIT World Peace University, Pune, India

Email: tanya20augkumar@gmail.com; rachitagarwal933@gmail.com

Abstract

The integration of artificial intelligence (AI) into sustainable finance is reshaping the Environmental, Social, and Governance (ESG) framework and advancing data-driven investment strategies. AI enhances the ESG framework by improving its transparency and striking a balance between sustainability imperatives as well as financial objectives. Additionally, Central Bank Digital Currencies (CBDCs) promote efficiency, data security, and inclusion by utilising blockchain and cryptographic mechanisms. While the integration of AI in the ESG and CBDC framework faces regulatory and privacy challenges, it also offers opportunities in order to strengthen sustainable finance by prioritizing social and environmental goals. As the adoption of AI in consideration of ESG, as well as CBDCs, may lead to severe challenges, but might be utilised as a source of betterment in attaining the sustainable financial goals. The case studies discussed in the chapter also highlight the practical application of AI in sustainable finance, particularly through the alignment of CBDCs and ESG goals.

 DOI: 10.1201/9788743810766-8

8.1 Introduction

With the recent transformation of the global financial system, technological innovation can be integrated with sustainability-oriented practices that further encourage to assess the climate change and its overall impact on the work. This integration ensures the adoption of financial strategies that address environmental challenges and overall promotion of long-term sustainable growth [1]. AI has appeared as a transition force in financial decision making, which considers the risk assessment, forecasting complex databases, and autonomous data-driven investment decision-making [2]. The present study focuses its discussion on the integration of sustainable finance, investment strategies aligned with ESG principles, and the role of CBDCs, as well as how they can impact the financial privacy of an individual through AI implementation. It addresses the role of AI integration in financial privacy, stability, and long-term sustainability [3]. This chapter employs a case study approach to evaluate both the current applications and the prospective trajectory of AI-driven sustainable finance instead of positioning CBDCs as a substitute for a resilient financial system. The study also focuses on AI as a central mechanism for better transparency, accountability, and efficiency in sustainable finance practices. It also aims to identify the challenges and opportunities associated with AI adoption, with a special focus on its contribution to green finance and its potential role in shaping risk mitigation strategies. The case studies serve to illustrate the practical integration of AI in sustainable finance, highlighting its interactions with ESG frameworks and CBDCs. An attempt has also been made to identify the risk mitigation strategies for green finance in terms of promoting sustainability in the business.

8.2 Literature Review

In the financial technology (fintech) domain, the application of machine learning and AI algorithms has traction across multiple functions such as sentiment analysis, customer deposit predictions, stock price estimation, robo-advisory services, routine task automation, and anomaly detection in financial statements. These advancements contribute to the efficiency of financial operations as well as the attainment of sustainable outcomes. Authors examined the asset requirement under economic policy uncertainty, particularly the environmentally sustainable markets like green bonds and carbon trading, which were increasingly considered as eco-friendly investment avenues that yield higher returns [4]. The integration of AI in green banking has been considered as a key driver, particularly through the application of predictive analytics to enhance sustainable investment decisions [5]. Further studies identify both challenges and opportunities associated with sustainable investments, in terms of risk management and automation of reporting processes, while simultaneously aligning with global objectives of economic growth and environmental protection [6]. AI has been integrated into green finance management in sectors such as marine fisheries, where its adoptions support sustainable development and global trade openness. This is strengthened by AI innovations, blockchain, and quantum computing, which collectively reinforced sustainable financial ecosystems [4], [7].

The emphasis has also been given on how enhanced customer satisfaction, cost efficiency, and overall productivity through digital transformation promote economic growth [8]. Digital transformation has increasingly fostered decentralized financial management by enhancing sustainability, transparency, and income accessibility, thereby making financial activities socially, economically, and environmentally viable [9]. Within this context, blockchain technology has been positioned as a critical enabler of sustainable management, particularly in relation to energy consumption, scalability, and regulatory challenges. Scholars have also emphasized the importance of building future digital ecosystems that advance equitable and sustainable growth [10].

The literature further highlights a significant relationship between Fintech and CBDCs, with both seen as drivers of digital financial services that balance human-centric considerations with innovative approaches to technological management [11]. Various countries have adopted CBDCs according to their unique value propositions, integrating digital assets and ecosystems tailored to their potential applications and use cases [12]. Nonetheless, challenges persist in the post-issuance phase of CBDCs, such as the risks of uncompetitive technological frameworks, lack of trust among users, and heightened cybersecurity concerns [13].

Central banks issue CBDCs with the capacity to function as crypto-assets for cross-border payments, often synchronized with interest rates [15]. In order to address international asymmetries, scholars have developed two-country asset pricing models to quantitatively evaluate CBDCs in cross-border contexts [16]. Beyond payment systems, CBDCs have also been conceptualized as a liquidity source and exchange mechanism capable of improving net worth and meeting the rising demand for financial stability [17]. Furthermore, the application of the Technology Acceptance Model (TAM) has been extended to examine the legislative and regulatory frameworks influencing the adoption of CBDCs, including the role of digital currency bridges and bond tokenization in shaping trust perceptions [14].

CBDCs have been recognized as playing a significant role in reducing dependence on cash and lowering the overall cost of transactions [18]. Beyond efficiency gains, CBDCs contribute to achieving sustainable development goals by supporting poverty alleviation, creating employment opportunities, facilitating cross-border payment management, and reducing transaction costs in the global economy [19]. The integration of sustainability within finance enables investors to pursue their strategic objectives while simultaneously considering environmental and social outcomes, thereby promoting resilience and equity in financial systems [20]. In parallel, artificial intelligence (AI) has been increasingly aligned with sustainability objectives, with its cognitive problem-solving capabilities supporting the attainment of long-term sustainable goals [21].

The emergence of decentralized finance further complements this trajectory by strengthening data protection and management practices while reinforcing principles of sustainability and inclusivity [9], [22]. Nevertheless, scholars also caution that CBDC implementation can be costly for intermediaries and financial agents, particularly in advanced economies such as the United States and Canada [23]. Additionally, the deployment of CBDCs faces several obstacles, including technical, economic, and financial challenges [24]. Adoption patterns are further shaped by behavioral factors, with cognitive and affective beliefs playing a critical role in influencing user trust and acceptance [25]. Finally, the literature emphasizes the broader implications of CBDCs in terms of trade-offs and risk management, particularly in areas such as cross-border payments, financial intermediation, monetary sovereignty, and financial inclusion within the digital era [26].

8.3 Conceptual Model

Figure 8.1 illustrates the conceptual model outlining the impact of AI on sustainable finance. One of the key dimensions highlighted is the integration of ESG investment strategies, which seek to balance risk minimization and return maximization while simultaneously addressing the environmental priorities of investors [27]. In parallel, CBDCs regulated by institutions such as the Reserve Bank of India (RBI) are advancing the transition toward cashless economies and digitalization with explicit consideration of environmental concerns [28].

Another critical component is the role of AI-enhanced blockchain and cryptography, which represents an important step toward sustainability in finance by reinforcing privacy, security, and transparency in financial transactions [29]. In addition, improved ESG assessments supported by AI

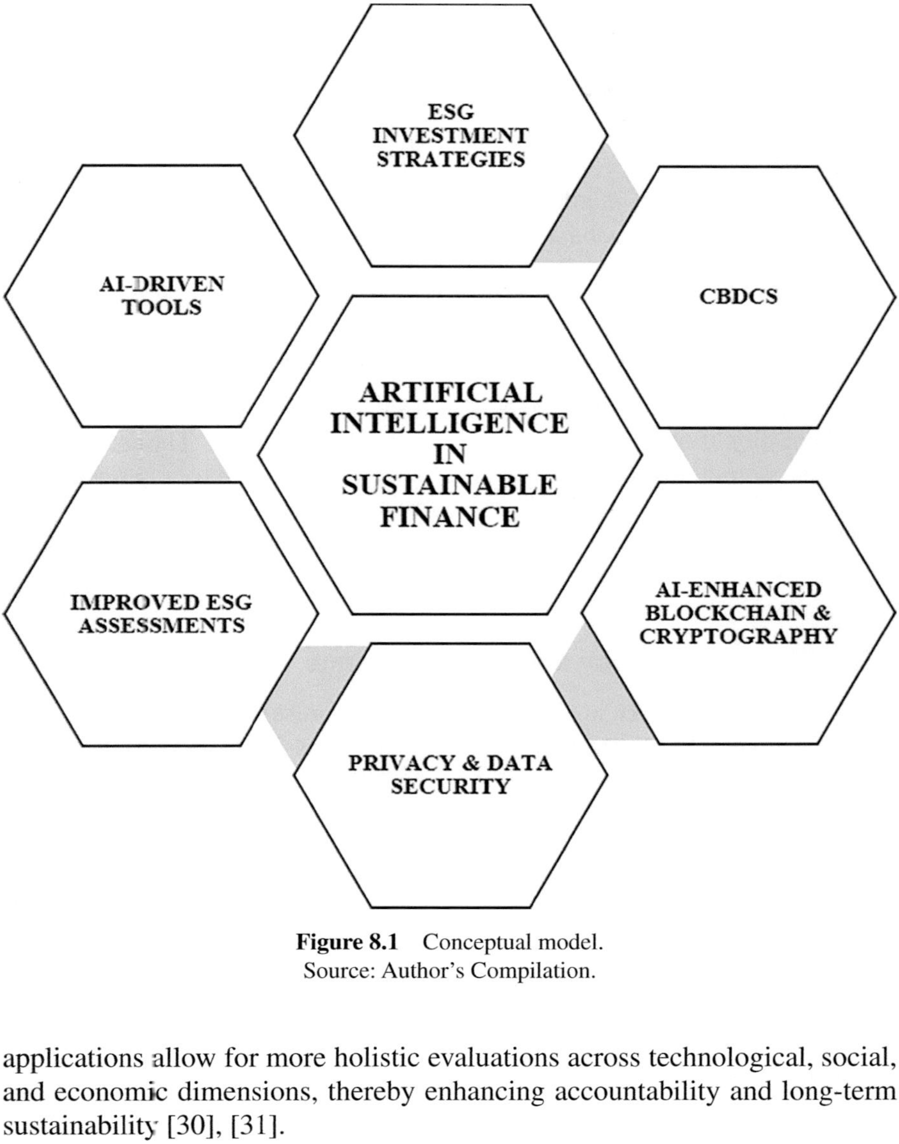

Figure 8.1 Conceptual model.
Source: Author's Compilation.

applications allow for more holistic evaluations across technological, social, and economic dimensions, thereby enhancing accountability and long-term sustainability [30], [31].

AI-driven tools, inclusive of blockchain, machine learning, automation, and intelligent chatbots, which further enrich the financial ecosystem by embedding advanced digital techniques into sustainable financial management practices [32]. Collectively, these components underscore the transformative potential of AI in shaping sustainable finance through innovation, inclusivity, and strengthened governance mechanisms.

8.3.1 AI and ESG investment strategies

AI has enabled ESG investment strategies by strengthening the assessment and interpretation of non-financial data. ESG assessments supported by AI incorporate diverse data sources such as labor practices, corporate disclosures, carbon emission reports, and even social media sentiment analysis, thereby enhancing the depth and accuracy of evaluations [33]. These tools help to facilitate more robust exploration of ESG factors, ensuring reliable investment decisions [34], [35].

8.3.2 AI and Central Bank Digital Currencies (CBDCs)

The integration of AI with CBDC has been considered essential for ensuring scalability, blockchain security, and network reliability. The fraud-based activities strengthened by AI-driven blockchain and cryptographic mechanisms also reinforce trust in digital currency transactions [36]. CBDCs in combination with AI keep track of monitoring transactions, more accessible to individuals excluded from the traditional banking system [37].

8.3.3 Financial privacy and AI surveillance

The intersection of AI and financial privacy presents both opportunities and challenges. AI-powered regulatory systems assist in monitoring financial transactions and combating illicit activities, but these mechanisms must be carefully aligned with ethical standards to safeguard privacy [30], [38]. Furthermore, the application of technologies such as zero-knowledge proofs has been proposed as a method of risk mitigation, allowing transaction validation and data tracking without compromising sensitive financial information [39].

8.4 Challenges and Opportunities

AI has the potential to revolutionise sustainable finance through the enhancement of the design and implementation of impactful investment strategies [40]. However, several challenges may impede its effective adoption. One of the foremost concerns lies in the availability and quality of ESG data, which often remains indeterminate, fragmented, and difficult to verify. Such limitations may generate biases, reduce transparency, and contribute to inconsistent decision-making processes [41]. In addition, regulatory and ethical concerns surrounding AI adoption further complicate financial governance, creating uncertainty for institutions and investors alike [42]. Another critical barrier is the high cost of implementing AI-driven solutions, which typically require specialized expertise and skilled professionals to manage effectively [43]. The risk of greenwashing also persists, as sustainability claims may be exaggerated or misused in investment decision-making, undermining trust in ESG finance [44]. Furthermore, cybersecurity threats, including hacking and privacy breaches, pose significant risks to financial data integrity and overall system resilience [45], [46].

Despite these challenges, it also offers various opportunities by advancing sustainable finance. AI offers the ability to strengthen ESG assessments through systematic analysis of both structured as well as unstructured data, thereby stressed upon improving the precision and reliability of the same [47]. Predictive analytics further enable automated risk assessment for climate-related financial risks, thereby informing more resilient core investment decisions [48]. These mechanisms also extend to fraud detection and regulatory compliance, ensuring adherence to financial governance frameworks [49]. Moreover, AI's predictive capabilities result in advanced climate risk modeling, portfolio optimization, and the forecasting of sustainable financial instruments such as carbon pricing or green bonds [50], [51]. By leveraging these capabilities, AI not only empowers investors to align with sustainability objectives but also generates broad benefits for businesses, communities, and society at large [35].

8.5 Role of AI in Green Finance

AI has emerged as a consistent enabler of green financial management, particularly in the domains of ESG analysis and reporting, where it supports companies in meeting regulatory compliance through real-time data handling [52]. AI-powered predictive models contribute to risk management by assessing environmental changes and guiding financial decision-making during uncertain events. In addition, AI-based tools play a significant role in market assessment by enabling trend analysis, evaluating financial viability, and conducting scenario modelling to ensure balanced investment strategies during uncertain conditions [53].

Beyond market evaluation, AI-driven applications enhance the identification of financial viability in sustainable projects and assist in the valuation of green bonds, thereby contributing towards portfolio optimization and more effective investment management. AI technologies also help to detect greenwashing practices by integrating global sustainability networks, thus improving the credibility of ESG-related claims [54]. Furthermore, AI enhances carbon trading mechanisms by tracking emissions and offset strategies with higher accuracy. Finally, AI-powered platforms expand financial accessibility in support of alternative credit assessments based on sustainability metrics, thereby facilitating the growth of start-ups and small businesses aligned with sustainable development goals [55].

8.6 AI Integration with CBDCs

The optimization of CBDCs has been found to enhance both security and financial inclusivity, providing a more resilient and accessible digital financial ecosystem. The integration of AI further strengthens this process by enabling real-time fraud detection and monitoring of day-to-day transactions, particularly in combating money laundering and other illicit financial activities through automated risk management systems [56]. AI-driven cybersecurity frameworks also play a critical role by incorporating biometric authentication measures, thereby addressing growing cyber threats and challenges in digital finance. In addition, smart contracts facilitated by AI enable automatic and efficient transactions through predictive analytics, which significantly improve operational efficiency [57].

Moreover, AI-enabled chatbots serve as a valuable tool for financial assistance, offering user-friendly credit scoring alternatives and enhancing overall accessibility to digital financial services. CBDCs also exert considerable macroeconomic influence by impacting inflation, interest rates, and broader financial stability within an economy [12]. Automated regulatory reporting, supported by AI, reduces the financial cost of compliance through mechanisms such as automated Know Your Customer (KYC) processes and anti-money laundering (AML) oversight [58]. Further, CBDC interoperability contributes to the streamlining of banking operations by facilitating efficient foreign exchange management and settlement in international trade. AI also supports privacy preservation in this domain by adopting encrypted techniques that balance transparency with data protection. Finally, the application of real-time monitoring tools enables policymakers to track consumer adoption behavior and adjust regulatory frameworks accordingly, ensuring the effective implementation of CBDCs [59].

8.7 Risk Mitigation Strategies

Risk mitigation has been increasingly recognized as a fundamental tool for sustainable financial management, ensuring both long-term stability and alignment with broader sustainability goals. One important dimension of this approach is the promotion of green investments, particularly in renewable energy and climate-resilient initiatives, which help to reduce the dependency on single sources of technology while diversification of sustainable financial portfolios [60]. Climate risk management further strengthens this framework through the application of scenario modeling and the adoption of mechanisms such as carbon pricing, which serve as strategic instruments for addressing financial risks associated with environmental uncertainty.

The case studies highlight the significance of introducing green insurance policies as hedging mechanisms to mitigate financial losses arising from environmental fluctuations, thereby safeguarding investors and institutions against volatility [61]. Importantly, sustainable investment strategies should not only prioritize short-term financial returns but also emphasize long-term socio-economic benefits, thereby fostering resilience and equity [7], [62]. In this regard, real-time risk management has emerged as a necessary practice, enabling dynamic portfolio adjustments in response to changing environmental and market conditions. Collectively, these strategies provide a pathway for responsible and sustainable growth at both national and global levels [63].

As shown in Table 8.1, the case studies of AI and sustainable finance with the implementation of CBDCs with respect to financial privacy and financial inclusivity. Four cases for different countries show the application and their outcomes.

Table 8.1 Case studies.

Case studies	Background	AI application	Outcome	Source
AI-Based CBDC for neutralised carbon state	The study was conducted in Singapore to reduce the carbon footprint in handling finance-related transactions.	The smart contracts can be used to fund the carbon-neutral economy. Blockchain technology and AI tracking have been used for the prevention of greenwashing. The carbon footprint was helpful for businesses to analyse their financial activities to attain the net-zero targets.	The cost of transaction can be reduced for a carbon-adjusted economy for green finance management. This further leads to monitoring of ESG compliance to reduce fraudulent sustainability claims.	[64]

(*Continued*)

Table 8.1 *Continued.*

Case studies	Background	AI application	Outcome	Source
Risk Mitigation using AI-Based Climate in the European Central Bank	The Central Bank of Europe integrated the CBDCs for risk assessment in combination with AI.	Real-time data adjustment used as per CBDC for financial risk management.	In handling the risk-based pricing models followed by green bonds, leading to sustainable returns for making financial decisions.	[65]
Canada's Carbon Credit Transaction	The Central Bank of Canada developed the AI-based marketplace with a carbon-credit state.	The focus was given on the verification of carbon offsets using CBDC transactions for the calculation of carbon offset for predicted price fluctuations for optimised trading of credit.	CBDC-based payment for enhanced ESG-based carbon credit risk management in terms of the sustainability of financial systems.	[66]
Disaster relief fund for the climate crisis	Japan adopted AI-based CBDCs for climatic relief from disaster through the swift allocation of funds during risky situations.	The real-time modeling for the prediction of disaster hotspots for the allocation of relief funds.	Speedy and efficient for equitable fund distribution for climatic conditions in terms of financial resilience.	[67]

8.8 Conclusion

The structure of sustainable finance is reshaped with the application of artificial intelligence by offering a clear insight into ESG outcomes, which further improves the state as well as the usage of CBDCs in the current financial world. The financial systems are for advanced analytics of data management, real-time management, and automation of investment techniques towards portfolio management. AI can also be used by investors to make effective investment decisions. The chapter also throws a light upon challenges in

AI applications for green finance management, as a risk of surveillance and uncertain consequences. Moreover, the opportunities ensure the AI deployment for inclusivity, transparency as well and accountability. The data quality insights may further lead to significant development of sustainable finance through CBDCs. The risk mitigation strategies with respect to CBDCs are also discussed in the study, which can be a source of significant results contributing towards the growth and development of the economy for global sustainability and economic well-being. The policies can be designed and implemented by the government through the adoption of AI in handling sustainable finance, in consideration of financial privacy and inclusivity.

References

[1] V. Jain and A. Mitra, "Enhancing Resilience in Business Continuity Management: Strategies and Best Practices," in *Enhancing Resilience in Business Continuity Management*, 2025, pp. 1–30. doi: 10.4018/979-8-3693-8809-9.ch001.

[2] C.-Q. Ma, X. Liu, T. Klein, and Y.-S. Ren, "Decoding the nexus: How fintech and AI stocks drive the future of sustainable finance," *International Review of Economics & Finance*, vol. 98, p. 103877, Mar. 2025, doi: 10.1016/j.iref.2025.103877.

[3] G. Degregori, V. Brescia, D. Calandra, and S. Secinaro, "Evaluating sustainability reporting in SMEs: insights from an ethical cooperative bank's approach," *Journal of Global Responsibility*, Mar. 2025, doi: 10.1108/JGR-10-2024-0197.

[4] D. Aboluwodi, P.-F. Muzindutsi, and B. Nomlala, "Investor sentiments and performance of selected ESG indices in BRICS markets during bull and bear conditions," *Investment Analysts Journal*, vol. 53, no. 3, pp. 231–248, Jul. 2024, doi: 10.1080/10293523.2024.2397889.

[5] M. Laboure, M. H.-P. Müller, G. Heinz, S. Singh, and S. Köhling, "Cryptocurrencies and CBDC: The Route Ahead," *Glob Policy*, vol. 12, no. 5, pp. 663–676, Nov. 2021, doi: 10.1111/1758-5899.13017.

[6] F. Abuamria and M. Ajouz, "Leveraging FinTech Innovations for Sustainable and Social Finance: A Comprehensive Analysis of Their Contributions to Social Impact Investment," in *From Digital Disruption to Dominance*, Emerald Publishing Limited, 2025, pp. 245–264. doi: 10.1108/978-1-83549-608-420251012.

[7] M. Pahwa, S. Agarwal, T. Choudhury, and V. Kandpal, "Analyzing the Role of DiFi on Income Distribution in Futuristic Green Indian Economy," 2025, pp. 329–352. doi: 10.1007/978-981-96-0843-0_17.

[8] J. A. Addae, S. Ahmed, and K. Simpe Ofori, "Learnings From Discontinued Central Bank Digital Currencies (CBDC)," 2023, pp. 165–186. doi: 10.4018/978-1-6684-6381-9.ch008.

[9] P. Trivedi, A. Ravisankar, G. P. Kumar, V. Krishnamoorthy, S. Shukla, and S. Boopathi, "Finance and Technology-Integrated Digital Economy: Circular Age of a Sustainable Digital Revolution," U. Tanveer, S. Ishaq, T. Q. Huy, and T. G. Hoang, Eds., IGI Global, 2024, pp. 91–120. doi: 10.4018/979-8-3693-2827-9.ch004.

[10] A. Kumar and V. Sikka, "International Lessons and Adaptations Examining Global CBDC Implementations and Extracting Insights for India's Digital Rupee," 2024, pp. 224–244. doi: 10.4018/979-8-3693-1882-9.ch014.

[11] J. B. Oleet, "Building a Better Future in the Fourth Industrial Revolution Through Blockchain," 2025, pp. 89–112. doi: 10.4018/979-8-3693-8664-4.ch005.

[12] A. Alora, P. Sahoo, and A. Sasidharan, "Central bank digital currency adoption challenges- The case of an emerging nation," *Financ Res Lett*, vol. 59, p. 104756, Jan. 2024, doi: 10.1016/j.frl.2023.104756.

[13] M. Wu, G. Subramaniam, Z. Li, and X. Gao, "Using AI Technology to Enhance Data-Driven Decision-Making in the Financial Sector," in *Artificial Intelligence-Enabled Businesses*, Wiley, 2025, pp. 187–207. doi: 10.1002/9781394234028.ch11.

[14] S. Alshammari, V. Serret, S. Tiwari, and K. Si Mohammed, "Industry 4.0 and AI amid economic uncertainty: Implications for sustainable markets," *Res Int Bus Finance*, vol. 75, p. 102773, Mar. 2025, doi: 10.1016/j.ribaf.2025.102773.

[15] Y. Wang, M. Shi, J. Liu, M. Zhong, and R. Ran, "The impact of digital-real integration on energy productivity under a multi-governance framework: The mediating role of AI and embodied technological progress," *Energy Econ*, vol. 142, p. 108167, Feb. 2025, doi: 10.1016/j.eneco.2024.108167.

[16] M. Ghaemi Asl, S. Ben Jabeur, and Y. Ben Zaied, "Analyzing the interplay between eco-friendly and Islamic digital currencies and green investments," *Technol Forecast Soc Change*, vol. 208, p. 123715, Nov. 2024, doi: 10.1016/j.techfore.2024.123715.

[17] A. I. Kato, E. G. Chiloane-Tsoka, and P. Mugambe, "Unlocking the potential: the influence of sustainable finance solutions on the long-term sustainability of small and medium-sized enterprises," *Cogent Business & Management*, vol. 11, no. 1, Dec. 2024, doi: 10.1080/23311975.2024.2391122.

[18] L. Ballester, A. González-Urteaga, and L. Shen, "Green bond issuance and credit risk: International evidence," *Journal of International Financial Markets, Institutions and Money*, vol. 94, p. 102013, Jul. 2024, doi: 10.1016/j.intfin.2024.102013.

[19] S. D. Shamurailatpam and M. Majeed, "The Autonomy of Central Banks and Digital Currency: A Macroeconomic Perspective," 2024, pp. 279–294. doi: 10.4018/979-8-3693-6321-8.ch012.

[20] M. Mani and R. Agarwal, "Payment Banks in India: Insights From the Customers' Perception," *International Journal of Asian Business and Information Management*, vol. 13, no. 1, pp. 1–15, Apr. 2022, doi: 10.4018/IJABIM.297851.

[21] K. Pancholi and P. Shukla, "Harnessing AI for Sustainability: Innovations, Policies, and Investment Paradigms," 2025, pp. 97–124. doi: 10.4018/979-8-3693-6011-8.ch005.

[22] V. D. Beloskar and S. V. D. Nageswara Rao, "Screening activity matters: Evidence from ESG portfolio performance from an emerging market," *International Journal of Finance & Economics*, vol. 29, no. 3, pp. 2593–2619, Jul. 2024, doi: 10.1002/ijfe.2798.

[23] Y. A. Waykar and S. Yambal, "AI and the Evolution of Green Finance: Transforming Banking for a Greener World," 2025, pp. 285–306. doi: 10.4018/979-8-3373-1917-9.ch013.

[24] Z. Yu, U. Farooq, M. M. Alam, and J. Dai, "How does environmental, social, and governance (ESG) performance determine investment mix? New empirical evidence from BRICS," *Borsa Istanbul Review*, vol. 24, no. 3, pp. 520–529, May 2024, doi: 10.1016/j.bir.2024 02.007.

[25] Q. Wang, T. Sun, and R. Li, "Does Artificial Intelligence (AI) enhance green economy efficiency? The role of green finance, trade openness, and R&D investment," *Humanit Soc Sci Commun*, vol. 12, no. 1, p. 12, Jan. 2025, doi: 10.1057/s41599-024-04319-0.

[26] M. Shehadeh and K. Hussainey, "Prelims," in *From Digital Disruption to Dominance*, Emerald Publishing Limited, 2025, pp. i–xxiii. doi: 10.1108/978-1-83549-608-420251016.

[27] B. Bertelli and C. Torricelli, "The trade-off between ESG screening and portfolio diversification in the short and in the long run," *Journal of Economics and Finance*, vol. 48, no. 2, pp. 298–322, Jun. 2024, doi: 10.1007/s12197-023-09652-9.

[28] A. Trotta, F. Rania, and E. Strano, "Exploring the linkages between FinTech and ESG: A bibliometric perspective," *Res Int Bus Finance*, vol. 69, p. 102200, Apr. 2024, doi: 10.1016/j.ribaf.2023.102200.

[29] H. Xia, Y. Gao, and J. Z. Zhang, "Understanding the adoption context of China's digital currency electronic payment," *Financial Innovation*, vol. 9, no. 1, p. 63, Mar. 2023, doi: 10.1186/s40854-023-00467-5.

[30] S. Brito-Ramos, M. C. Cortez, and F. Silva, "Do Sustainability Signals Diverge? An Analysis of Labeling Schemes for Socially Responsible Investments," *Bus Soc*, vol. 63, no. 6, pp. 1380–1425, Jul. 2024, doi: 10.1177/00076503231204613.

[31] E. G. Carayannis, R. Dumitrescu, T. Falkowski, G. Papamichail, and N.-R. Zota, "Enhancing SME resilience through artificial intelligence and strategic foresight: A framework for sustainable competitiveness," *Technol Soc*, vol. 81, p. 102835, Jun. 2025, doi: 10.1016/j.techsoc.2025.102835.

[32] P. K. Ozili, "Central Bank Digital Currency in India: The Case for a Digital Rupee," in *Revolutionizing Financial Services and Markets Through FinTech and Blockchain*, 2023, pp. 1–14. doi: 10.4018/978-1-6684-8624-5.ch001.

[33] D. Curcio, I. Gianfrancesco, G. Onorato, and D. Vioto, "Do ESG scores affect financial systemic risk? Evidence from European banks and insurers," *Res Int Bus Finance*, vol. 69, p. 102251, Apr. 2024, doi: 10.1016/j.ribaf.2024.102251.

[34] S. Das, "Significance of Digital Currencies in Sustainable Finance and Investment—An Indian Perspective," in *Fintech for ESG and the Circular Economy*, Wiley, 2025, pp. 225–245. doi: 10.1002/9781394234035.ch12.

[35] H. Sisodia, "Case Study on the Sand Dollar CBDC of the Bahamas," 2024, pp. 298–314. doi: 10.4018/979-8-3693-1882-9.ch018.

[36] S. M. Davoodalhosseini, "Central bank digital currency and monetary policy," *J Econ Dyn Control*, vol. 142, p. 104150, Sep. 2022, doi: 10.1016/j.jedc.2021.104150.

[37] Q. Yang, M. Zheng, and Y. Wang, "The Role of CBDC in Green Finance and Sustainable Development," *Emerging Markets Finance and Trade*, vol. 59, no. 15, pp. 4158–4173, Dec. 2023, doi: 10.1080/1540496X.2023.2185096.

[38] S. Dewangan and S. Kumar, "Frontiers of Innovation: Unveiling the Future Opportunities in Fintech," in *Financial Landscape Transformation: Technological Disruptions*, Emerald Publishing Limited, 2025, pp. 153–165. doi: 10.1108/978-1-83753-750-120251008.

[39] P. Pant, K. K. Mishra, and A. Singh, "AI for Sustainable Personal Finance and Green Lifestyles," 2025, pp. 307–332. doi: 10.4018/979-8-3373-1917-9.ch014.

[40] G. Singh and A. Verma, "RBI's Digital Currency and Its Significance in the Global Trade," in *Digital Currencies in The New Global World Order*, Singapore: Springer Nature Singapore, 2024, pp. 247–263. doi: 10.1007/978-981-97-4810-5_16.

[41] P. Fegatelli, "Monetary policy and reserve requirements with a zero-interest digital euro," *J Macroecon*, vol. 80, p. 103597, Jun. 2024, doi: 10.1016/j.jmacro.2024.103597.

[42] I. U. Haq, "Time-frequency comovement among green financial assets and cryptocurrency uncertainties," *Economic Notes*, vol. 52, no. 1, Feb. 2023, doi: 10.1111/ecno.12216.

[43] A. B. Sarin and S. Sharma, "The Synergy of Artificial Intelligence and Green Finance for Sustainable Investment," 2024, pp. 83–100. doi: 10.4018/979-8-3693-7570-9.ch006.

[44] L. Hupel, "Interoperability aspects of central bank digital currency across ecosystems and borders," *Journal of Payments Strategy & Systems*, vol. 17, no. 4, p. 422, Dec. 2023, doi: 10.69554/MBDJ6710.

[45] M. Irfan, S. Parameswaran, K. A. Singh, and E. R. Kismawadi, "Cutting-Edge Technologies for Economic Well-Being: The Transformative Power of AI and Blockchain," in *Driving Socio-Economic Growth With AI and Blockchain*, 2025, pp. 229–248. doi: 10.4018/979-8-3693-8664-4.ch010.

[46] A. J. Nair, S. Manohar, and A. Mittal, "AI-enabled FinTech for innovative sustainability: promoting organizational sustainability practices in digital accounting and finance," *International Journal of Accounting & Information Management*, vol. 33, no. 2, pp. 287–312, Apr. 2025, doi: 10.1108/IJAIM-05-2024-0172.

[47] S. Taneja, N. Bansal, and E. Özen, "The Future of the Indian Financial System," in *Finance Analytics in Business*, Emerald Publishing Limited, 2024, pp. 125–143. doi: 10.1108/978-1-83753-572-920241006.

[48] R. Jafar, B. Basuki, W. Windijarto, R. Setiawan, and Z. Yaacob, "Environmental, social and governance (ESG) disclosure and cost of equity: the moderating effects of board structures," *Cogent Business & Management*, vol. 11, no. 1, Dec. 2024, doi: 10.1080/23311975.2024.2429794.

[49] S. Karau, "Central bank digital currency competition and the impossible trinity," *Financ Res Lett*, vol. 54, p. 103723, Jun. 2023, doi: 10.1016/j.frl.2023.103723.

[50] W. Wu, X. Chen, R. Zvarych, and W. Huang, "The Stackelberg duel between Central Bank Digital Currencies and private payment titans in

China," *Technol Forecast Soc Change*, vol. 200, p. 123169, Mar. 2024, doi: 10.1016/j.techfore.2023.123169.

[51] D. Kirby, C. H. MacMahon, and S. Thompson, "The co-evolution of sustainable finance stakeholders under the EU taxonomy for sustainable activities: an exploratory study of Irish disclosure experiences," *Sustainability Accounting, Management and Policy Journal*, vol. 15, no. 6, pp. 1257–1285, Nov. 2024, doi: 10.1108/SAMPJ-11-2023-0842.

[52] E. M. Lange and N. G. Banadaki, "ESG consideration in venture capital: drivers, strategies and barriers," *Studies in Economics and Finance*, vol. 41, no. 3, pp. 724–739, Jun. 2024, doi: 10.1108/SEF-06-2023-0380.

[53] Y. Zhang, B. Gong, and P. Zhou, "Centralized use of decentralized technology: Tokenization of currencies and assets," *Structural Change and Economic Dynamics*, vol. 71, pp. 15–25, Dec. 2024, doi: 10.1016/j.strueco.2024.06.006.

[54] P. Makhija, M. Kukreja, and R. T. Kumar, "CBDC's FinTech Innovations: Socioeconomic Implications and the Need for Digital Detox," in *Business Drivers in Promoting Digital Detoxification*, 2024, pp. 25–35. doi: 10.4018/979-8-3693-1107-3.ch003.

[55] O. Boiral, M. Brotherton, and D. Talbot, "What you see is what you get? Building confidence in ESG disclosures for sustainable finance through external assurance," *Business Ethics, the Environment & Responsibility*, vol. 33, no. 4, pp. 617–632, Oct. 2024, doi: 10.1111/beer.12630.

[56] M. Manning, E. A. Akartuna, and S. Johnson, "Opportunities to future crime: Scoping the future of money laundering and terrorist financing through cryptoassets," *Technol Forecast Soc Change*, vol. 210, p. 123894, Jan. 2025, doi: 10.1016/j.techfore.2024.123894.

[57] G. A. Ogunmola and U. Das, "Analyzing consumer perceptions and adoption intentions of central bank digital currency: a case of the digital rupee," *Digital Policy, Regulation and Governance*, vol. 26, no. 4, pp. 450–471, Apr. 2024, doi: 10.1108/DPRG-09-2023-0136.

[58] M. Pirgmann and P. Wawrosz, "Assessing the Effective Lower Bound in the Context of Introducing the Digital Euro," *Economies*, vol. 12, no. 6, p. 143, Jun. 2024, doi: 10.3390/economies12060143.

[59] S. C. Rajpurohit, B. Palande, J. Kalal, and S. Parkhi, "Sustainable Development in the Digital Age: The Role of CBDCs in Achieving the SDGs," in *Green Finance and Energy Transition*, 2024, pp. 491–502. doi: 10.1007/978-3-031-75960-4_45.

[60] V. K. Sadanand and T. Sadanand, "Artificial Intelligence in India: Navigating Social Justice, Environmental Ethics, and Legal Governance," in *Exploring AI Implications on Law, Governance, and*

Industry, S. Chakraborty, Ed., 2025, pp. 85–116. doi: 10.4018/979-8-3373-3384-7.ch004.

[61] D. Tercero-Lucas, "Central bank digital currencies and financial stability in a modern monetary system," *Journal of Financial Stability*, vol. 69, p. 101188, Dec. 2023, doi: 10.1016/j.jfs.2023.101188.

[62] J. Wang, G. Chen, P. Hsieh, and W. Chen, "Physical climate change risk and ESG green premium," *Appl Econ*, pp. 1–14, Oct. 2024, doi: 10.1080/00036846.2024.2421456.

[63] U. Kayani and F. Hasan, "Unveiling Cryptocurrency Impact on Financial Markets and Traditional Banking Systems: Lessons for Sustainable Blockchain and Interdisciplinary Collaborations," *Journal of Risk and Financial Management*, vol. 17, no. 2, p. 58, Feb. 2024, doi: 10.3390/jrfm17020058.

[64] L. Insights, "Singapore to develop wholesale CBDC. Live pilots in 2024," Ledger Insights. Accessed: Sep. 17, 2025. [Online]. Available: https://www.ledgerinsights.com/singapore-wholesale-cbdc-pilots-2024/

[65] European Central Bank, "Managing climate-related risks," European Central Bank. Accessed: Sep. 17, 2025. [Online]. Available: https://www.ecb.europa.eu/ecb/climate/managing_mitigating_climatel_risk/html/index.en.html

[66] A. DiCaprio, "Central banks already use AI and CBDC, why not together?," r3. Accessed: Sep. 17, 2025. [Online]. Available: https://r3.com/central-banks-already-use-ai-and-cbdc-why-not-together/

[67] M. Kenjiro, "Next-Gen Disaster Tech: AI Transforms Social Media and Big Data into Life-Saving Insights," The Government of Japan. Accessed: Sep. 17, 2025. [Online]. Available: https://www.japan.go.jp/kizuna/2025/03/next-gen_disaster_tech.html

9

Ethical Considerations in AI-driven Finance: Balancing Innovation and Responsibility

Ayushi Arora

AyushI Arora, Assistant Professor, Chandigarh College of Technology, CGC Landran & Research Scholar, Punjabi University, Patiala

Email: arorasayushi@gmail.com

Abstract

Artificial Intelligence (AI) is rapidly transforming the financial services landscape, driving significant advancements in credit scoring, fraud detection, investment management, and customer service. However, this technological progress also brings complex ethical challenges related to fairness, transparency, accountability, and data privacy. This chapter offers a novel perspective by arguing that truly ethical AI cannot be achieved through checklists or regulatory compliance alone. Instead, it emphasizes that an organization's cultural values and shared norms play a decisive role in shaping how AI systems are designed, implemented, and governed. By drawing on insights from ethics, finance, technology, and organizational behavior, the chapter demonstrates that many ethical failures stem from misaligned organizational priorities and weak ethical cultures rather than technical flaws alone. This work highlights how cultivating a robust ethical culture – where ethical reflection, open dialogue, and accountability are embedded across functions – can help financial institutions build customer trust, mitigate regulatory risks, and ensure that AI-driven innovation supports fairness and social responsibility. By moving the conversation beyond compliance to culture, the chapter provides practical pathways for financial firms to navigate the ethical complexities of AI and to act responsibly in an increasingly digital financial ecosystem.

 DOI: 10.1201/9788743810766-9

9.1 Introduction

In the last few years, the financial services industry has been transformed deeply by Artificial Intelligence (AI). Banks and financial institutions now benefit from algorithmic trading, automatic approval of loans, detection of fraud, and chatbots that offer customized service to customers. As the World Economic Forum stated in a report from 2021, more than 80% of financial services companies already use AI in their operations, and most anticipate that it will boost their income and decrease costs [15]. Most AI's allure is how rapidly it can manage massive collections of data, and with a high accuracy rate. Because of technology, institutions can act more swiftly and wisely, improve how they operate, and deliver customized financial offers to many people. Models leveraging AI are considered more effective at evaluating borrower risk than conventional credit scoring systems, which may lead to increased financial inclusion through broader loan accessibility. On the same note, machine learning systems spot fraud quickly and more efficiently than humans can do on their own. Still, these new technologies create many ethical questions. As more responsibilities are given to AI at these institutions, some important problems have appeared. These include:

- Since AI products are based on information from the past, they may process and judge in ways that favor some and put others at a disadvantage on issues like getting a loan or buying insurance.
- Most Deep Learning models, which are common AI systems, do not easily explain what decisions they make.

The use of AI depends on gathering lots of data, raising questions about people's privacy and telling them to use their data. With automated decision making, it is not always known who is to be held accountable for the outcomes: developers, executives, or the algorithm.

In the financial area, these risks stand out since decisions can bring huge and life-changing effects to both people and communities. Giving credit unfairly to some demographic groups and not to others can cause inequality to increase, setting back the sector's goal to assist many members of society.

9.2 Beyond Compliance: The Critical Role of Organizational Culture

Responding to similar concerns, regulators from different parts of the world are now designing frameworks for ethical AI use. The proposed AI Act from the European Union (2021) categorizes AI tools for credit and fraud-risk evaluation as being at high risk and puts in place security measures that include transparency, supervision by humans, and sufficient robustness. AI and machine learning systems are viewed by both the U.S. Federal Reserve and the Office of the Comptroller of the Currency as important areas to address model risk management [15]. Even so, regulatory compliance alone is not enough. Issues in AI ethics can change, depend on the situation, and happen where no specific rules apply. Organizations that depend only on rules may be unable to stop problems from occurring. The effort to comply with rules does not always lead people to regard ethics as something they value inside themselves.

Building trust and managing ethical risks related to AI means financial institutions should do more than use checklists and risk matrices. They need to foster an ethical environment for AI – a collective belief system where everyone uses ethical guidelines for their work with AI. The culture needs to address and control risks as well as encourage creativity centered on respecting people.

9.3 The Effect of Organizational Culture

Organizational culture consists of the common values, customs, and approaches that control how people behave in a company. Culture helps decide how ethical matters are handled in various parts of an organization, including engineering, analytics, law, and top management. A good ethical culture helps employees address wrongdoings, brings different groups together, and makes sure ethical thinking is applied throughout the development of AI technology. Having good intentions is not enough; an organization needs a strong moral culture to avoid failure. Various cases have proven that mistakes in ethics, such as those seen in biased facial recognition or uncertain credit algorithms, may happen because of unintentional errors caused by internal shortcomings and little evaluation of plans. In a book, Weapons of Math Destruction, software algorithms may fail or cause issues without careful checks [8]. Doing business ethically with AI often helps a company retain loyal consumers, attract responsible investors, and dodge both lawsuits and disapproving public opinion. Most importantly, it is morally important to realize that financial institutions can largely decide who gets access to credit, housing, and insurance. They should make certain that their tools support justice, fairness, and equal chances for people – not only help the business succeed. At the close of the chapter, learners will realize that ethics in AI demands regular effort, careful consideration, and involves many voices. Those organizations in the financial industry that follow good principles will benefit most as AI becomes more involved.

9.4 Culture as the Lens Through Which AI is Interpreted and Applied

AI systems do not function in a vacuum. They are designed, trained, tested, and deployed by humans within institutional contexts. Each decision along the AI lifecycle – from selecting datasets and defining objectives to calibrating model thresholds and responding to model outputs – reflects underlying cultural assumptions. If an organization prioritizes speed and profitability above all else, ethical considerations may be sidelined or treated as afterthoughts. Conversely, if an organization values accountability, fairness, and transparency, those principles are more likely to be embedded into the design and use of AI systems.

What drives AI designers and how problems are addressed both depend on culture. A strong ethical culture helps organizations spot and solve risks quickly, rewards those who report wrongdoing within the company, and keeps moving forward with improvements. But organizations that have a poor work culture may overlook or hide their ethical issues, causing the company to fail and bring on public criticism.

Technological systems are built for and by our social lives [13]. Artificial intelligence (AI) behaves ethically depending on the qualities of the organization that designs and uses it. Big ethical mistakes are often problems with a culture rather than individuals [12]. Many of the biggest failures in the financial sector, such as those related to culture, are often at their root because of organizational culture challenges, not solely due to technical errors.

9.4.1 Loans and credit scoring

Algorithmic bias in credit scoring is an example of this problem. AI models deployed by financial organizations have been criticized because they have led to discrimination against minority groups in credit judgment. The same year, it was alleged that Apple and Goldman Sachs' AI-based credit card system granted lower credit limits to women when their income levels and credit histories matched those of men. Even though the companies claimed to have acted without bias, the incident caused worry over unclear facial recognition behavior and no ethical checks in place for this technology.

Often, fairness was not a key concern in the organization as a whole, so the driving force was not the bias in AI but in unclear or unfair company cultures. They show that teams working in AI design and governance are not being taught proper ethics.

9.4.2 Automatic declines for loans and unfair treatment for groups of people

It is also worth noting that fully automated loan systems depend on historical data, some of which shows a history of unequal lending. If the biases are not removed, the AI teaches itself to continue existing inequities, which only further hurts populations in need. An organization with caring values would need a thorough review, confirmation from people outside the organization, and input from various team members to stop such problems.

Weapons of Math Destruction points out that because these systems appear fair, when introduced without proper controls, they may become tools for oppression. O'Neil believes that because AI makes hard-to-understand choices, it is very dangerous in areas of finance where things can go wrong for individuals and last for a long time. The way a culture is shaped affects a company's ethical behavior and risk control.

Institutions respond to ethical risks in a certain fashion due to their culture. Those companies with developed ethical cultures not only respond when the law or media bring them change. Instead, they blend ethical perspectives into their planning for the future and into risk handling. The ECI's research confirms that companies with a strong ethical culture find wrongdoing more quickly, encourage staff to report it, and see fewer cases of retaliation. Many times, these groups react ahead of problems by setting up ethics groups, describing clear rules for ethical AI, and planning for potential risks that AI might create.

Having a good ethical culture helps the company deal quickly and effectively with things that did not go as planned. Such a company will also have the structure, leadership support, and methods to check, apologize, and correct the issue if an unexpected harm takes place.

9.4.3 Cross-functional ethical alignment begins with culture

Ethical AI governance cannot reside solely within technical teams or compliance departments. It requires buy-in and coordination across diverse roles:

a. Data scientists and engineers must be trained to detect algorithmic bias and consider the social implications of model outputs.

b. Legal and compliance professionals must ensure that AI systems align with both regulatory frameworks and ethical standards.

c. Executives and board members must allocate resources, set priorities, and establish performance metrics that include ethical outcomes.

d. Customer-facing employees must be empowered to raise concerns when automated decisions appear unfair or unexplainable.

Only a strong and shared ethical culture can align these disparate functions around a common set of values and practices. Culture serves as the "glue" that binds organizational efforts into a coherent approach to ethical AI.

9.4.4 Ethical culture as a strategic asset

Beyond risk mitigation, an ethical culture can be a strategic differentiator in a competitive financial marketplace. As AI adoption becomes ubiquitous, firms that can demonstrate responsible innovation may be better positioned to earn the trust of customers, regulators, and investors. A study by Deloitte (2022) found that 62% of consumers are more likely to remain loyal to financial services providers that are transparent about how they use AI and personal data [17].

Financial institutions that promote ethical AI practices through branding, thought leadership, and transparency reports can shape public discourse and influence regulatory standards. Just as firms once competed on the basis of data security, today they increasingly compete on the basis of AI ethics.

9.4.5 Core principles of ethical AI culture in finance

Building a culture of ethical AI in financial institutions requires more than an abstract commitment to "doing the right thing." It involves integrating specific, actionable principles into every stage of the AI development and deployment process. These principles should serve as the foundation for governance frameworks, employee training, risk management policies, and cross-functional collaboration.

Below are five widely recognized ethical principles that financial firms must internalize to institutionalize an ethical AI culture, supported by scholarly literature, international standards, and real-world cases.

9.4.5.1 Fairness and non-discrimination

At the heart of AI ethics in finance is the principle of fairness – the idea that AI systems should make decisions equitably, without systematically disadvantaging any individual or group. This is especially critical in financial services, where AI is used to make high-impact decisions such as credit approval, insurance pricing, and loan underwriting.

Bias is a problem
Since AI reads information from prior situations, it can identify social biases in our past. If neglected, this approach could increase the presence of biases. A credit scoring model created with data that showed unfair loan denials to minorities might repeat the same biased results, even for people who otherwise deserve approval.

Ways to be fair
There are several ways to describe what makes an algorithm fair.

- Equal results for all groups of people,
- Both methods have the same positive predictive value.
- People who are alike should also get the same results.

Every definition has advantages and disadvantages, so institutions have to choose which idea of fairness fits with their mission and the law [1].

Real-world case
The people who mortgage lending algorithms need to be in line with ECOA. This points out that fairness in financial AI is required by both law and ethics [4].

9.4.5.2 Transparency and explainability

The principle of transparency refers to the openness of AI systems regarding how they function, what data they use, and how decisions are made. Explainability, a closely related concept, refers to the degree to which AI decisions can be understood and interpreted by humans – particularly end users and impacted stakeholders.

Importance in financial contexts
In finance, explainability is essential for building trust, complying with regulations, and ensuring that users can contest or appeal automated decisions. For example, the European Union's *General Data Protection Regulation (GDPR)* includes a "right to explanation" under Article 22, particularly relevant to automated credit decisions [7].

Technical and organizational dimensions

Explainability is not solely a technical challenge. Organizations must determine:

1. Who needs to understand the model (e.g., regulators, clients, internal auditors),
2. What level of explanation is sufficient, and
3. How explanations are communicated.

Recent work in XAI (Explainable AI) includes methods such as:

1. LIME (Local Interpretable Model-Agnostic Explanations),
2. SHAP (SHapley Additive exPlanations), and
3. Counterfactual explanations.

These techniques help uncover why a model made a certain prediction, enabling financial institutions to provide clearer justifications.

9.4.5.3 Accountability

Accountability in ethical AI ensures that there are clear lines of responsibility for every decision and action taken by or through an AI system. It answers the critical question: *Who is responsible when an AI system causes harm or fails to act ethically?*

Institutional responsibility

Accountability must be enforced at multiple levels:

1. Developers are responsible for building systems aligned with ethical guidelines.
2. Managers must ensure these systems are properly vetted.
3. Executives and boards must establish governance structures that include AI ethics as a strategic priority.

The IEEE's *Ethically Aligned Design* (2019) initiative argues that human accountability must be maintained even when AI systems operate autonomously, to prevent the diffusion of responsibility [16].

AI governance structures

Financial institutions are increasingly creating AI governance boards or ethics committees that oversee AI projects, evaluate ethical risk, and ensure compliance with policies. Some firms, like HSBC and JPMorgan Chase, have established dedicated roles such as "AI Risk Officer" to manage oversight.

9.4.5.4 Privacy and consent

The idea of privacy and consent is key to protecting our personal information. Always, privacy and being informed are central to any ethical system about personal data. Since computerized financial analysis touches on sensitive matters of income, habits of spending, and credit details, it is both right and necessary to look after privacy. AI is able to get info from data that users might not know they provide. Data from a transaction might suggest someone's health or relationship status, which can lead to debates about whether they had consent.

Privacy by Design (PbD) principles should be used so that privacy is considered early in the process, rather than only later.

9.4.5.5 Robustness and security

Any AI solution in finance has to be secure and strong enough not to be manipulated or stopped accidentally. It is especially necessary in financial services because errors from AI can set off problems throughout the market or allow for hacker attacks.

Adversarial risks

AI models are vulnerable to adversarial attacks, where small, deliberate perturbations in input data can lead to incorrect outputs – such as wrongly flagging a legitimate transaction as fraud.

Operational resilience

Financial institutions must ensure their AI systems:

1. Function reliably under varying conditions,
2. Include safeguards against manipulation, and
3. Offer fail-safe options in case of malfunction.

The ISO/IEC TR 24028:2020 framework outlines key concepts and models for trustworthiness in AI, including reliability, resiliency, accuracy, and safety [19].

9.4.6 Steps to build a culture of ethical AI

9.4.6.1 Leadership commitment and ethical tone at the top

Change starts with leadership. Board members and C-suite executives must set the ethical tone by explicitly stating their commitment to responsible AI. Initiatives such as appointing Chief AI Ethics Officers or creating AI oversight committees send a strong signal across the organization.

Leaders should also incorporate AI ethics into organizational vision statements, investor reports, and strategic planning documents.

9.4.6.2 Embedding ethics into AI governance frameworks

An ethical culture must be institutionalized through robust governance. This includes:

1. AI ethics committees: Multidisciplinary teams to oversee high-risk AI systems.
2. Model risk management: Integrating AI models into existing MRM protocols as outlined by the Federal Reserve (SR 11-7 guidance).
3. Third-party audits: Engaging independent evaluators to assess AI fairness, transparency, and compliance.

9.4.6.3 Training and capacity building

Training programs are essential to build ethical literacy across all functions. These should include:

1. AI ethics workshops for developers and data scientists
2. Compliance-focused training for legal and risk teams
3. Executive education for ethical leadership in AI

Academic institutions like Stanford's Institute for Human-Centered AI and MIT Sloan offer online modules tailored to financial services. Internal certifications and ongoing workshops help reinforce learning and adaptation.

9.4.6.4 Fostering cross-functional collaboration

Ethical AI is not solely a technical issue. It requires diverse perspectives:

1. Data scientists: To detect and correct algorithmic bias.
2. Legal teams: To ensure compliance with privacy and financial regulations.

3. Social scientists: To understand societal impacts of automated decisions.
4. Customer representatives: To bring user-centric insights.

Cross-functional teams improve ethical foresight and prevent tunnel vision in AI development.

9.4.6.5 Encouraging ethical innovation

Firms should incentivize innovation that aligns with ethical values. This includes:

1. Ethical-by-design toolkits: Embedding fairness and explainability during model development (e.g., IBM AI Fairness 360, Microsoft Responsible AI Toolbox).
2. Internal hackathons: Focused on creating transparent, inclusive AI solutions.
3. Funding ethical AI research: Collaborations with academia and think tanks.

A case in point is Mastercard's AI Garage, which integrates responsible AI practices into every development phase.

9.4.6.6 Whistleblower protection and ethical reporting mechanisms

To truly encourage ethical conduct, institutions must create safe spaces for reporting concerns:

1. Anonymous hotlines for unethical AI deployment
2. Formal processes for internal review of AI model risks
3. Protection policies for ethical whistleblowers

Organizations with robust reporting mechanisms experience 60% fewer ethical violations [7].

9.4.6.7 Metrics and continuous improvement

Firms should define and track metrics related to AI ethics, such as:

1. Percentage of models audited for bias annually
2. Number of staff trained in AI ethics
3. Number of AI-related customer complaints or regulatory incidents

Feedback loops help improve model performance and cultural alignment over time. Benchmarking against industry standards like OECD AI Principles or ISO/IEC 23894:2023 ensures continuous relevance [17].

9.5 Case Examples

Case 1: JP Morgan Chase
JPMC established an AI Governance Council that includes legal, risk, compliance, and data science experts. They implemented a model documentation protocol ensuring every AI model meets explainability and fairness thresholds before deployment.

Case 2: ING Bank
ING adopted a Responsible AI framework with four key tenets: explainability, human oversight, fairness, and privacy. Their "AI ethics dashboard" helps visualize fairness metrics in real time.

Case 3: BBVA
BBVA's AI Factory includes an ethics unit that assesses social impact before greenlighting projects. The unit works closely with regulatory teams to align with EU AI regulations.

9.6 Challenges in Building an Ethical AI Culture

While many financial institutions are taking initial steps toward responsible AI adoption, embedding a truly ethical AI culture remains a complex and multifaceted challenge. These difficulties arise from both internal organizational dynamics and external structural constraints, ranging from economic incentives to regulatory uncertainty. Understanding and addressing these challenges is crucial for ensuring that ethical AI principles move beyond policy statements and into actionable practice.

9.6.1 Commercial pressures: Speed-to-market vs. ethical caution

In the financial services industry, competitive advantage and rapid innovation are key drivers. The promise of AI in automating tasks, detecting fraud, personalizing services, and optimizing decision-making has made it a focal point for fintech startups and established institutions alike. However, this innovation race can incentivize speed over scrutiny.

9.6.1.1 The "move fast" dilemma

Many firms operate under the logic of "move fast and iterate," which may be suitable for product development but incompatible with the time-consuming demands of ethical review, impact assessments, and model audits. Ethical risks such as algorithmic bias or privacy violations are often discovered only after deployment, when harm has already occurred. AI ethics teams are sometimes sidelined in favor of product development units, reducing their practical influence.

9.6.2 Complex AI supply chains: Misalignment with third-party vendors

Financial institutions frequently outsource AI solutions or integrate third-party components – from machine learning APIs to analytics platforms. These external vendors may not share the same ethical values, data handling standards, or accountability structures.

9.6.2.1 Ethical risks in outsourcing

1. Opacity in vendor algorithms makes it difficult for banks to understand and audit decision logic.
2. Contractual gaps may fail to specify responsibilities in the event of AI-related harm.
3. Geopolitical risks arise when vendors operate in jurisdictions with weaker data protection laws.

"Ethics washing" is common among tech vendors, where ethical principles are marketed but not operational. Without strong due diligence, financial firms risk delegating ethical responsibilities to less accountable partners [14].

9.6.3 Ambiguity in regulation: Evolving and inconsistent frameworks

The global regulatory landscape for AI in finance is fragmented, dynamic, and often ambiguous. While jurisdictions like the EU have developed comprehensive frameworks (e.g., AI Act, GDPR), other regions lack enforceable AI-specific regulations.

9.6.3.1 Impacts on ethical culture

1. Uncertainty leads to inconsistent compliance efforts and risk-averse behavior.

2. Lack of harmonization across borders complicates ethical governance in multinational firms.

3. Reactive enforcement (e.g., post-breach penalties) often discourages proactive ethical innovation.

9.6.4 Cultural resistance: Ethics as a low priority

Even with top-level support, ethical AI adoption often meets resistance at the cultural level, especially among employees focused on technical efficiency, compliance, or revenue generation.

9.6.4.1 Underlying factors

1. Rewarding the wrong things: Personnel may be rewarded if they pay enough attention to ethical matters, rather than if they focus on delivery and lowering expenses.

2. Some data scientists and engineers have not had instruction on ethical or social topics.

3. Showing generic ethics messages is likely to cause employees to tune out and become less involved.

According to a study, even though the vast majority of executives feel their financial services AI is ethical, just one-third of customers trust the technology [2]. Moral machines also require considering incentives and governance among institutions and social technology [10]. If AI developers are not given attention to responsible behaviors within metrics, they are unlikely to care about ethics.

9.6.5 Overcoming the challenges: Strategic integration of ethics

To move past these challenges, financial institutions need a strategic and systemic approach to ethical AI. This includes embedding ethical considerations across the entire AI lifecycle and aligning them with business incentives and governance structures.

9.6.5.1 Key strategies

1. Ethics-integrated performance metrics: Include ethical KPIs (e.g., fairness scores, model audit completeness, explainability ratings) in performance evaluations for developers, managers, and product leads.

2. Vendor selection and due diligence: Incorporate AI ethics criteria – such as bias testing, data lineage documentation, and third-party audits – into procurement processes and contractual obligations.
3. Ethical product lifecycle management:
   a. Embed ethical risk reviews at each stage: ideation, development, deployment, and decommissioning.
   b. Use tools like *algorithmic impact assessments (AIA)* and *ethics checklists*.
4. Training and education: Provide ongoing training to AI practitioners, product managers, and executives on legal, social, and ethical implications of AI in finance.
5. Interdisciplinary ethics boards: Establish cross-functional ethics councils including ethicists, data scientists, legal advisors, and business leaders to vet AI use cases.

9.7 Conclusion

Artificial Intelligence is already reshaping financial services – from loan approvals and fraud detection to portfolio management and customer interaction – but its rapid adoption raises critical ethical concerns such as algorithmic discrimination, invasion of privacy, lack of transparency, and unchecked automation. These issues go beyond technical limitations, posing challenges to societal trust, regulatory oversight, and vulnerable populations. While most AI ethics efforts focus on compliance with existing guidelines, the fast-paced nature of finance demands a deeper cultural shift; laws lag behind technology, and legality does not always align with morality. A strategic culture of ethics must be embedded throughout every phase of the AI lifecycle – from ideation and data collection to model development, deployment, and retirement. Leadership must demonstrate ethical commitment as a core value and be assessed with relevant KPIs; developers and product teams need continuous training in fairness, explainability, and social impact, with ethics taught as part of technical fluency. Organizations should create multidisciplinary teams – spanning IT, law, ethics, and customer service – to review AI projects collaboratively, integrating ethical perspectives at every stage. In today's competitive financial marketplace, trust is a strategic asset: consumers increasingly value honesty and fairness in AI, employees prefer working at ethically conscious firms, and ethical innovation supports long-term sustainability. To develop a resilient culture, institutions must prioritize trust over short-term profits, invest in tools for ethical auditing, and foster continuous learning anchored in clear values and leadership by example.

References

[1] Barocas, S., Hardt, M., & Narayanan, A. (2019). *Fairness and machine learning: Limitations and opportunities.*

[2] Capgemini Research Institute. (2020). *AI and the ethical conundrum: How organizations can build ethically robust AI systems and earn trust.*

[3] Cavoukian, A. (2009). *Privacy by design: The 7 foundational principles*. Information and Privacy Commissioner of Ontario.

[4] Deloitte. (2022). *AI ethics in financial services: Winning trust through responsible AI.*

[5] Doshi-Velez, F., & Kim, B. (2017). Towards a rigorous science of interpretable machine learning. *arXiv preprint arXiv:1702.08608.*

[6] Ethics & Compliance Initiative. (2020). *Global Business Ethics Survey Report.*

[7] European Union. (2018). *General Data Protection Regulation (GDPR).*

[8] Hao, Karen. 2019. "The Future of AI Research Is in Africa." MIT Technology Review (blog). June 21, 2019.", contributed by Angela Okune, *Research Data Share, Platform for Experimental Collaborative Ethnography*

[9] O'Neil, C. (2016). *Weapons of math destruction: How big data increases inequality and threatens democracy*. Crown Publishing.

[10] Papernot, N., McDaniel, P., Goodfellow, I., Jha, S., Celik, Z. B., & Swami, A. (2017). Practical black-box attacks against deep learning systems using adversarial examples. *arXiv preprint arXiv:1602.02697.*

[11] Rahwan, I., Cebrian, M., Obradovich, N., Bongard, J., Bonnefon, J. F., Breazeal, C., ... & Lazer, D. (2019). Machine behaviour. *Nature*, 568(7753), 477–486.

[12] Raji, I. D., & Buolamwini, J. (2019). Actionable auditing: Investigating the impact of publicly naming biased performance results of commercial AI products. *Proceedings of the AAAI/ACM Conference on AI, Ethics, and Society.*

[13] Vallor, S. (2018). *Technology and the virtues: A philosophical guide to a future worth wanting*. Oxford University Press.

[14] Wachter, S., Mittelstadt, B., & Russell, C. (2017). Counterfactual explanations without opening the black box: Automated decisions and the GDPR. *Harvard Journal of Law & Technology*, 31(2), 841–887.

[15] Wagner, B. (2018). Ethics as an escape from regulation: From ethics-washing to ethics-shopping? In *Being Profiled* (pp. 84–89). Amsterdam University Press.

[16] Chatila, Raja & Havens, John. (2019). The IEEE Global Initiative on Ethics of Autonomous and Intelligent Systems. 10.1007/978-3-030-12524-0_2.

[17] World Economic Forum. *The New Physics of Financial Services,* Retrieved from https://www3.weforum.org/docs/WEF_New_Physics_of_Financial_Services.pdf

[18] Deloitte. *Increasing Consumer Privacy and Security Concerns in the Generative AI Era,* Retrieved from https://www.deloitte.com/us/en/about/press-room/increasing-consumer-privacy-and-security-concerns-in-the-generative-ai-era.html

[19] International Organization for Standardization. *Information technology — Artificial intelligence — Overview of trustworthiness in artificial intelligence.* ISO/IEC TR 24028:2020,Retrieved from https://www.iso.org/obp/ui/#iso:std:iso-iec:tr:24028:ed-1:v1:en

10

AI-driven Strategies for Risk Assessment and Management in Banking

Gurpreet Kaur[1*] and Puneet Singh[2]

[1*]Manav Rachna University, India
[2]SAVP, EXL Services, India

Email: Phd.gurpreet@gmail.com; Puneetsingh.juc@gmail.com

Abstract

In the era of advanced technological developments and the financial landscape, banks have increasingly facing and fraud and are exposed to several risks. Therefore, the identification, assessment, and management of banking risk have become essential for the sustainable growth and long-term stability of banking institutions. Besides this, early detection and prevention of fraud are also important to ensure sustainable banking practices. AI has emerged as a very effective tool for enhancing the bank's effectiveness and overall performance. One of the advanced techniques is AI predictive analytics, which is used by banks to address the key challenges in managing assets and liabilities, including liquidity risk, capital adequacy, and interest rate risk. An AI-powered system has proved very effective in the early detection and prevention of fraud. Many banks these days are using predictive analysis tools. While predictive analysis is fundamental to business operations, AI is a key driver of success. On one hand, where predictive analysis is used for collecting data, the integration of AI will allow corporations to use their large volume of data effectively and quickly. AI enables banks to implement robust fraud detection by leveraging advanced predictive analytics and real-time monitoring. The present study provides a comprehensive insight into how AI systems are combating fraud using advanced behavioral analytics and adaptive learning, reducing the risk in the financial sector. This chapter looks into the financial world and explores the use of AI in risk management and

 DOI: 10.1201/9788743810766-10

automated credit assessments. Furthermore, the chapter explores the strategic role of AI and predictive analysis in preventing liquidity risk by applying early warning systems, stress testing, forecasting, etc.

10.1 Introduction

Banking has always been at the forefront of technology adoption, whether it is for digitizing contact centres and back office operations or for creating cutting-edge automation through high-frequency trading platforms used by hedge funds for profit maximization. Moreover, in such a quickly evolving technological landscape, banks find themselves dealing with two seemingly opposing forces – innovation and vulnerability [2], [7]. While banks continue on their march towards technology-driven operational efficiency, they are continuously threatened by fraudsters who continue to find backdoors to exploit banks' system glitches. Moreover, while external fraudsters come armed with sophisticated tools and tactics, there are equally grave concerns arising out of internal threats of collusion or oversight and from third-party manipulation. And what used to be isolated events of fraud are now becoming large-scale operations, almost mimicking the bank's risk department with a man-to-man marking. This kind of scale in fraud rings is creating fraud threats that have the potential to escalate into a liquidity crisis, aside from damaging reputations and inviting regulatory scrutiny.

This chapter explores the linkage between fraud, whether it happens through digital scamsters or through large institutional players, and liquidity and capital adequacy risks in a bank. There are multiple examples like scamsters exploiting naïve customers on UPI launch day or billion-dollar hacks that almost crippled a nation's central bank through a state-sponsored operation. These examples throw light on the evolving capacity of fraud to bring entire banking systems to a halt. The case studies included in this chapter, be it incidents that occurred at Punjab & Maharashtra Bank, Yes Bank, or Bangladesh's Central Bank, highlight the fact that what starts as a reputation issue quickly boomerangs into a complete catastrophe, leading to financial instability.

Faced with such threats that pose existential questions, this chapter explores the power of predictive analytics in dealing with these threats through risk detection, mitigation, and forecasting. Modern-day risk managers are empowered with AI-driven predictive models that shift through real-time streams of ever growing number of data points of customer transactions, behavior, market trends, sovereign events, etc, to predict possibilities of fraud events, provide fraud prevention warnings, and even forecast the level of contingency funds needed to cover the risk profile that the bank is dealing with. Case studies included in this section cover HSBC and Google's partnership for real-time monitoring, JP Morgan's transformative AI adoption, and Bank of America's unique monetization opportunity with CashPro. All these case studies showcase that predictive analytics has gone mainstream in areas of detecting and preventing fraud and has a direct bearing on the enhancement of operational efficiency and financial forecasting.

Through this assessment, predictive analytics can be seen as not only a tool for preventing risk events from happening but also as an enabler of sustainable banking. Bankers now have modelling platforms that empower them with control that makes their institutions trustworthy allies in their clients' financial journeys.

10.2 Mechanism Through Which Bank Fraud Leads to Liquidity Risk

Frauds in the banking system are almost as old as the banking system itself. If a system is putting in place to improve efficiency, compliance or even customer experience, there are always going to be bad actors ready to pounce on that system and take advantage of either a gap in the system or process or by directly defrauding a naïve customer who may be unaware of a new feature and may fall prey to a sophisticated fraudster and end up giving into some enticement that may lead to loss of a lot of money. For example, on the very day when UPI was launched by the government of India, fraudsters started sending requests to random UPI IDs to get Re 1 from random strangers [11]. In some cases, the random UPI ID may be wrong, and in others, the recipient of the request may have been cautious and denied the request. However, there were thousands of people who either did not pay attention or thought they were receiving money, or the bank was probably testing the system with low-value transactions. Either way, they unwittingly deposited these small amounts into the fraudsters' accounts. Moreover, while these were low-value transactions, for a fraudster who could execute these requests at scale, these successful transactions meant earning thousands in a day. And due to the sheer distributed nature and randomness of the defrauded people, these transactions were not even reported till someone saw a pattern at a bank.

This was an example of a small fraud done at a limited scale and was caught before it became any kind of sizeable risk.

However, there are multitudes of customer-facing frauds, internal frauds, and third-party frauds that can put the entire banking system at risk. And as fraudsters become more and more skilled at using technology to their advantage, they are getting closer to executing frauds at a scale that can cause serious Liquidity and Capital Adequacy risks. For Instance, North Korean state-sponsored hackers came within inches of success in executing a $ 1 billion fraud on Bangladesh's Central Bank by breaking into the bank's computer system and taking control of a printer that was used for printing out records of multi-million dollar transactions every day [12]. This created a liquidity scare for not just a bank but the entire banking system of the nation.

In this chapter, we will evaluate how predictive analytics helps detect and prevent large-scale fraud that can create liquidity and capital adequacy risks for banks. But before we do that, it is critical to understand some of the ways in which frauds are creating these risks:

10.2.1 Direct financial losses

- **Unrecoverable funds**: When fraudulent transactions like unauthorized wire transfers and credit card fraud, occur at scale in a bank, it can create a short-term liquidity risk by reducing the bank's available cash and liquid assets, as these transactions tend to happen in a short span, creating an unusual event leading to a cash shortage in the bank. This can then lead to a severe impact on the bank's ability to take care of its short-term obligations. This will further cause the bank to look for expensive short-term borrowings.
- **Impaired assets**: Fraudsters can come in any garb and take an entire banking system for a ride. And while banks have been able to successfully curb small retail credit frauds by putting scalable detection and prevention technology in place, it is the big sharks and their often pretentious and layered big business reputations that put liquidity pressures on banks. And these things can happen due to multiple reasons, like implicit trust due to the big borrower's reputation, internal collusion with some high-ranking bank officials, or simple greed in officials arising out of the lure of commissions and promotions they may earn by closing such humongous debt deals.

However, once these loans, which can at times be bigger than a small nation's entire GDP, become non-performing assets, they can cause a liquidity scare for the bank and can even lead to insolvency proceedings if not handled carefully. There are some glaring examples of this, as is evident from the case of how Vijay Mallya defrauded an entire consortium of Indian banks.

10.2.2 Reputational damage and loss of confidence

- **Deposit runs**: As fraud incidents become part of public knowledge, it leads to severe damage to the bank's reputation. This leads to a loss of trust in the bank's ability to maintain enough cash to honor its customers' withdrawal requests. This trust erosion can then create a situation of a "run on the bank", as a large number of depositors start lining up to withdraw funds simultaneously, as they start fearing the bank's insolvency. The massive and sudden fund outflow makes way for an immediate and severe liquidity crisis, as there may be a limit to the bank's liquid assets to meet all the withdrawal requests. Take the case of Punjab and Maharashtra Bank, which came under RBU scrutiny in 2019, as its fraudulent loans to the real estate company HDIL came to light. Huge lines of retail depositors formed outside the bank's ATMs, with the hopes of withdrawing money before the bank went under [11]. Such events often spiral out of control, leading to restrictions on withdrawal limits, which can lead to even more chaos.
- **Difficulty in raising funds:** A bank that goes through a fraud event of any significant size finds itself in further tight spots when it finds it challenging to raise funds in interbank markets or from institutional investors. This is naturally inevitable as the bank's credit or funding requests are evaluated at a high credit risk. This further increases the liquidity issues as it restricts the bank's ability to secure the required short-term and long-term funds. This is what Yes Bank went through in 2020 when the Reserve Bank of India placed the bank under moratorium, restricting not only withdrawals from the bank, but also curtailing the bank's ability to raise funding until its board and leadership were changed through the setup of an overseeing administrative council. [10]

10.2.3 Regulatory penalties and fines

On the one hand, banks suffer financial losses and liquidity risks due to fraudulent activities. To top it all, regulatory bodies, such as central banks and financial intelligence units, are also seen taking severe action by charging substantial fines and penalties if banks are seen having inadequate fraud prevention and detection mechanisms. Not just that, as seen in the Yes Bank case, regulatory scrutiny also brought with it significant restrictions on the bank's operations and growth, affecting revenue generation, which is critical for maintaining the much-needed liquidity buffer.

10.2.4 Operational disruption

Another indirect impact of fraud on liquidity arises out of operational disruptions as the bank diverts resources from core activities to fraud management. This significantly reduces the bank's ability to run day-to-day operations such as customer service, credit disbursement, etc., with efficiency impacting the bank's financial performance and indirectly affecting liquidity.

10.3 How Predictive Analytics is Helping Banks in Mitigating These Risks

10.3.1 Use of predictive analytics for fraud prevention

10.3.1.1 Prevention of retail fraud

- **Real-time monitoring**: Through the use of large swathes of data on customer behavior pertaining to spending patterns, transactions, locations, login times, etc., predictive models first baseline the normal customer behavior. Now, with the help of real-time transaction monitoring, these sophisticated models can spot any deviation from this baseline and start flagging it as suspicious. If these deviations are significant or if there is a pattern of deviations, these are either flagged for real-time customer review and validation or are declined outright. This reduces the risk of fraudulent transactions fairly significantly.
- **Behavioral biometrics**: Each customer has a unique pattern of interacting with the bank's online platform. This can include fundamental parameters like login times, device, and location, but behavioral biometrics takes it a step beyond these parameters to baseline much more sophisticated user behavior parameters like typing speeds, mouse movements, app navigation patterns, etc. If the fraud prevention system sees a deviation from these patterns, it starts tracking the activity on this account and flags the account for review of any type of changes, even if those changes are being initiated on a different channel. This reduces the risk of account takeover fraud and prevents unauthorized changes to customer accounts, which may be a prelude to other large financial transactions that may prove irreversible, given that they would seemingly come from legitimate authorized customer access.
- **Transaction scoring**: Within the banking ecosystem, every transaction is a data point. Moreover, this data point further has various associated parameters, which are linked with customer behavior, the bank's risk

parameters, network analysis, and even market forces. Each transaction is thus scored based on parameters linked to areas.

With a baseline established for this transaction score, transactions keep getting approved as long as the transaction score is below the risk threshold. This ensures that the overall operational efficiency of the system is maintained and there is no disruption in day-to-day banking.

But the moment a transaction occurs to have a transaction score above the risk threshold, it gets flagged for review and validation by the customer and is also flagged for review by the risk team. Once cleared by both, the transaction is allowed to go through; otherwise, fraud has been prevented successfully.

10.3.1.2 Case study: HSBC's dynamic risk assessment

While proprietary banking models need to be kept confidential, not only to maintain a competitive edge but also to avoid misuse of the model by fraudsters for sidestepping or breaking the very model, banks often highlight the impact of predictive analytics in fraud prevention.

HSBC partnered with Google Cloud to transition from a rules-based anti-money laundering system to an AI solution that recognizes suspicious activity on its own, without the need to manually set any rules or thresholds [5].

They trained the model on their vast customer transaction data and let it scan a billion-plus monthly transactions.

The new AI model has impacted both efficiency and effectiveness. Overall, it has reduced the total number of alerts by 60% by not flagging transactions that would come out as "false positives" upon investigation after being flagged by the previous system. But, at the same time, the effectiveness of the AML team has also improved as the AI system now spots two to four times as much actual suspicious activity as the previous system, meaning HSBC investigation teams are spending much more time reviewing genuinely suspicious cases.

10.3.1.3 Enhancements in loan scoring

It has been observed that retail credit scoring has been revolutionized in the last couple of decades, with the use of a humongous amount of customer data like income, credit history, spending patterns, and even alternative data like social media behavior. All this data, along with the power of predictive analytics, helps assess the creditworthiness of borrowers and predict the likelihood of default with much more accuracy. Overall, it means that retail credit decisions are completely data-driven and more or less aligned with the risk appetite of the banking industry.

However, the same cannot be said about institutional lending practices, which continue to be subjective and have risks associated with them. And there are several factors that lead to this subjectivity.

Institutional borrowers have an army of financial consultants who can help them package their loan proposal much more favorably than their company's fundamental financials may deserve. Secondly, institutional borrowers, by virtue of their financial heft, can influence the bank's board or senior leadership to sign off on slightly higher risk, too. Thirdly, the sheer size of institutional borrowing creates a vested interest for the very team that is reviewing the creditworthiness, and even the bank's incentive structure lures them into approving the loan even if it comes at the risk of personal scrutiny in case of a default.

In all these scenarios, all parties are acting under the assumption that debt taken by such a reputed organization or institution would not default, whether it is the board or the chairman who is making a decision under some influence, or it is the senior leaders who are tasked with evaluating creditworthiness and are more concerned about the incentives they will receive if they approve this loan.

More can be said about collusion under any kind of influence, but that is not really the subject of this chapter.

However, if the regulators and banking institutions are motivated enough, they can use all of this data for fraud detection. And whatever can be used for fraud detection can also be used for fraud prevention.

- **Predictive analysis of unstructured data for loan fraud prevention**: While institutional borrowers have the wherewithal to hire sophisticated financial consultants to beef up their case in front of bankers, there is no escaping what independent analysts or the press may analyze about such borrowers. And increasingly, it is becoming mandatory for case managers, who in such scenarios can be senior leaders of the bank, to submit detailed external and third-party analysis of the borrower's well-being and creditworthiness. And this is where sophisticated AI tools come in handy in analyzing the borrower's trustworthiness, creditworthiness, and overall market segment. Without these qualitative and quantitative assessments, the documents submitted by the borrower have almost no value, as they do not stand the test of corroboration with trusted external data. These predictive analyses include natural language processing to predict markers of financial stress, cashflow issues, or any other leading indicators that point towards potential for credit defaults at the very least or complete fraud at its worst. The analysis and assessment that were earlier dependent on only documentation and reports submitted by the enterprise can be corroborated with external sources and predictive analytics for validation [1–2].

- **Internal threat prevention**: Banks, these days, have to be aware and vigilant about internal fraud and threats as they are about bad actors from the external world. Predictive analytics solutions can help with this kind of internal behavior monitoring without compromising privacy regulations and obligations towards bank employees.
- **Employee behavior analysis**: Behavioral biometrics is a digital fingerprint that is not only applicable to customers but is more useful for analyzing anomalies in employee behavior and can provide early warning signals of internal fraud threats. There are loads of internal data points like login times, access to sensitive data, trading patterns, etc., which create an employee's behavioral biometrics. Any unusual or anomalous outlier in this pattern can indicate a high-risk event and trigger enhanced vigilance on employee behavior, especially during the time they may be working on a critical deal or a report that could prove significant for a large enterprise.
- **Communication analysis**: Internal communication, like emails or chat logs, is as much of a work product as the reports that an employee may produce while being employed by a bank. Hence, these communications can be used to scrutinize employee integrity and avoid financial losses in a fraud event. The system can identify suspicious patterns and keywords in such communications that might indicate illicit activities through the use of overtly cryptic language or collusion through an uncharacteristically large volume of communication between related or unrelated individuals.
- **Transaction monitoring**: When the stakes are as high as those that are seen when funding institutional borrowers, no measure should be left unused to avoid internal fraud, which usually is a part of the issue when there is a lack of due diligence in the case of institutional borrowing. These measures go up to the extent of analyzing transactions from their expense claims and even personal accounts to spot any anomalies and take proactive action to fix due diligence reports that the employee may have been working on.
- **Anticipating fraud-related outflows:** One of the critical functions of the fraud prevention team at a bank is also to provide their assessment

regarding the likelihood of fraud occurring in the bank and allow the bank to create a sufficient buffer to enable it to tide through the financial impact of a fraud-related event, even though there will still be reputational loss and other kinds of impacts.

Predictive analytics helps banks by forecasting the likelihood of fraud-related activities based on the overall risk profile of the banking operations and the potential impact of such fraud-type activities. By doing this, banks can incorporate these potential losses into their liquidity forecasts. This enables the bank to have cash flow projections that are much more realistic and helps the bank in its liquidity buffer by keeping away contingency funds.

- **Case study: JP Morgan's broad AI investments:** JP Morgan has made enterprise-wide AI investments to empower leaders with data-led insights for more objective decision-making [13]. These investments have included applications in fraud detection, fraud forecasting, and risk optimization strategies, too. These applications let them not only detect and prevent fraud but also let them forecast the likelihood, the key philosophy being that banks can only minimize fraud, not completely eliminate it.

This has helped them create relevant contingency funds for a scenario in which fraud ends up happening.

10.3.2 Managing liquidity risk through predictive analytics

While predictive analytics has played a critical role in fraud detection and prevention, it also finds direct applications in the area of liquidity risk management at banks through the use of ever-sophisticated models. Here are some of the ways in which banks are mitigating liquidity risks and creating much more efficient fund usage strategies.

10.3.2.1 Real-time liquidity forecasting

Banks that have started using predictive analytics realize the power of real-time data usage and have moved on from the usage of traditional liquidity forecasting methods, which relied solely on static historical data sources.

This real-time data includes not only customer behavior and transaction data but also takes into account market parameters such as stock prices and exchange rates, macro-economic indicators, social media trends, and even unlikely data sources like weather patterns that may have an impact on cash demand in certain sectors and regions.

The real-time liquidity forecasting models are not only adept at using real-time data but are also designed to continuously learn and adapt from data anomalies as new data keeps coming in, and can adjust the forecasts to keep those relevant and accurate even in the face of rapidly changing market scenarios.

- **Case study:** The Digital First Bank Sofi is using sophisticated AI models for the creation of 6-hour rolling forecasts for cash flow requirements and sees the models working with 91% accuracy [9]. This improves their capital deployment efficiency and reduces idle cash by over $15 million every year.

10.3.2.2 Cash flow prediction

Banks have had to deal with cash flow issues since the very inception of the banking system, where a lack of accurate forecasting of cash flow has always created risks of either overstocking of cash or underserving customers.

However, with the use of predictive analytics, banks can now go as granular as they need to forecast cash flow needs at the level of specific customer segments or product lines based on seasonality in that segment. For example, during the time of the year when most of the new car launches are supposed to happen, banks would see a rise in cash flow needs as the auto sector will need to beef up production to meet new model demand. But that is not all. Predictive analytics models are allowing banks to go as granular as forecasting cash flow needs at the individual branch level to ensure optimum efficiency in cash flow usage.

This kind of granularity also feeds into the bank's ability to predict cash flow needs across different time horizons, too. With the power of predictive analytics, banks now have the ability to forecast cash flow changes that may happen intraday to forecasts that help plan cash flow needs in the short term, i.e., days and weeks, to medium-term predictions that may take into account business cyclicity and seasonality.

- **Case study:** Bank of America created a platform for predicting cash movement trends that helped them predict the bank's cash flow needs with such accuracy, granularity, and efficiency that the bank decided to commercialize the platform. Named CashPro, the platform leverages predictive analytics and enables Bank of America's corporate clients to manage liquidity and cash flow, not just at an enterprise level but also at the level of various segments and factories. This is a unique example of a bank that has been able to monetize a non-financial product [9].

10.3.2.3 Early warning systems

Cash management applications monitor 100s of internal and external parameters continuously. These parameters include internal transactional data and data streams coming in from non-transactional systems like digital applications or even social media listening posts. From an external standpoint, these data points can include data points related to markets, exchange rates, corporate results, supply chains, and even weather situations.

Suppose the system sees a sudden shift in the data trends, it is bound to react and trigger an alert. However, such systems are also sophisticated enough to sport minute deviations from the pattern and can trigger early warnings, which can indicate a potential stress point in the system before it becomes a full-blown catastrophe.

Such systems are designed to trigger alerts to treasury and risk managers, early enough to allow them to implement course corrections before things become unmanageable.

- **Case study:** Another digital native neobank, Chime, has implemented liquidity protocols that use auto, which have helped them gain improvements in liquidity management as compared to their peer group [8]. This system works by leveraging Chime's blockchain-based network to monitor the routing of funds through smart contracts. The moment cash volume at a network level goes below a certain threshold, it creates trigger warnings for risk managers to arrange for fund sources at an intraday and short-term level.

10.3.2.4 Dynamic stress testing

Beyond monitoring and alerting, predictive analytics platforms also help risk managers in other key areas. This is by creating multitudes of "what–if" scenarios and simulating the impact that such scenarios can have on the bank's cash flow.

These scenarios can include market disruption simulations, such as the announcement of generative AI applications, which could impact diverse areas of industry. These can also be simulations of credit rating downgrades of big corporations or nations, and the exposure they can create for the bank.

These systems help provide quantitative insights into the impact of such events and can enable risk managers to prepare proper contingency plans.

The systems are now further evolving into prescriptive platforms that also provide several action path recommendations to risk managers, so that they can evaluate those and choose the best path to tread during such scenarios.

- **Case study:** Santander Bank has implemented a predictive analytics system to generate early default predictions and simulate scenarios if multitudes of such events were to coincide with each other [6]. Not only did it help the bank improve its prediction accuracy by 43%, but it also triggered actions towards contingency plans for likely scenarios with high probability.

10.4 Tangible Results from the Use of Predictive Analytics in Fraud Prevention and Liquidity Risk Management

Any change that has enterprise-wide implications does not come easily, especially in the banking sector, where the cost of failure can be very high. When dealing in an area as sensitive as risk management, bankers can become even more change-averse. Thus, it is important to highlight that the movement from traditional risk management methods to predictive analytics models has shown very tangible benefits, due to which banks continue to remain excited about such applications. Here are some instances where a significant tangible impact is seen:

10.4.1 Improvement in forecasting accuracy

A number of industry reports and analyst studies have indicated that banks that use advanced predictive models for cash management are able to forecast their cashflow needs with a 25–40% better accuracy, making them better positioned to create more reliable financial plans [3-4].

10.4.2 Reduced cost of funds

With better accuracy in cashflow forecasting, banks are able to avoid scenarios of overstocking, where excessive idle cash leads to overall lower return on assets, and are also able to mitigate scenarios of underserving, where cash shortages can create the need for emergency, costly short-term borrowing. The banks with more reliance on predictive analytics are able to avoid these scenarios more frequently, thereby reducing their overall cost of funds.

10.4.3 Operational efficiency gains

With the implementation of predictive analytics platforms, data collection, processing, and analysis have all become completely automated. This means that risk management and treasury teams at banks are spending more time strategizing about mitigation plans and can better prepare for failure events. Thus, such platforms are providing direct efficiency gains through automation and are also giving a more effective and strategically oriented risk department.

10.4.4 Better investment and lending decisions

Better cash flow prediction creates an environment of certainty, which allows managers to create a cash flow deployment strategy for the surplus available and look for profitable investments or expand their lending operations, both ways maximizing returns on assets.

10.4.5 Improvement in regulatory compliance

Better forecasting capability, by design, comes with better real-time data visibility, improving overall transparency and the added benefit of real-time data availability. Banks have now gained better availability as the platforms enable risk managers to create liquidity risk reports in real time. This has significantly reduced the cost of compliance.

10.5 Conclusion

In the present dynamic and volatile environment, AI-driven risk management and predictive analytics strategies have brought immense transformation in the banking sector. These emerging technologies have empowered the banks to act proactively in managing liquidity and credit risk. Not only this, but it has also enhanced the fraud detection and prevention capabilities of banks. The transition from the traditional system to the AI-driven system has led to the introduction of operational resilience in the banking sector. The present chapter provides in-depth insights into AI applications in banking through the case studies of Global banks such as JP Morgan, Bank of America, HSBC, and neobanks like SoFi and Chime. These banks have applied AI to reduce detection and prevent fraud, improve decision-making, and boost trust among stakeholders. Thus, it can be concluded that AI and predictive analytics are important strategic tools for driving sustainable banking operations, enhancing customer engagement, mitigating financial risk, and bringing resilience to the disruption. The adoption of advanced technology in banking will provide a competitive advantage to the banks in this rapidly changing financial landscape.

References

[1] D. J. Hand, "Statistical challenges of administrative and transaction data," *J. R. Stat. Soc.: Ser. A*, vol. 181, no. 3, pp. 555–605, 2018.

[2] E. W. T. Ngai, Y. Hu, Y. H. Wong, Y. Chen, and X. Sun, "The application of data mining techniques in financial fraud detection: A classification framework and an academic review of literature," *Decis. Support Syst.*, vol. 50, no. 3, pp. 559–569, 2011.

[3] P. Jorion, *Value at Risk: The New Benchmark for Managing Financial Risk*, New York, NY, USA: McGraw-Hill, 2007.

[4] Basel Committee on Banking Supervision, *Principles for Sound Liquidity Risk Management and Supervision*, Basel, Switzerland: Bank for International Settlements, 2010.

[5] McKinsey & Company, "Artificial Intelligence in Banking: Winning the AI Race," 2021. [Online]. Available: https://www.mckinsey.com. [Accessed: Jul. 9, 2025].

[6] Deloitte, "2023 Banking and Capital Markets Outlook," 2023. [Online]. Available: https://www2.deloitte.com. [Accessed: Jul. 9, 2025].

[7] PwC, "AI in Financial Services: How Artificial Intelligence is Reshaping Risk and Compliance," 2020. [Online]. Available: https://www.pwc.com. [Accessed: Jul. 9, 2025].

[8] World Economic Forum, "The Future of Financial Infrastructure: An Ambitious Look at How Blockchain Can Reshape Financial Services," 2020. [Online]. Available: https://www.weforum.org. [Accessed: Jul. 9, 2025].

[9] Accenture, "The Future of Banking: AI and Predictive Analytics as Key Drivers," 2022. [Online]. Available: https://www.accenture.com. [Accessed: Jul. 9, 2025].

[10] Reserve Bank of India (RBI), "Press Release on Yes Bank Moratorium and Reconstruction Scheme," 2020. [Online]. Available: https://www.rbi.org.in. [Accessed: Jul. 9, 2025].

[11] *The Economic Times*, "PMC Bank Fraud Case Timeline," 2019. [Online]. Available: https://economictimes.indiatimes.com. [Accessed: Jul. 9, 2025].

[12] *Reuters*, "How the Bangladesh Bank Was Hacked in $81 Million Heist," 2016. [Online]. Available: https://www.reuters.com. [Accessed: Jul. 9, 2025].

[13] JPMorgan Chase & Co., "Annual Report: Investment in AI and Risk Management Systems," 2023. [Online]. Available: https://www.jpmorganchase.com. [Accessed: Jul. 9, 2025].

11

Ensuring Fair Access and Ethical Considerations in Artificial Intelligence

Amandeep Kaur

Chitkara Business School, Chitkara University, India

Email: akak101280@gmail.com

Abstract

The study brings forth a stringent need for the use of artificial intelligence and big data analytics to be done safely and securely. AI simplifies the work, specifically by automating the claims processes in Health insurance, but at the same time, there is a need for a backup plan in case of failures in technological support services. The study highlights the dire need of the hour to adopt technologically stout and safe AI systems with transparent operations. Further study brings forth the need for a thorough understanding of the benefits and limitations attached to the use of artificial intelligence systems. This research design adopts a theoretical approach to the study of technologically stout and safe AI systems with transparent operations. By using content analysis for the study and by undergoing an in-depth literature review of previous case studies, research papers, reports, the level of transparency in operations, benefits, and limitations attached with the use of artificial intelligence systems, and to further propose fair access to AI and its applications. More stringent use of artificial intelligence and big data analytics needs to be done safely and firmly, with transparency in operations and by generating awareness with respect to the benefits and limitations attached with the use of artificial intelligence systems. By use of content analysis, a systematized analysis of content was conducted to gain an understanding of the benefits and limitations attached with the use of artificial intelligence systems and the need for fair access to AI and its applications for all stakeholders at large.

 DOI: 10.1201/9788743810766-11

11.1 Introduction

Artificial Intelligence-based applications are transforming the health insurance sector at a rapid pace. Being ethical and responsible in its use is still in its nascent phase. AI has improved the relationship between the insured and the insurer. It provides an aid in performing multiple health-related tasks at a substantial pace with accuracy. One of the aftermaths of Covid has been to bring the insurer and the insured closer with the help of technological advancement. Chatbots have made the requirement of an optimum health plan a reality for users by providing easy interaction with health insurance companies to understand the customized requirements of the insurers. Each stratum of people these days has 24×7 access to the internet and smartphones for such interactions. Every query related to policy switching cost, claim ratios, and networked hospitals covered by the schemes is all answered in simple language, thereby reducing the role of the traditional agent to explain the schemes, which was for him purely a commission-linked explanation session. It was hard to identify fair cases for claim settlements. It took a long time to physically access each case for authenticity, checking of previous claims and many more, but with AI, the turnaround time has been reduced thus, resulting in speedier claim settlements. Conventional data is utilized to check the genuineness and in the release of cashless claims for its users, thereby gaining customers' delight. AI has brought an improvement in the health plans framed and offered. With the advancement in technology, AI is constructively working towards checking of frauds and speedier operations. It works constructively towards avoiding of duplication of efforts. There is a stringent need to draft AI-based regulations, after conducting thorough professional brainstorming sessions for cost effective, user friendly and accuracy accompanied results.

11.2 Literature Review

Chatbots are an easy way to handle discussions and add value to the insurance sector [1]. AI is becoming a valuable aid in making the insurance industry cost-efficient by gaining the capability to estimate losses. Furthermore, AI has been revolutionary in helping insurance companies to come up with new designs of insurance products, on the grounds of changed risk scenarios [2]. AI algorithms are being used to seek medical forecasts and opinions, but external validation can enhance and match to real-world scenarios [3]. AI has simplified, and at the same time increased, the pace, accuracy, and authenticity of the work. It is very helpful in distinguishing between justified and unjustified filing of claims [4-5]. By adhering to five principles as transparency, fairness, safety, privacy, and accountability, universal convergence can be reached. AI will bring a significant impact on jobs globally and will lead to social inflation [6]. AI is basically a universal solution for multiple problems, in multiple sectors and areas, where large-scale innovations pose multiple challenges for professionals to cope with. [7] AI will turn a routine phenomenon, in times to come, in the health insurance services, thereby requiring more rigorous attention towards investments in AI-based applications [8]. Ever-growing population demands automated and innovative solutions with respect to healthcare services. AI is proficient to add speed and effectiveness to human-based operations. Optimum management and speedy processing of insurance claims, greater fraud detection rates are the zones getting an advantage, with the aid of AI-based applications [9]. Algorithms, which are based on AI, are catering in an effective way to the customized needs of the clients. Such insurance products are thereby facilitating their users by providing real-time assistance by considering their unique touchpoints. It is a road towards enhanced customer delight and satisfaction [10]. With the aid of AI technologies, insurance companies have gained competence and are easily able to cope with technological advancements for the ease of the stakeholders and at the same time provide hassle-free and effective communications [11]. It is vital to comply with the legal and ethical codes for the fair access and usage of AI in the health insurance sector, particularly when we are driving our efforts towards meeting of sustainable development goals. Further generation of awareness, with respect to positive outcomes, is vital for a fruitful return [12]. People engaged in positions of regulators or policy makers, or guides, need to be vigilant about the AI practices and regulations worldwide, for optimal output in health insurance in India. The impact of big data and artificial intelligence (AI) in the insurance sector is humongous [13]. To cater to rising community needs, efficiency and accuracy need to be encouraged at reduced costs. It can play a constructive role in minimizing human error and negligence [14]. AI-backed virtual helpers have streamlined customer interaction routes and thus have contributed to the formation of a trustworthy bond between the insurer and the insured. [13–14] As per a study, Researchers are taking up fair practices in the application of AI very seriously on the grounds of risk of data leakage, accountability, and to reflect being transparent in operations [15].

11.3 Objectives

1. To ensure the use of technologically stout and ethically safe AI systems with transparent operations in the health insurance sector.

2. To generate awareness regarding the benefits and limitations attached to the use of artificial intelligence-based health insurance systems.

3. To ensure fair access to AI and its applications in health insurance is a must for all.

11.4 Safe, Transparent, and Ethical AI Systems

There is a need to adhere to and promote the principle of ethical use of Artificial Intelligence (AI) in the health insurance sector. AI has eased the human work by matching the profile of the people with optimum health insurance plans as per their suitability. Ethical AI refers to the responsible use of AI for the benefit of stakeholders. For an effective AI at health insurance companies' end, it needs to be bias-free, holistic in approach, and by maintaining data privacy, transparency in operations can be well justified while meeting the customized requisite interests and complying with the government's interest of growth in multiple disciplines [16].

On one hand, AI would add to the performance of service delivery by medical practitioners, as there is no emotional, social, or physical component involved, but at the same time, it is all the more challenging that AI applications are based on algorithms, where empathy has no role to play [17]. A decision based upon AI should be supported by justification and elaboration [18]. Data security is a vital point of concern in the case of health insurance companies. To overcome such limitations, in-depth research into technical aspects and modifications in the existing norms is in progress [3, 19]. Community involvement, faith, not being rigid, coordinative, and cohesive are a few of the vital parameters that were incorporated in the US regulations with respect to AI-based applications [20]. AI-based applications should be reliable and safe from every perspective, to form faith and trust of the users in their applications. Word of mouth marketing will do wonders for fruitful and reliable AI-based results. Since AI is still in its progressive, yet nascent stage, awareness, robustness, transparency, and reliability are constructive pillars for long-term growth and stability. Though AI policy framers and constructors are working constructively with respect to numerous challenges in its working. Still, matters related to data confidentiality, lack of adequate faith amongst the insurer and the insured, and fraudulent experiences are some of the issues on the way towards successful working of AI in health insurance. For optimum output, a collaborative approach of all the stakeholders in the development of the AI-based health insurance policies is of utmost concern. There is an equal probability of AI in making faulty decisions; furthermore, the impact of such poor decisions cannot be imagined.

11.5 Understanding the Advantages and Limitations Attached with the Use of Artificial Intelligence Systems

Every health insurance company with artificial intelligence-based applications is bound to subsist with a protective cover from the probability of cybercrimes, data security, and accountable transactions with a better customer experience [21]. AI-based health insurance systems are productive in the design of customized health insurance products and services [22]. In Indonesia, the AI-based healthcare structure is proving very beneficial by providing sophistication and privacy [23].

The ease of operations gained with the aid of artificial intelligence is proving beneficial to all the stakeholders and providing protection to the regulations provided by the Indonesian government [21–23]. With the aid of AI, the client's claim processing cycle has improved, leading to better customer experience with minimal manual work involved [24]. AI is a brainy computer and can outperform humans, as it is adjustable to new settings and works on the basis of informational and productive sources [25]. AI-enabled automotive claims settlements, customer query handling, and underwriting procedures would result in enhanced customer satisfaction levels and a positive impact on customer retention levels [24–25]. AI-based operations have added pace to the profitability rates and act as an emotional and social support for the users [26]. AI has the capability to aid in enhanced customer experience [27].

Apart from the benefits attached to the use of artificial intelligence, it is equally challenging to frame accurate algorithms. Even the programmers remain unsure about the outputs to be generated with respect to the use of AI-based applications [28]. Due to the dependency on humans for Automated underwriting, its optimum working is highly prone to errors, but at the same time, its sampling techniques are of immense aid in searching for prospective future customers [7, 28]. There is a constant need among the companies working with the aid of AI systems to study and further explain the working, use, and limitations attached with the AI-based application for the benefit of all [21] [28]. AI aids health insurance companies and other stakeholders in getting acquainted with the latest trends going on in the market and has thus added to the efficiency and speed of the operations [4–5]. There is a stringent need to understand the governance of AI-based applications in healthcare, though being responsible AI is a must for the long-term success of the operations [8]. Some valuable discussions in legitimate and virtuous contexts would constructively resolve the challenges of data safety, justified algorithms, bias, effectiveness, and accountability in the US and Europe [20]. The corporations working with the aid of AI need to be more cautious and well-defined, in the benefits and repercussions attached with the use of AI-based applications.

While AI aids in easy, quick, and fair extraction of useful and required information, at times, the misunderstanding of similar and related data or conditions results in quick but unreliable extraction of information. AI although aids in accurate and quick analysing of the danger associated with health insurance parameters, as the claim settlement time period, proportion of settlement, cashless settlement or previous settlement history as a base for future decision making but at the same time the regulatory and compliance code needs to be strict, clear and uniform for all, which AI should also suggest to be complied with.

11.6 Ensuring Fair Access to AI and Its Applications in Health Insurance

In order to enhance and explore the potential of AI in health insurance, there is a need to regard access to AI as a complementary rather than a substitute tool [29]. The accelerating role of AI has posed numerous sorts of risks as ethical, physical, mental, etc, which has turned into a cause of concern for many rich countries. Further, fair and ethical access aims not to be risk-averse but to be well aligned with human rights and cultural values to add further to the quality of life being led [30]. Being fair means ethical and many times more than non-discrimination, where the focus should lie on for social good [30]. There is an utmost need to generate awareness with respect to the scenarios and situations where the aid of AI can be fruitful [31]. Complying with ethics, with respect to AI-based applications, is vital to gain the trust of the users. There is a vital need for a universal AI Framework to be developed, for the benefit of different stakeholders [32]. Developing a well-embedded framework can help in solving tedious complications among the minds of customers, on the grounds of discomfort and lack of trust in AI-based applications [33].

Collaborative brainstorming of professionals to develop productive and innovative criteria with thorough research understanding and analytical skills is vital for optimum and sustainable AI-based solutions. Advancement in technologies in the era of drones, Fitbit, and other similar technologies requires thorough applications and access to AI-based technologies for all [7]. There is a stringent need for AI-based applications to be value-based and focused on community problem solvers with globalized access for all. There is a need

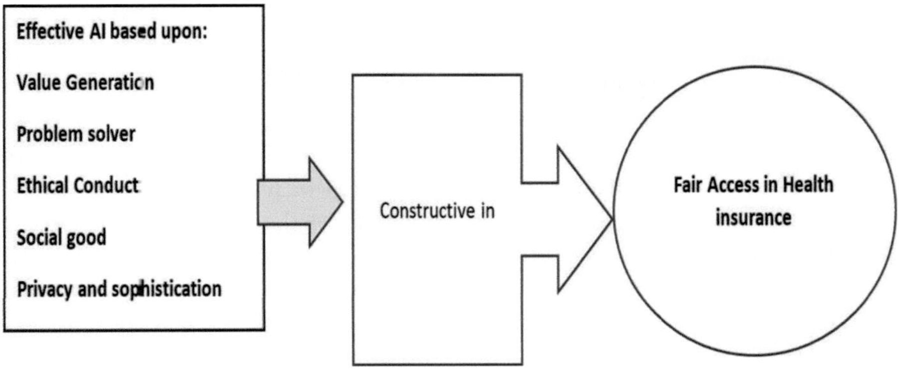

Figure 11.1 Effective and fair access to AI in health insurance.
Source: Author's creation.

to draw a sketch of the future challenges in its futuristic operations for the universal good. It is the need of the hour to rely on artificial intelligence after thoroughly exploring the pros and cons associated with its use [34]. Incorporating the principle of justice in the application of AI-aligned processes and procedures, for increased convenience and delight in customer service, is essential [35]. An interactive connection between the AI algorithm makers and ultimate implementers, and users is vital. Continuous interactions and feedback of the AI policy framers and their ultimate users aid in polishing and adding ease to respective operations. Thus, for technological advancement and organizational growth, reliance on AI is turning more obvious but should be aligned with ethical conduct.

AI usage has been successfully incorporated and promoted at an accelerating pace by health workers to gain people's trust and confidence. The positive outputs of AI in meeting the customized needs of the insurers as per the requirements of the company, with easy claim processing procedures and switching to other schemes or to a different health insurance company on comparative grounds, are all possible with the aid of AI. Apart from the ease of the health insurance services to the users, it has been successful in improving the access, confidence, and trust of the people.

11.7 Conclusion

AI has added speed to the operations in the health insurance sector by not only acting as a substitute but also as a complementary aid in health insurance operations. AI-based operations are adding to the reputation of the organizations by offering customized services with accuracy and speed. It had been constructive in reducing the cost of operations and adding speed to the claim procedures and processes. In times to come, AI will be revolutionizing risk assessments, customer response, and will add to customers' delight. But technological advancements are attached to fear and distrust with respect to applications of AI. There is a need to frame accurate algorithms for optimum results. There is also a need for the development of regulations with respect to AI and its applications, and to further sensitize the rule makers to define thoroughly the specific risks attached and the ways to reduce them. So, for the growth and future success of the organizations, it is vital to frame internal policies within the organizational work structures, which imparts awareness with respect to the risk and return trade-off attached with the use of AI-based applications. Actuarial fairness rate can be checked by the involvement of data analysts, policy developers, scientists, managers, and engineers. Apart from internal policy framing, compliance with government structures is vital. Organizations are accountable to the government for their fairness in policy framing, development, and implementation. Discrepancies and challenges in the ways towards successful implementation of AI-based applications can be resolved by providing internal training sessions. These training and development sessions can familiarize and smooth up the AI-based operations and thereby reduce the probability of failures in risky operations.

References

[1] Riikkinen, Mikko, Hannu Saarijärvi, Peter Sarlin, and Ilkka Lähteenmäki. "Using artificial intelligence to create value in insurance." International Journal of Bank Marketing 36, no. 6 (2018): 1145-1168.

[2] Eling, M., Nuessle, D., & Staubli, J. (2021). The impact of artificial intelligence along the insurance value chain and on the insurability of risks. The Geneva Papers on Risk and Insurance-Issues and Practice, 1-37.

[3] Park, S. H., Choi, J., & Byeon, J. S. (2021). Key principles of clinical validation, device approval, and insurance coverage decisions of artificial intelligence. Korean journal of radiology, 22(3), 442.

[4] Singh, J., & Urolagin, S. (2021). Use of artificial intelligence for health insurance claims automation. In Advances in Machine Learning and Computational Intelligence: Proceedings of ICMLCI 2019 (pp. 381-392). Springer Singapore.

[5] Sood, K., Dhanaraj, R. K., Balusamy, B., Grima, S., & Uma Maheshwari, R. (Eds.). (2022). Big Data: A game changer for insurance industry. Emerald Publishing Limited.

[6] Kelley, K. H., Fontanetta, L. M., Heintzman, M., & Pereira, N. (2018). Artificial intelligence: Implications for social inflation and insurance. Risk Management and Insurance Review, 21(3), 373-387.

[7] Singh, S. K., & Chivukula, M. (2020). A commentary on the application of Artificial Intelligence in the insurance industry. Trends in Artificial Intelligence, 4(1), 75-79.

[8] Reddy, S., Allan, S., Coghlan, S., & Cooper, P. (2020). A governance model for the application of AI in health care. Journal of the American Medical Informatics Association, 27(3), 491-497.

[9] Owens, E., Sheehan, B., Mullins, M., Cunneen, M., Ressel, J., & Castignani, G. (2022). Explainable artificial intelligence (xai) in insurance. Risks, 10(12), 230.

[10] Adeoye, O. B., Okoye, C. C., Ofodile, O. C., Odeyemi, O., Addy, W. A., & Ajayi-Nifise, A. O. (2024). Integrating artificial intelligence in personalized insurance products: a pathway to enhanced customer engagement. International Journal of Management & Entrepreneurship Research, 6(3), 502-511.

[11] Erem Ceylan, I. (2022). The effects of artificial intelligence on the insurance sector: Emergence, applications, challenges, and opportunities. The Impact of Artificial Intelligence on Governance, Economics and Finance, Volume 2, 225-241

[12] Mishra, Y., & Shaw, A. (2023). Artificial Intelligence in the Health Insurance Sector: Sustainable or Unsustainable from the Lens of Ethical-Legal and Socio-Economic Standards. The Impact of Climate Change and Sustainability Standards on the Insurance Market, 57-74.

[13] Mamiko, Y. A. (2020). The impact of big data and artificial intelligence (AI) in the insurance sector.

[14] Sunarti, S., Rahman, F. F., Naufal, M., Risky, M., Febriyanto, K., & Masnina, R. (2021). Artificial intelligence in healthcare: opportunities and risk for future. Gaceta sanitaria, 35, S67-S70.

[15] Ueda, D., Kakinuma, T., Fujita, S., Kamagata, K., Fushimi, Y., Ito, R., ... & Naganawa, S. (2024). Fairness of artificial intelligence in healthcare: review and recommendations. Japanese Journal of Radiology, 42(1), 3-15.

[16] Larsson, S., & Heintz, F. (2020). Transparency in artificial intelligence. Internet Policy Review, 9(2).

[17] Shuaib, A., Arian, H., & Shuaib, A. (2020). The increasing role of artificial intelligence in health care: will robots replace doctors in the future?. International journal of general medicine, 891-896.

[18] Ho, C. W., Ali, J., & Caals, K. (2020). Ensuring trustworthy use of artificial intelligence and big data analytics in health insurance. Bulletin of the World Health Organization, 98(4), 263.

[19] Mensah, G. B., Mijwil, M. M., & Abotaleb, M. (2024). Examining Ghana's National Health Insurance Act, 2003 (Act 650) to Improve Accessibility of Artificial Intelligence Therapies and Address Compensation Issues in Cases of Medical Negligence. Mesopotamian Journal of Computer Science, 2024, 28-33.

[20] Gerke, S., Minssen, T., & Cohen, G. (2020). Ethical and legal challenges of artificial intelligence-driven healthcare. In Artificial intelligence in healthcare (pp. 295-336). Academic Press.

[21] Riyanti, R. (2023). Legal status of artificial intelligence-based health insurance services: Challenges, opportunities for customer protection.

[22] Amerirad, B., Cattaneo, M., Kenett, R. S., & Luciano, E. (2023). Adversarial artificial intelligence in insurance: from an example to some potential remedies. Risks, 11(1), 20.

[23] Kaplan, A., & Haenlein, M. (2020). Rulers of the world, unite! The challenges and opportunities of artificial intelligence. Business Horizons, 63(1), 37-50. https://doi.org/10.1016/j.bushor.2019.09.003

[24] Chummun, I., Bhaw-Luximon, A., & Jhurry, D. (2018). Modulating matrix-multicellular response using polysucrose-blended with poly-L-lactide or polydioxanone in electrospun scaffolds for skin tissue regeneration. Journal of Biomedical Materials Research Part A, 106(12), 3275-3291.

[25] Ali, O., Abdelbaki, W., Shrestha, A., Elbasi, E., Alryalat, M. A. A., & Dwivedi, Y. K. (2023). A systematic literature review of artificial intelligence in the healthcare sector: Benefits, challenges, methodologies, and functionalities. Journal of Innovation & Knowledge, 8(1), 100333.

[26] Johnson, M., Albizri, A., & Harfouche, A. (2023). Responsible artificial intelligence in healthcare: Predicting and preventing insurance claim denials for economic and social wellbeing. Information Systems Frontiers, 25(6), 2179-2195.

[27] Ameen, N., Tarhini, A., Reppel, A., & Anand, A. (2021). Customer experiences in the age of artificial intelligence. Computers in human behavior, 114, 106548.

[28] Asatiani, A., Malo, P., Nagbøl, P. R., Penttinen, E., Rinta-Kahila, T., & Salovaara, A. (2020). Challenges of explaining the behavior of black-box AI systems. MIS Quarterly Executive, 19(4), 259-278.

[29] Goldberg, C. B., Adams, L., Blumenthal, D., Brennan, P. F., Brown, N., Butte, A. J., ... & Kohane, I. S. (2024). To do no harm—and the most good—with AI in health care. Nejm Ai, 1(3), AIp2400036
[30] Giovanola, B., & Tiribelli, S. (2023). Beyond bias and discrimination: redefining the AI ethics principle of fairness in healthcare machine-learning algorithms. AI & society, 38(2), 549-563.
[31] Angerschmid, A., Zhou, J., Theuermann, K., Chen, F., & Holzinger, A. (2022). Fairness and explanation in AI-informed decision making. Machine Learning and Knowledge Extraction, 4(2), 556-579.
[32] Karimian, G., Petelos, E., & Evers, S. M. (2022). The ethical issues of the application of artificial intelligence in healthcare: a systematic scoping review. AI and Ethics, 2(4), 539-551.
[33] Jeyaraman, M., Balaji, S., Jeyaraman, N., & Yadav, S. (2023). Unraveling the ethical enigma: artificial intelligence in healthcare. Cureus, 15(8).
[34] Benjamins, R. (2021). A choices framework for the responsible use of AI. AI and Ethics, 1(1), 49-53.
[35] Rajkomar, A., Hardt, M., Howell, M. D., Corrado, G., & Chin, M. H. (2018). Ensuring fairness in machine learning to advance health equity Annals of internal medicine, 169(12), 866-872.

12

Integrating Microcredit, Fintech, and Social Safety Nets for Holistic Financial Inclusion: Empirical Insights from Urban Slums in India

J. Singh[1*], S. K. Chatrath[2], Jyoti Verma[3] and G.S. Batra[4]

[1] ICSSR, Ministry of Education, India
[2]School of Business, University of Canberra, Australia
[3]Chitkara Business School, Chitkara University, Punjab, India
[4]Jagat Guru Nanak Dev Punjab State Open University, India

Email: Jasky786@gmail.com; sarvjeetkaur.chatrath@canberra.edu.au; Jyoti.verma@chitkara.edu.in; batra.gurdip@gmail.com

Abstract

Against the backdrop of accelerating urbanization, the persistence of entrenched poverty in India's burgeoning slum settlements raises important questions about the reach and efficacy of financial inclusion efforts. Although microcredit, fintech, and social safety nets each show promise individually, scholars have seldom analysed how these instruments function in tandem to shape the financial and socio-economic outcomes of marginalized communities. This chapter proposes and applies a multi-layered conceptual framework that interweaves (i) a refined Microcredit Utilization Model, (ii) an extended Technology Acceptance Model (TAM), (iii) the capabilities approach, and (iv) a Social Safety Net Model. Drawing on empirical data compiled from peer-reviewed published studies conducted in urban slums across Punjab, India, we examine nuanced patterns of microcredit usage, fintech adoption, and reliance on welfare benefits. Our findings highlight the high prevalence of unproductive credit consumption – spurred by constrained financial literacy, immediate household needs, and suboptimal monitoring – yet also reveal

 DOI: 10.1201/9788743810766-12

encouraging signs of fintech's capacity to enhance banking engagement and efficiency in welfare distribution. We further demonstrate that strengthening human capabilities and tightening social safety net delivery produce synergistic effects, magnifying the overall impact on poverty reduction. Policy recommendations underscore the necessity of a comprehensive approach that simultaneously addresses microcredit policy, digital readiness, entrepreneurial capacity, and social welfare governance. This holistic perspective, we argue, holds considerable promise for achieving inclusive growth and advancing key Sustainable Development Goals (SDGs) that target poverty, inequality, and sustainable urban development.

12.1 Introduction

Despite India's robust strides in economic growth, the proliferation of urban slums underscores the country's persistent challenges in ensuring equitable development. Recent estimates place the number of Indians living in informal settlements at over 80 million [1], [2]. These neglected pockets are often characterized by precarious housing, lack of reliable sanitation, and minimal formal employment prospects. In this context, financial inclusion emerges as a strategic lever for improving living conditions and enhancing socio-economic mobility.

Traditionally, microcredit – providing small loans primarily to under-resourced populations – has been viewed as the linchpin of inclusive finance [3]. Some success stories suggest that microcredit can foster entrepreneurship and raise household incomes, effectively combating poverty [4]. However, more nuanced analyses reveal a complex, and at times contradictory, picture. Instances of unproductive utilization, in which households divert loans for daily consumption or ceremonial expenses, are far from rare [5], [6]. Such patterns often saddle families with debt, undercut the promise of microcredit, and create a cycle of dependency.

Simultaneously, fintech has gained momentum as a powerful catalyst for financial innovation. By leveraging digital solutions (e.g., mobile banking, e-payment platforms), fintech aspires to reduce transaction costs, broaden coverage, and tighten financial monitoring mechanisms [7]. Notably, India's JAM Trinity (Jan Dhan accounts, Aadhaar identification, and mobile connectivity) has already propelled significant leaps in digital finance use among low-income individuals [8]. Yet the potential of fintech to transform financial inclusion remains tempered by persistent obstacles such as poor digital literacy, limited internet infrastructure, and distrust of digital platforms [9].

Beyond market-based instruments, government social safety nets represent another vital dimension in safeguarding the poorest households from economic shocks. India operates extensive welfare programs, for instance, the public distribution system (PDS), the Mahatma Gandhi National Rural Employment Guarantee Act (MGNREGA), and various pension schemes [10]. These programs can function as stabilizers when households face urgent expenses, thereby staving off unproductive borrowing and mitigating the risk of debt. Nevertheless, challenges related to leakage, corrupt practices, and administrative complexity frequently blunt the effectiveness of these interventions [11].

While scholars have studied microcredit, fintech, and social safety nets individually, research integrating these strands under one conceptual umbrella remains relatively sparse. Without a holistic view, policy interventions risk missing the intricate feedback loops in the lives of slum residents, where digital finance might interplay with welfare distribution, or where weak human capabilities might obstruct otherwise beneficial credit usage [12]. Our study addresses this research gap by proposing and empirically applying a consolidated conceptual framework that comprises: (i) a microcredit utilization model; (ii) an extended TAM for fintech adoption; (iii) the capabilities approach; and (iv) a Social Safety Net Model. We subsequently examine the utility of this integrated lens using data synthesized from seven peer-reviewed studies based in Punjab's urban slums.

Following this introduction, the next section offers a comprehensive review of the extant literature. We then introduce our expanded theoretical framework, highlight our methodology, and present the empirical findings. Subsequently, we engage with those results in a deeper discussion focused on policy implications, connecting them explicitly to emerging SDG mandates. Our conclusion summarizes the core contributions and proposes future research trajectories.

12.2 Literature Review

12.2.1 Microcredit and the pitfalls of unproductive utilization

Microcredit's promise has been chronicled widely, from Grameen's groundbreaking model in Bangladesh to various self-help groups across South Asia [4], [3]. Early proponents hailed microloans as transformative, particularly for empowering women and fostering small enterprises. But subsequent randomized evaluations reveal that benefits are neither universal nor guaranteed [13]. Microcredit may spur modest entrepreneurship in certain contexts, yet in others, unproductive consumption sharply weakens its potential to reduce poverty [5]. Several recent works in the Indian setting, including [6], highlight how loan usage patterns can be highly context-dependent, subject to immediate household pressures, cultural norms, and suboptimal monitoring by microfinance institutions (MFIs).

12.2.2 Fintech adoption: Promise and caveats

In parallel, fintech-driven innovations – from mobile money (e.g., M-Pesa) to digital payment platforms and app-based lending – have gained strong traction in low- and middle-income countries [14]. Prominent scholarship underscores how fintech can dismantle geographic barriers, minimize overhead costs, and accelerate financial inclusion [7]. In India specifically, the JAM Trinity architecture laid the groundwork for digital IDs linked with bank accounts and mobile phones, thereby facilitating direct benefit transfers and e-payments [8]. Still, trust deficits, poor internet connectivity, low digital literacy, and security concerns impede mass uptake [9]. Extending the classic TAM, scholars emphasize perceived usefulness, perceived ease of use, perceived trustworthiness, and social norms as critical antecedents for adopting digital financial tools [15].

12.2.3 The capabilities approach

Amartya Sen's [12] capabilities approach adds another layer by shifting analytical focus beyond resource provision to the actual freedoms and functioning that individuals can attain. Within financial inclusion, capabilities influence whether borrowers can harness credit effectively or adopt fintech meaningfully [16]. Factors such as literacy, entrepreneurial skill, and community support networks shape how well individuals can capitalize on newfound credit or technological solutions. Empirical evidence [17] suggests that where participants have higher educational levels and are empowered by skill training, they are more likely to invest loans productively and employ fintech channels, yielding stronger poverty reduction outcomes. The growing use of technologies like chatbots in financial services also plays a role here, as explored by [32], where the humanization of such technologies can influence consumer perceptions and behaviors.

12.2.4 Social safety nets as stabilizers

Social protection initiatives – ranging from cash transfers to public works programs – aim to reduce vulnerability, especially for households prone to income shocks [18]. India's PDS, MGNREGA, and pension schemes illustrate large-scale interventions intended to strengthen food security, provide temporary income support, or enable old-age subsistence [10]. When effectively designed, such programs can buffer households from catastrophic expenditures and curb the lure of high-interest debts. However, widespread leakages, limited administrative coordination, and corruption can undermine these welfare measures [11]. In some slum pockets, a share of borrowed funds covers the informal bribes needed to secure entitlements – paradoxically entrenching debt rather than alleviating poverty. In the context of economic stability and social welfare, [33] examined the dynamic nexus between economic growth, environmental degradation, and public health in Pakistan, which indirectly relates to the effectiveness of social safety nets.

12.2.5 Toward an integrated lens

Recent debates underscore that exclusive reliance on one instrument – be it microcredit or cash transfers – often fails to address the multifaceted realities of urban poverty. A synergy of strategies might be more impactful, as microfinance can spur enterprise, fintech can reduce friction and expand usage, capabilities building can ensure more optimal decision-making, and social welfare can act as a safety net. Building on this premise, our study synthesizes four pillars – microcredit, fintech, capabilities, and social safety nets – into one cohesive framework. We posit that ignoring any of these dimensions risks undermining the collective effect, particularly in urban slum contexts marked by tenuous livelihoods and complex social networks [12].

Table 12.1 situates these streams of literature, illustrating not only their individual contributions but also the potential synergy when viewed in combination.

By systematically interweaving these four strands, we strive for a comprehensive understanding of how slum communities can leverage financial instruments more productively. In turn, this synthesis reveals novel insights on how local and national policymakers might target interventions to maximize sustainable impact.

12.3 Research Objectives

i. To develop an integrated conceptual framework that accounts for microcredit utilization, technology adoption, capabilities development, and social welfare schemes.

Table 12.1 Core perspectives on financial inclusion instruments.

Perspective	Key focus	Strengths	Limitations	Illustrative sources
Microcredit	Small loans to marginal groups	Can promote self-employment; fosters financial discipline	Risk of unproductive consumption; potential over-indebtedness	[3]; [13]; [6]
Fintech solutions	Digital platforms, e-payments	Reduces transaction costs; improves reach and transparency	Digital literacy gaps; trust, security concerns	[7]; [9]; [8]
Capabilities approach	Focus on real freedoms & functioning	Emphasizes multi-dimensional well-being, empowerment	Practical measurement challenges; requires supportive infrastructure	[12]; [16]; [17]
Social safety nets	Welfare programs, subsidies	Mitigates vulnerability; boosts resilience to shocks	Leakages, corruption, poor targeting	[18]; [10]; [11]

ii. To empirically examine how these dimensions interact, using evidence drawn from multi-site studies in Punjab's urban slums.

iii. To identify policy implications and strategies that support holistic financial inclusion in contexts similar to Punjab's urban underprivileged clusters.

12.4 Integrated Theoretical Framework

12.4.1 Rationale for a multi-pillar approach

Many prior investigations prioritize either the microfinance sector or fintech advancement, but few systematically incorporate social welfare dynamics and human capabilities. Our conceptual framework begins with the premise that (i) microcredit usage patterns are contingent on borrowers' abilities to manage funds effectively, (ii) fintech can amplify or constrain people's access to and deployment of financial services, (iii) human capabilities shape not only the uptake of credit/technology but also the entrepreneurial capacity to transform borrowed funds into stable livelihoods, and (iv) social safety nets can buffer families against shocks, diminishing the impulse to take on debts that cannot be repaid productively.

12.4.2 Conceptual model

We propose an enhanced integrative diagram (Figure 12.1) that visually expresses the reciprocal nature of these pillars. Rather than simplistic arrows, we integrate feedback loops and mediating elements.

This framework shows the interlocking relationships among microcredit utilization, fintech adoption, human capabilities, and social safety nets.

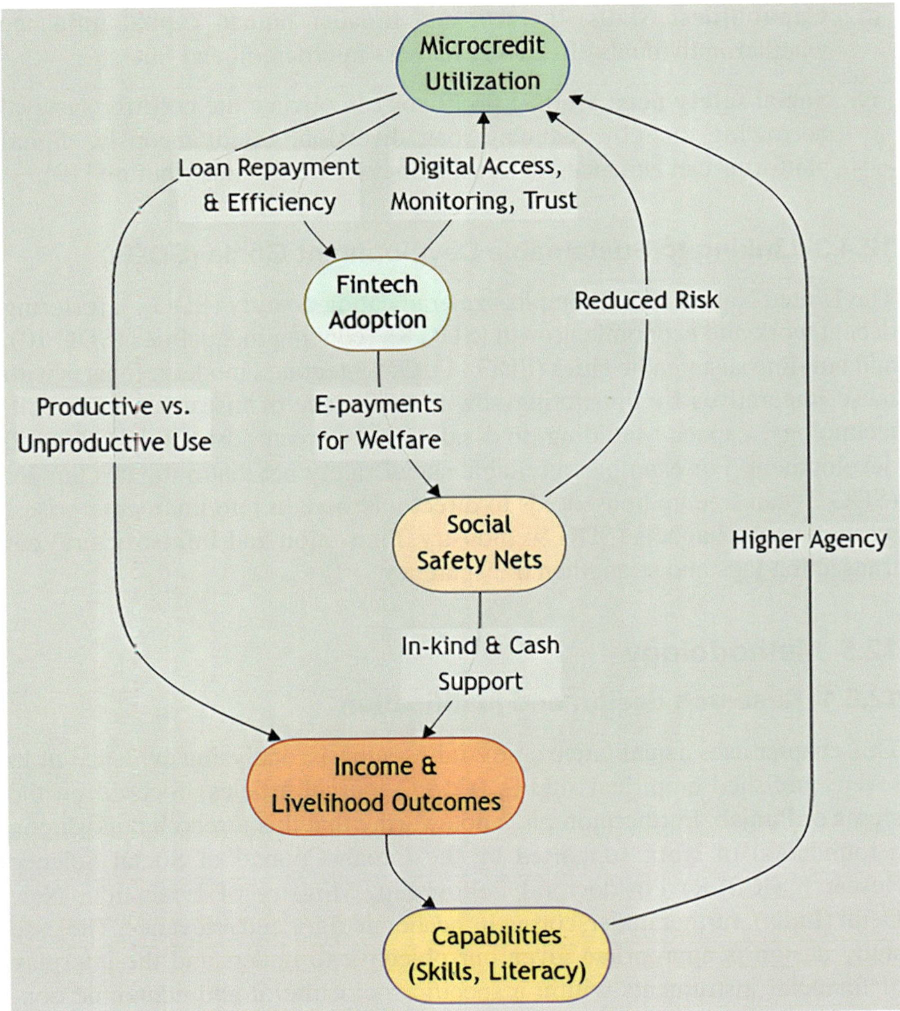

Figure 12.1 Proposed multi-pillar framework.

Feedback loops indicate potential synergies and mediating factors in achieving inclusive financial outcomes.

i. **Microcredit utilization:** Central to the model is how low-income households deploy credit – whether for genuinely productive investments or urgent consumption.

ii. **Fintech adoption:** Fintech can streamline loan disbursal, offer continuous usage monitoring, and facilitate rapid transfers [7].

iii. **Capabilities:** Skills, literacy, and broader human capital influence whether individuals effectively harness microcredit and fintech.

iv. **Social safety nets:** Welfare programs can obviate the need for survival borrowing, thereby reducing loan diversion. Simultaneously, digital platforms can enhance the transparency of welfare distribution [19].

12.4.3 Linking to Sustainable Development Goals (SDGs)

The United Nations SDGs emphasize eradicating poverty (SDG 1), fostering decent work and economic growth (SDG 8), reducing inequalities (SDG 10), and building sustainable cities (SDG 11). Our integrated model resonates with these imperatives by illustrating how a confluence of instruments – credit, technology, capacity-building, and safety nets – can advance broad-based development. For example, a reliable social safety net that mitigates hunger (SDG 2) can free up households to direct microcredit into microenterprises, while fintech channels (SDG 9: Industry, Innovation and Infrastructure) cut transaction lags and strengthen transparency.

12.5 Methodology

12.5.1 Research design and justification

This chapter uses a qualitative case study synthesis, analysing evidence from seven published empirical studies (Q1/Q2 journal articles) focused on the slums of Punjab. Furthermore, it is noteworthy that this research builds upon a foundation of work supported by the Indian Council of Social Science Research (ICSSR) Postdoctoral Fellowship, Ministry of Education, New Delhi (India), further underscoring its academic rigor and relevance. The case study design is appropriate given our objective to understand the interplay of financial instruments within a specific sociocultural and economic context [20]. Punjab's urban slums serve as a pertinent laboratory: it is an economically advanced state, yet it hosts extensive slum populations that reflect the broader challenges of urban marginalization in India [11].

12.5.2 Data sources and scope

We incorporate data from seven peer-reviewed pieces of research conducted between 2021 and 2024 (see Table 12.2). These investigations collectively surveyed thousands of respondents across multiple districts, providing robust cross-sectional insights into credit usage, e-payment adoption, skill training, and welfare receipt. Each study used validated instruments (factor analysis, SEM models) and had been screened by reputable editorial processes, underscoring data quality and credibility.

All these studies employed structured surveys with a combination of Likert-scale items and demographic data, supplemented by limited qualitative interviews in certain instances [11]. The compiled database thus furnishes an expansive picture of financial practices and constraints among Punjab's urban slum dwellers.

12.5.3 Analytical strategy

We undertook an iterative cross-study synthesis, combing through each paper's results on (i) microcredit patterns, (ii) fintech usage rates, (iii) welfare entitlements, and (iv) links to educational or skill-building interventions. Patterns that recurred across multiple samples – e.g., high rates of

Table 12.2 Overview of empirical studies and methodological profiles.

Study and ranking	Sample size	Urban locations	Core methods	Focus areas
Singh et al. [21]	346	Amritsar, Jalandhar, Ludhiana	EFA, SEM	Microcredit usage patterns
Singh et al. [6]	598	Major urban centers, incl. Chandigarh	EFA, CFA, SEM	Loan utilization and poverty impact
Singh & Singh [19]	525	Five major cities	EFA, CFA, SEM, ANOVA, t-test	Social safety nets and socio-economic stability
Singh & Singh [22]	433	Five districts (urban pockets)	SEM	Fintech adoption and classic TAM extension
Singh & Singh [8]	605	12 cities, 9 districts	EFA, CFA, SEM	E-payments, JAM Trinity linkage
Singh & Singh [11]	546	Municipal corporations of Punjab	EFA, CFA, SEM	Welfare program leakages, unproductive borrowing
Singh & Singh [17]	515	Slums in major cities	SEM	Capabilities, entrepreneurship, and poverty reduction

consumption-driven borrowing – were highlighted, while outlier findings were also noted. This approach respects each dataset's methodological independence yet extracts broader thematic convergences consistent with our framework [16].

12.5.4 Ethical considerations and limitations

The original studies adhered to ethical protocols, including informed consent and privacy measures. Our synthesis inherits those safeguards and accurately cites primary findings. Nonetheless, reliance on secondary data restricts our ability to re-verify or elaborate on certain nuances. Furthermore, though Punjab's slums are socioeconomically diverse, caution must be exercised when extending these insights to other Indian states or countries.

12.6 Findings

12.6.1 Microcredit utilization: A persistent consumption bias

A striking commonality is the significant fraction of unproductive credit usage among slum households. For instance, [6] revealed that roughly 62.5% of respondents channelled loans into daily household expenses or cultural obligations, rather than entrepreneurial activities. The reasons cited included immediate health bills, urgent family needs, or inadequate business acumen – aligning with earlier critiques of microcredit's limited poverty-alleviation impact when usage patterns lean heavily toward consumption [5].

Figure 12.2 graphs the credit utilization split from aggregated data, underscoring how consumption-driven borrowing often dwarfs livelihood investments.

Aggregating data from [21], [6], [11], and [17]. Consumption, at 61%, eclipses productive use.

12.6.2 Fintech adoption: Promising yet uneven

In contrast to the pessimistic findings on microcredit, the fintech narrative appears more varied. Two main aspects emerged:

i. **Rising awareness:** Between 57% and 60% of slum respondents were aware of e-payment platforms or mobile wallets, signifying an expanding familiarity with digital finance [22], [8].

ii. **Limited usage:** Actual adoption rates trailed behind awareness, hovering around 45–47%. Key barriers included mistrust of digital systems,

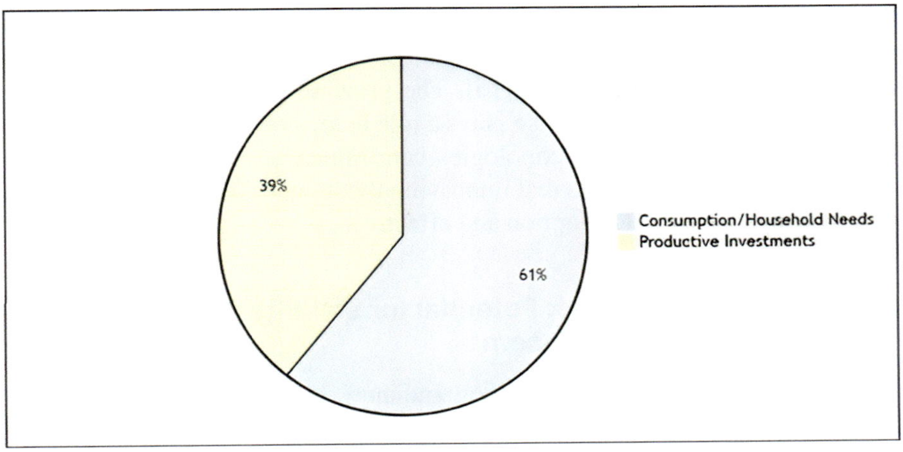

Figure 12.2 Weighted average breakdown of microcredit usage.

irregular internet connectivity, and the inability to troubleshoot technical glitches [9].

Interestingly, these studies suggested that households that overcame these hurdles experienced faster loan repayment cycles, saved on transportation costs, and received government benefits more efficiently. Fintech thus underscores the Extended TAM proposition that perceived usefulness and trust heavily condition actual uptake [15]. The presence of Aadhaar-linked bank accounts also played a central role, as direct benefit transfers from government schemes were credited promptly without the usual red tape [8].

12.6.3 Capabilities and entrepreneurship

In [17], the correlation between borrowers' educational backgrounds, vocational skills, and the likelihood of channelling loans into microenterprises is specifically tested. They discovered:

- Respondents with secondary education or above were 2.3 times more likely to pursue an income-generating venture ($p < 0.05$).
- Households engaged in basic financial literacy or business training modules reported higher self-efficacy in using digital tools and broader confidence in navigating credit terms.

Furthermore, the presence of social support systems (neighborly advice, local success stories) seemed to reinforce positive financial behaviors [12]. These findings confirm the central premise of the capabilities approach: targeted skill development and support networks can enable more strategic credit utilization and stable livelihood formation [16]. The growing use of technologies like chatbots in financial services also plays a role here, as explored by [32], where the humanization of such technologies can influence consumer perceptions and behaviors. This suggests that improving the human-like aspects of fintech could further enhance its adoption and effectiveness among these populations.

12.6.4 Social safety nets: Potential for stability, but corruption concerns

Two studies dedicated attention to how Indian welfare schemes intersect with microfinance usage [19], [11]. Key observations included:

- **Welfare as a safety valve:** Households receiving regular PDS rations or pension payments appeared less compelled to divert microloans into emergency consumption. In effect, they had a modest buffer against health shocks and hunger.
- **Leakages and informal fees:** Notably, around 42% of welfare beneficiaries admitted paying "tips" or bribes to local intermediaries, which they sometimes financed through short-term credit. This irony underscores how corruption can subvert the intended stabilizing role of social protection [10].

The synergy between digital transfers (via Aadhaar-linked bank accounts) and consistent welfare entitlements emerged as pivotal for improving household cash flows [8]. However, these potential gains could be undermined if local officials or middlemen demand illicit payments. In the context of economic stability and social welfare, [33] examined the dynamic nexus between economic growth, environmental degradation, and public health in Pakistan, which indirectly relates to the effectiveness of social safety nets in reducing poverty and improving living standards. This highlights the importance of integrating environmental considerations into social welfare programs to achieve long-term sustainable development.

12.6.5 Integrated view: Reinforcing or undermining factors

When mapped onto our conceptual framework (Figure 12.1), the data affirm several synergy points:

i. **Fintech + Microcredit:** Where e-payments and digital interfaces simplified loan repayment, the burden of unproductive usage declined.

Borrowers had fewer chances to divert funds because disbursements and installments were transparent.

ii. **Safety nets + Capabilities:** Households with reliable welfare support had more freedom to invest in capacity-building and entrepreneurial ventures, as they were not perpetually firefighting immediate consumption crises.

iii. **Barriers + Negative loops:** High corruption, poor digital awareness, and minimal skill training locked many families in cyclical debt, with repeated reliance on microloans just to patch daily or monthly deficits.

Overall, the findings illustrate the critical importance of coordinated interventions that address microcredit policies, digital readiness, skills enhancement, and robust welfare oversight in tandem.

12.7 Discussion

12.7.1 Revisiting the four pillars

Our results indicate that microcredit alone struggles to deliver transformative outcomes in slum contexts where high consumption needs and limited entrepreneurial know-how prevail [5], [6]. However, layering in fintech solutions introduces efficiencies that potentially curb misuse – provided trust-building initiatives and basic digital training are in place [9].

Capabilities emerge as a cross-cutting enabler, without which even well-designed programs often fail to spur income diversification or meaningful asset accumulation [12]. Meanwhile, social safety nets can serve as the bedrock preventing households from sliding into deeper vulnerability, though only if the programs are administered with integrity and transparency [18], [10].

12.7.2 Theoretical implications and alignment with literature

The interplay among these pillars suggests that integrated frameworks are essential for unpacking the realities of financial inclusion in informal urban settlements. While previous studies often analysed microcredit or fintech in isolation, our approach resonates with calls for a broader lens capturing multiple policy levers and societal conditions [13]. We reinforce the argument that capabilities (literacy, skill development, social support) are not peripheral but central to how effectively financial innovations achieve poverty-reducing outcomes [16].

Furthermore, we observe that the extended TAM perspective is critical in slum environments, where perceived usefulness alone may not suffice to trigger fintech adoption. Trust, digital literacy, and cultural acceptance become key catalysts. This underscores the significance of local champions, government-led campaigns, and NGO-led training to dispel apprehensions and clarify user benefits [7].

12.7.3 Policy relevance and SDG linkages

Our findings bear direct relevance to SDGs focused on ending poverty (SDG 1), promoting decent work (SDG 8), reducing inequalities (SDG 10), and advancing sustainable cities (SDG 11) (as mentioned in Table 12.3). By highlighting both micro-level actions (e.g., skill-building, digital awareness drives) and macro-level governance reforms (e.g., corruption clampdown in welfare distribution), we outline a path toward more equitable financial systems. This resonates with broader global agendas that encourage integrated approaches rather than piecemeal solutions [23].

12.8 Limitations and Caveats

Despite the robustness of our multi-study synthesis, certain caveats remain:

- **Regional specificity:** Punjab's socio-economic context, featuring better-than-average infrastructure and a strong diaspora, may not reflect slum conditions in less industrialized states or smaller towns.

Table 12.3 Key SDG dimensions and policy entry points

SDG	Policy entry points
SDG 1 – No Poverty	Strengthen synergy between welfare programs and microcredit to reduce survival borrowing Offer capacity-building modules to boost productive loan use
SDG 8 – Decent Work and Economic Growth	Encourage micro-entrepreneurship among slum residents through targeted training Leverage digital platforms to formalize small businesses
SDG 10 – Reduced Inequalities	Expand coverage of digital finance across underserved slum clusters Integrate anti-corruption frameworks in welfare distribution
SDG 11 - Sustainable Cities	Collaborate with urban local bodies to mainstream financial inclusion in city development plans Allocate spaces for skill centers within or near slums

- **Lack of longitudinal data:** Most of the underlying studies rely on cross-sectional survey snapshots, limiting our ability to infer causal relationships or track credit usage changes over time.
- **Underlying cultural factors:** The interplay of gender norms, caste hierarchies, and local power dynamics warrants deeper ethnographic inquiry to understand why some households consistently avoid or misuse credit.

12.9 Policy Implications

To maximize the impact of financial inclusion efforts in urban slums, policymakers and practitioners must tackle the four pillars – microcredit, fintech, capabilities, and welfare – concurrently. Below, we propose a multi-level approach (refer Table 12.4).

12.9.1 Micro-level: Borrowers, households, and MFIs

i. **Mandatory financial literacy:** Incorporate short modules on budgeting, entrepreneurial basics, and the dangers of over-indebtedness as a prerequisite for loan disbursal [11].

ii. **Personalized loan products:** Encourage MFIs to design specialized products that tie lending conditions to business planning. For example, a portion of the loan might be "locked" for productive assets (machinery, inventory).

iii. **Tech-focused mentorship:** Link borrowers with peer mentors who have successfully integrated fintech into small enterprises. This fosters trust and demystifies digital usage.

Table 12.4 Holistic policy framework for financial inclusion in urban slums.

Level	Policy actions
Micro (Household, MFI)	Financial literacy as a precondition for loans Specialized credit products earmarked for production Local mentorship for digital finance
Meso (Community, NGOs)	Resource centers for skill/digital training Community committees to track welfare and credit usage Cluster-based enterprise development
Macro (National)	Strengthened fintech regulations and data security Anti-corruption audits for welfare distribution "One-stop" integrated service centers

12.9.2 Meso-level: Community organizations and local governance

i. **Skill and digital literacy hubs:** Municipalities can partner with local NGOs to create "slum resource centers," offering ongoing training sessions on e-payments and entrepreneurial management.

ii. **Community monitoring committees:** Set up local monitoring groups to keep track of welfare distribution, microloan usage, and emerging tech adoption. This fosters transparency and reduces corruption at the grassroots.

iii. **Cluster-based enterprise zones:** Identify and promote clusters of slum-based microenterprises (e.g., tailoring, handicrafts) through local fairs or digital marketplaces. Such initiatives can harness fintech for inventory tracking and sales payments.

12.9.3 Macro-level: National policy, donor agencies, and regulatory bodies

i. **Regulatory oversight on fintech:** Strengthen guidelines around data privacy, user protection, and dispute resolution to build confidence in digital platforms among vulnerable groups [9].

ii. **Enhanced anti-corruption protocols:** Mandate real-time audits of welfare transfers using digital dashboards, with clear redress mechanisms for beneficiaries who face extortion.

iii. **Incentivizing capacity-building:** Link central government credit subsidies or interest subventions to tangible improvements in borrower skills (e.g., completion of recognized entrepreneurship training).

iv. **Integrated "One-Stop Shop":** Foster integrated service centers at the city or ward level where slum residents can access multiple resources – e.g., health services, skill training, microcredit sign-ups, Aadhaar updates – under a single administrative roof.

Ensuring policy synergy is essential. Reforms must be jointly pursued – no single measure will resolve the deep-seated constraints faced by slum dwellers. Monitoring and evaluation systems that track progress on each dimension – loan utilization, fintech usage, training outcomes, welfare efficacy – help stakeholders adjust their strategies in real time.

12.10 Conclusion and Future Research

This study contends that financial inclusion in urban slums necessitates an integrative framework that combines microcredit, fintech, human capabilities, and social safety nets. Drawing on seven empirical investigations in Punjab's slums, we find that unproductive credit usage, digital adoption barriers, and administrative leakages in welfare programs are not merely isolated phenomena; rather, they reflect deeper structural and capability-related challenges. Yet the evidence also suggests that well-coordinated interventions can lead to tangible improvements in living standards, entrepreneurship, and overall financial resilience among slum communities.

12.10.1 Key contributions

i. **Conceptual advancement:** By weaving together four theoretical pillars, we present a blueprint for integrated financial inclusion scholarship that transcends single-dimensional analysis. This multi-pillar lens clarifies the interactions of microcredit policies with digital platforms, welfare governance, and educational investments.

ii. **Empirical insights:** Punjab's urban slums serve as an illustrative vantage point for understanding the multi-layered realities of credit usage, e-payment uptake, and social safety net reliance in an emerging economy. The findings underscore how local conditions – such as the presence of industrial clusters and high levels of internal migration – further complicate the application of universal financial models.

iii. **Policy relevance:** Our recommendations, grounded in both quantitative and qualitative evidence, highlight the necessity of synergistic approaches. Specifically, we call for mandatory financial literacy modules, digital trust-building, skill hubs, and robust anti-corruption measures that encourage more productive borrowing and consistent welfare delivery.

12.10.2 Study limitations

- **Geographical focus:** While Punjab's slums are socioeconomically diverse, they may not capture regional variations across India's diverse states or other Global South settings.
- **Secondary data dependence:** Our synthesis is only as comprehensive as the original studies' designs and data scope. Unmeasured

variables – such as cultural nuances or gender-based power structures – might yield fresh insights if investigated through future research.

- **Cross-sectional snapshots:** Without extensive longitudinal data, it remains challenging to ascertain whether households move from unproductive loan usage to more constructive investments over time, or vice versa.

12.10.3 Future research directions

i. **Comparative regional studies:** Extending this framework to other Indian states (e.g., Bihar, Maharashtra) or internationally (e.g., sub-Saharan Africa, Southeast Asia) can verify its robustness and uncover context-specific modifications.

ii. **Longitudinal tracking:** Establishing multi-year cohort studies that monitor households' credit usage, fintech adoption, and social welfare participation can illuminate dynamic shifts and causal impacts more precisely.

iii. **Gender-focused analysis:** Microcredit historically targeted women, yet our data show no explicit breakdown by gender. Future work could dissect how gender roles interact with digital literacy, entrepreneurship choices, and family-level financial decisions.

iv. **In-depth ethnographies:** Beyond surveys and SEM models, qualitative studies capturing the lived experiences of slum residents – particularly narratives around empowerment, trust, and reciprocity – could deepen our understanding of how intangible cultural factors influence the success of integrated financial inclusion interventions.

12.10.4 Final thoughts

Ultimately, pursuing an integrated financial inclusion ecosystem aligns directly with core Sustainable Development Goals (SDGs) and the broader aim of empowering the urban poor to claim agency over their economic futures. The synergy among microcredit, fintech, capabilities, and social safety nets can help break cyclical patterns of debt and vulnerability, especially if accompanied by strong governance mechanisms and cultural sensitivity. Achieving this vision, however, requires coordinated efforts by policymakers, civil society, and the private sector, underpinned by rigorous, data-driven evaluations and a steadfast commitment to ethical, equitable provision of financial tools and social services.

References

[1] Planning Commission, "Press Note on Poverty Estimates, 2011-12," Government of India, 2014.

[2] World Bank, "Urban population (India)," The World Bank, 2022.

[3] M. Yunus, *Creating a world without poverty: Social business and the future of capitalism*, PublicAffairs, 2007.

[4] B. Armendáriz and J. Morduch, *The economics of microfinance*, MIT Press, 2010.

[5] D. Roodman, *Due diligence: An impertinent inquiry into microfinance*, Center for Global Development, 2012.

[6] J. Singh, D. Sharma, and G. S. Batra, "Does credit utilization pattern promote poverty alleviation? An evidence from India," *Global Business Review*, vol. 24, no. 6, pp. 1227–1250, 2023. https://doi.org/10.1177/0972150920918967

[7] T. Suri and W. Jack, "The long-run poverty and gender impacts of mobile money," *Science*, vol. 354, no. 6317, pp. 1288–1292, 2016.

[8] J. Singh and M. Singh, "Accelerating Financial Inclusion of the Urban Poor: Role of Innovative e-Payment Systems and JAM Trinity in Alleviating Poverty in India," *Global Business Review*, 09721509231222609, 2024. https://doi.org/10.1177/09721509231222609

[9] J. Aron and V. Murinde, "Fintech in sub-Saharan Africa: A review and research agenda," *Journal of African Economies*, vol. 28, no. 4, pp. 377–412, 2019.

[10] J. Drèze and R. Khera, "Recent social security initiatives in India," *World Development*, vol. 98, pp. 555–572, 2017.

[11] J. Singh and M. Singh, "Addressing unproductive credit consumption and beneficiary malpractices in social welfare programs for slum-dwellers: A study from India," *Cities*, vol. 145, p. 104729, 2024. https://doi.org/10.1016/j.cities.2023.104729

[12] A. Sen, *Development as freedom*, Oxford University Press, 1999.

[13] A. V. Banerjee, E. Duflo, R. Glennerster, and C. G. Kinnan, "The miracle of microfinance? Evidence from a randomized evaluation," *American Economic Journal: Applied Economics*, vol. 7, no. 1, pp. 22–53, 2015.

[14] R. P. Buckley and L. Malady, "Fintech and the future of finance," *Journal of Financial Transformation*, vol. 42, pp. 14–21, 2015.

[15] V. Venkatesh, M. G. Morris, G. B. Davis, and F. D. Davis, "User acceptance of information technology: Toward a unified view," *MIS Quarterly*, vol. 27, no. 3, pp. 425–478, 2003.

[16] D. A. Clark and C. D'Ambrosio, "Capabilities, poverty and the measurement of well-being," in *The Oxford Handbook of Well-Being and Public Policy*, Oxford University Press, 2019, pp. 467–492.

[17] J. Singh and M. Singh, "Alleviating urban poverty in India: The role of capabilities and entrepreneurship development," *International Journal of Social Economics*, vol. 51, no. 10, pp. 1314–1335, 2024. https://doi.org/10.1108/IJSE-07-2023-0514

[18] S. Devereux and R. Sabates-Wheeler, "Transformative social protection," *IDS Working Paper 232*, Institute of Development Studies, 2004.

[19] J. Singh and M. Singh, "Does financial inclusion impact socio-economic stability? A study of social safety net in Indian slums," *International Journal of Social Economics*, vol. 50, no. 8, pp. 1060–1084, 2023. https://doi.org/10.1108/IJSE-04-2022-0261

[20] R. K. Yin, *Case study research and applications: Design and methods* (6th ed.). Sage, 2018.

[21] J. Singh, G. S. Batra, D. Sharma, and V. Singh, "Microcredit Usage Pattern and its Impact on Economic Activities of the Urban Deprived: A Study of Punjab State, India," *South Asian Journal of Management*, vol. 28, no. 1, p. 128, 2021. Retrieved from https://openurl.ebsco.com/contentitem/gcd:150904866?sid=ebsco:plink:crawler&id=ebsco:gcd:150904866

[22] J. Singh and M. Singh, "Fintech applications in social welfare schemes during Covid times: An extension of the classic TAM model in India," *International Social Science Journal*, vol. 73, no. 250, pp. 979–998, 2023. https://doi.org/10.1111/issj.12406

[23] A. Demirguc-Kunt, L. Klapper, D. Singer, and S. Ansar, "The Global Findex Database 2017: Measuring financial inclusion and the Fintech revolution," World Bank, 2018.

[24] M. Chaba, P. Tyagi, D. Dembla, Y. Chaba, and S. K. Chatrath, "Ensuring data integrity in the cloud computing using hash algorithms based data auditing techniques," in *Data Science and Security*, V. H. C. de Albuquerque and G. S. Batra, Eds. Singapore: Springer Nature Singapore, 2024, pp. 291–306.

[25] A. Kumar, B. Maheshwari, M. Bala, S. K. Chatrath, A. K. Saini, and I. H. Ting, "How social entrepreneurship transform into sustainable development goals of women via m-commerce and smart cities in Southeast Asia: Mediating effect of value creation," *Technological Forecasting and Social Change*, vol. 200, p. 123198, 2024, doi: https://doi.org/10.1016/j.techfore.2023.123198.

[26] F. Allen, E. Carletti, R. Cull, J. Q. Qian, L. Senbet, and P. Valenzuela, "The foundations of financial inclusion: Understanding ownership and use of formal accounts," *Journal of Financial Intermediation*, vol. 26, pp. 1–30, 2016.

[27] R. P. Buckley and L. Malady, "Fintech and the future of finance," *Journal of Financial Transformation*, vol. 42, pp. 14–21, 2015.

[28] V. Venkatesh, M. G. Morris, G. B. Davis, and F. D. Davis, "User acceptance of information technology: Toward a unified view," *MIS Quarterly*, vol. 27, no. 3, pp. 425–478, 2003.

[29] A. Demirguc-Kunt, L. Klapper, D. Singer, and S. Ansar, *The Global Findex Database 2017: Measuring financial inclusion and the Fintech revolution*. Washington, DC: World Bank, 2018.

[30] D. A. Clark and C. D'Ambrosio, "Capabilities, poverty and the measurement of well-being," in *The Oxford Handbook of Well-Being and Public Policy*, E. Diener, S. Oishi, and L. Tay, Eds. Oxford, UK: Oxford University Press, 2019, pp. 467–492.

[31] R. K. Yin, *Case study research and applications: Design and methods* (6th ed.). Thousand Oaks, CA: Sage Publications, 2018.

[32] J. K. Fatima, M. I. Khan, S. Bahmannia, S. K. Chatrath, N. F. Dale, and R. Johns, "Rapport with a chatbot? The underlying role of anthropomorphism in socio-cognitive perceptions of rapport and e-word of mouth," *Journal of Retailing and Consumer Services*, vol. 77, p. 103666, 2024, doi: https://doi.org/10.1016/j.jretconser.2023.103666.

[33] R. Firdous, S. K. Chatrath, A. K. Jadoon, M. Iqbal, S. A. Batool, and Z. Ul Hasan, "Exploring dynamic nexus between economic growth, environmental degradation, and public health in Pakistan: a moderated mediation approach," *International Journal of Energy Economics and Policy*, vol. 13, no. 1, pp. 241-249, 2023.

Index

About the Editors

Dr. Jyoti Verma is a faculty member at Chitkara Business School, Chitkara University, Punjab, India. With more than 30 research papers to her credit published in various journals and conferences at national and international levels, Dr. Verma has developed her core expertise in the area of service quality, blockchain, and behavioral finance. She has authored one book titled 'Accelerating the Development of Quality of IT-Enabled Banking Services' for international publishers. She has published many book chapters in edited books at the international level and published two edited books. She is a Subject Matter Expert and Course Planner for MOOC courses of SWAYAM and UGC CEC. She is an Associate Editor (Finance & International Business) for Journal of Technology Management for Growing Economies, Chitkara University Publications.

Dr. Sarvjeet Kaur Chatrath is an award-winning scholar of management and leadership. She has over 28 years of distinguished experience in higher education, strategic financial planning, marketing, and institutional development. She has consistently demonstrated excellence in curriculum design, research leadership, and fostering industry-academia collaboration. An award-winning educator, she was honoured with the Faculty of Business, Government & Law Executive Dean's Award for Excellence in Teaching (2024), reflecting her commitment to innovative pedagogy and student success. Dr Chatrath is the Council Member, The Australia and New Zealand Section of the Regional Science Association International (ANZRSAI).

Dr. Chatrath's research expertise is led by her work in Social marketing, with a strong focus on consumer vulnerability, gender psychology, and the use of technology and social media to drive behavioural change. Her broader research interests include strategic financial management, marketing analytics, leadership, human resource management, and corporate social responsibility (CSR) in marketing. She is actively engaged in exploring environmental degradation, alignment with Sustainable Development Goals (SDGs), fintech for poverty alleviation, public sector innovation, chatbot rapport-building, service technology, and blockchain applications for social welfare. She is also deeply involved in higher education policy, institutional development, and the application of artificial intelligence in business and governance. Her work contributes to public sector performance, international business, cross-cultural management, and the development of innovation ecosystems. Dr. Chatrath has successfully secured competitive research grants, mentored Ph.D. and DBA candidates to completion, and published extensively in high-impact Q1Scopus and ABDC-ranked journals, Technological Forecasting and Social Change, Cities, Journal of Cyber Security and Privacy, Scientific reports, Journal of Service Theory and Practice, Journal of Retailing and Consumer Services.

With a global perspective and a strong commitment to continuous improvement, Dr. Chatrath is dedicated to advancing academic excellence, impactful research, and international collaboration across dynamic academic environments.

Dr. Gagandeep, a highly accomplished academic with a Ph.D. in management, brings over 15 years of teaching experience to the table. He earned his M.B.A. in marketing and completed his Ph.D. in marketing and international business at Panjab University's University Business School. With a strong background in marketing and a track record of publications in reputable journals, including Scopus indexed ones, Dr. Gagandeep's expertise spans research methodology, marketing research, and strategic management. Holding notable positions at prominent institutions like Chitkara University, Dr. Gagandeep has excelled as both a dedicated educator and a researcher. Additionally, his involvement in faculty development programs, mentoring of students, and contributions to various webinars and conferences underscore his commitment to the academic community.

For Product Safety Concerns and Information please contact our EU representative GPSR@taylorandfrancis.com Taylor & Francis Verlag GmbH, Kaufingerstraße 24, 80331 München, Germany